Administrator's
COMPLETE
SCHOOL
DISCIPLINE
GUIDE

Techniques & Materials for Creating an Environment Where Kids Can Learn

ROBERT D. RAMSEY, Ed.D.

PRENTICE HALL
Paramus, New Jersey 07652

Library of Congress Cataloging-in-Publication Data

Ramsey, Robert D.
     Administrator's complete school discipline guide : creating an environment
where all kids can learn / Robert D. Ramsey.
          p.   cm.
     Includes bibliographical references.
     ISBN 0-13-079401-5
     1. School discipline—United States—Handbooks, manuals, etc.   2. School
administrators—United States—Handbooks, manuals, etc.   I. Title.
LB3012.2.R35   1995   94-31881
371.5—dc20   CIP

Printed in the United States of America

10   9   8   7   6   5   4   3

To all those teachers who put *children first* every day.

ISBN 0-13-079401-5

PRENTICE HALL
Career & Personal Development
Paramus, NJ 07652
A Simon & Schuster Company

On the World Wide Web at http://www.phdirect.com

Prentice-Hall International (UK) Limited, *London*
Prentice-Hall of Australia Pty. Limited, *Sydney*
Prentice-Hall Canada Inc., *Toronto*
Prentice-Hall Hispanoamericana, S.A., *Mexico*
Prentice-Hall of India Private Limited, *New Delhi*
Prentice-Hall of Japan, Inc., *Tokyo*
Simon & Schuster Asia Pte. Ltd., *Singapore*
Editora Prentice-Hall do Brasil, Ltda., *Rio de Janeiro*

About the Author

Dr. Robert D. Ramsey is a life-long educational leader and author who has served in three award-winning school districts in two different states. His professional preparation includes B.S., M.S., and Ed.D. degrees from the University of Kansas. Dr. Ramsey's front-line experience spans 35 years as a teacher, counselor, supervisor, curriculum director, assistant, and associate and acting superintendents.

Dr. Ramsey's previous publications include the *Educator's Discipline Handbook* (Parker Publishing Company, 1981); *Secondary Principal's Survival Guide* (Prentice Hall Publishing Company, 1992); and *501 Ways to Boost Your Child's Self-Esteem* (Contemporary Books, 1994). He is currently a freelance writer living in Minneapolis, MN.

Acknowledgments

Writing may be a solitary act, but it takes teamwork to produce a finished work. My team consisted primarily of Connie Kallback, who served as editor, advisor, and encourager; Joyce Ramsey, who produced the manuscript and nurtured the author; and Sue Thomas, who helped with production during the early phases and served as cheerleader throughout. Without their expertise, support, and assistance, you wouldn't be reading this book.

WHY ANOTHER DISCIPLINE HANDBOOK NOW?

Ask teachers anywhere and they'll tell you that "today's kids are different!" Student discipline in our nation's schools has taken a new, and sometimes dangerous twist. Problems of disrespectful, disruptive, and damaging behavior, which were once the exclusive province of a few secondary schools, are now becoming commonplace at all levels of education.

As new threats menace learning from kindergarten through high school in districts of all sizes, traditional disciplinary techniques aren't enough anymore. School leaders everywhere are beginning to rethink discipline practices and to seek new ways to address today's unprecedented behavior problems.

The *Administrator's Complete School Discipline Guide* is a one-of-a-kind comprehensive handbook for dealing with the new generation of behavior problems in elementary and secondary schools. The guide is designed to provide all principals, assistants, and other school leaders responsible for discipline with state-of-the-art techniques for maintaining safe, productive, and nurturing schools. This resource is a hands-on manual offering specific school-tested methods for handling all of today's new threats to school order including gangs, violence, drugs, and sexual harassment. Straightforward suggestions and solutions that can be put to work immediately in your school are spelled out through the entire handbook in key sections such as:

- What doesn't work anymore and why?
- Trust-building programs that can turn your school around
- Guidelines for a successful peer counseling program
- What it takes to have a curriculum where all students succeed
- How to make your school a safe-zone from gangs
- New ways to keep weapons out of your school
- How to plan an antiviolence education program
- What's new in drug education
- How to have a drug-free education
- How to have a drug-free school
- How to handle sexual harassment in school
- New approaches to traditional discipline problems
- What teaching strategies work best with today's students
- How to rejuvenate the partnership between home and school

—and much more.

In every chapter, you'll find a variety of practical examples, sample policies, position descriptions, checklists, illustrations, and step-by-step procedures that can be adapted to fit any school situation. Today's school leaders are being called on to meet discipline challenges unheard of a few years ago. The *Administrator's Complete School Discipline Guide* tells you how. The down-to-earth tips, information and advice offered in this unique guide are derived from the real-world experiences of winning schools and school leaders in all parts of the nation. If you want an up-to-date resource for managing all of today's different and difficult discipline problems in your school, this handbook will become a favorite addition to your professional library.

Robert D. Ramsey, Ed.D.

CONTENTS

CHAPTER FIVE
HOW TO DEAL WITH GANGS IN SCHOOL • 83

CHAPTER SIX
WHAT TO DO TO CURB VIOLENCE IN SCHOOL • 103

C H A P T E R   S E V E N

THE BEST OF THE BEST IN DRUG PREVENTION MEASURES • 121

C H A P T E R   E I G H T

HOW TO HANDLE SEXUAL HARASSMENT IN SCHOOL • 141

CHAPTER NINE
New Approaches to Traditional Discipline Problems • 161

CHAPTER TEN

HELPING TEACHERS LEARN THE SECRETS OF SUCCESSFUL CLASSROOM MANAGEMENT • 199

CHAPTER ELEVEN

HOW TO REJUVENATE THE PARTNERSHIP BETWEEN HOME AND SCHOOL • 215

CHAPTER TWELVE

LITTLE THINGS THAT MAKE A DIFFERENCE IN DISCIPLINE • 231

CHAPTER THIRTEEN

A FINAL WORD • 247

Appendices • 252

KIDS AREN'T BUYING

WHAT WE'RE SELLING

ANYMORE

When adults return to visit their childhood elementary or secondary school, they almost always comment that "Everything's changed!" What they usually mean is that the library is now a media center or that the rows of student desks they remember so well have been replaced by computer stations and learning centers. They're struck with the transformation of the physical plant and the external trappings of the school. What they don't observe, however, is that the greatest changes have occurred in student attitude, expectations and behavior. What's changed the most about schools today is *discipline*.

Daily headlines herald student behavior problems in schools at all levels. Based on media portrayals of violence, weapons, and gangs, many in the public have been led to believe that the nation's schools have become lawless wastelands. Many parents fear that their children are no longer safe in school. It is true that some schools have lost control. Others are losing it. *But it doesn't have to be that way.*

The best schools and the best administrators across the country continue to create a safe, orderly environment in which all kids can learn. You can too. This guide will help show you how to do it. The first step is to understand what's going on with kids in school today.

It's a New Ball Game in School Discipline

Teachers everywhere are quick to tell you that "Today's kids are different." Rudeness and defiance are commonplace in many classrooms. Compliance isn't automatic. Respect has to be earned. (It doesn't just come automatically with being a teacher anymore.) More and more students come to school with an attitude which noted educator-psychiatrist Dr. William Glasser describes as, "I don't want to do it and you can't hurt me." The old models of discipline aren't working. As one veteran teacher has stated, "Kids aren't buying what we're selling anymore."

Today's students are more outspoken and assertively protective of their rights than they have been in previous years. Likewise both students and parents are increasingly willing to challenge the authority of the school. Many administrators now feel that they discipline students not only to establish a common code of conduct and improve behavior, but also to protect themselves and their district from liability.

It's a new ball game in school discipline. Some of the old problems are getting worse and starting to occur at earlier ages. At the same time, new problems are emerging which were unheard of in schools a few years ago.

Modern Threats to Every School

Schools mirror society and sometimes the images are ugly. As the nation struggles with problems of sexual misconduct, racial tensions, and violence, these issues are acted out daily in classrooms, hallways, and school grounds in every community.

Many of yesterday's discipline concerns seem innocuous compared to the intensity and escalation of today's major problems. Inappropriate and unacceptable behavior in schools is shifting dramatically toward more violent, destructive and dehumanizing activity as illustrated in the diagram below.

Continuum of Discipline Problems

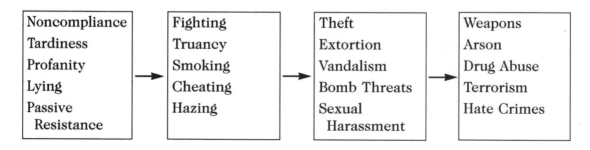

Drugs, gangs, and weapons have been relatively recent problems for school personnel. "Gun-totin' kids" in school are a new phenomenon. However, in 1992, the Justice Department reported that 100,000 students brought guns to school every day and that teenagers were three times more likely to be crime victims than adults. In that same year, the St. Paul Minnesota Public Schools conducted a survey of students in grades 7–12 with the following chilling results:

63% had been crime victims

43% had something stolen

29% had brought weapons (guns, knives, razors) to school

5% had brought guns to school

4% had been forced to have sexual contact

9% had obtained drugs and alcohol on school grounds

2% had spent lots of time in gangs

3% had spent some time in gangs

St. Paul is no worse than most urban areas and probably is better than many. The point is that, in many schools and communities, crime is common and violence has become an acceptable way to settle disputes and solve problems among children.

Most likely, the situation was not like that when you were a student. Likewise, your administrative training probably didn't prepare you to deal with situations such as this. It takes creative new approaches to maintain positive discipline in today's schools, to recapture schools that are out of control and to reclaim the lives of many at-risk students who have become alienated from education as we traditionally have "sold it." The old ways just don't work with today's problems.

WHAT DOESN'T WORK ANYMORE AND WHY

Traditional techniques are no longer enough to solve modern student behavior problems. If you ask veteran teachers about what doesn't work anymore, they'll often tell you, "Almost everything."

The list of failed and failing traditional discipline measures includes the following:

- *Verbal Reprimands.* Many students have become immunized by years of verbal abuse at home.
- *Physical Punishment.* Rapidly disappearing in the wake of lawsuits against teachers and administrators.

- *Corporal Punishment.* Now outlawed in most states.
- *Calling Parents.* Growing numbers of parents don't have the time or energy for, or interest in, addressing their child's discipline problems at school. For many parents, "It's the school's problem. Let the school handle it."
- *Suspension.* No longer a threat for many students who treat it as "time off" to enjoy the arcade, the mall or MTV.
- *Expulsion.* In many states, true expulsion no longer exists because schools are required to provide an alternative educational program even when students are dismissed for extreme behavior. Likewise, expulsion is prohibited by the *Individual Educational Plan* (IEP) for many special education students.

There are lots of reasons why the old models of discipline don't work today. One of the principal factors which has diffused the effect of traditional discipline measures is confusion about the role of the school. In many ways, we have become a nation that doesn't know what it wants to do with its schools. Constant calls for reform reflect a growing disaffection for traditional educational programs and the way schools are run. Teachers and administrators often don't know what they're supposed to do or what they can do to meet societal expectations.

In addition to this confusion, society's hypocrisy is catching up with us in terms of influencing the attitude and behavior of young people. Repeated incidents of role models in trouble and of corruption and scandal involving leaders in all fields make cynics out of students. When adults cheat, it's difficult to convince students to be honest. Its hard to impose discipline in an atmosphere of double standards.

Other significant factors contributing to the breakdown of school discipline include the following:

- Growing diversity and racial tension in schools.
- The impact of drugs.
- Shifting family values and structures.
- Advent of a gang culture in many communities.
- Loss of school as the centerpiece of the community. (Widespread consolidation has led to hyphenated school districts with a loss of community identity and loyalty to the school.)
- Normalization/glamorization of violence by the media.
- Growing poverty affecting children.
- Availability of weapons (particularly guns).
- Fear of litigation and liability by school authorities.

- Overlabeling of students which has created a class of "throw-away kids."
- Misunderstanding of the law by administrators (i.e. "We can't do anything about discipline anymore").
- The "choice" movement ("If we don't like it here, we'll go to school someplace else").

These developments have altered the attitudes which students bring to school, the way students react and behave in the classroom, the nature and level of parental support and involvement, and the options open to school authorities. In short, they've changed forever the rule book for dealing with student discipline.

As if these changes weren't enough, school leaders must also deal with the fact that students today are coming to school with a completely different agenda than students of the past.

THE NEW AGENDA FOR TODAY'S YOUTH

When teachers say that today's kids are different, they don't just mean the way students talk or dress or act. It goes deeper than that. Newspaper editors, educators, ministers, and others who work with young people (and read their writings and listen to what they say), all report a new level of pain, anxiety, and apprehension among children of all ages. Growing up has never been easy. Now it's a scary and sometimes life-threatening "trial by ordeal."

Today's children and youth are experiencing unprecedented societal pressures, confusion about society's polarization of values, uncertainty about the future, and feelings of profound loneliness in a crowded land. These fears, concerns, and uncertain dreams constitute a new agenda of youth issues.

In safer, simpler times, the worries children had were reflected in questions such as:

- Will people like me?
- Where will I go to college?
- What will I major in?
- What kind of job will I have?
- How much money will I make?
- When will I be out on my own?
- Who will I marry?
- How many children will I have?
- Where will I live?

- What kind of house and car will I have?
- Will I be happy?

The questions provoked by the new youth agenda are far more critical and troubling:

- Will I be safe?
- Will I be raped?
- Will I get AIDS?
- Will I be killed?
- Will my parents stay together?
- Will our planet survive in spite of us?
- Will I be able to afford college?
- Will I be able to make a living?
- Will anyone care?

In most ways, the basic nature of children has not changed. Nevertheless, in adapting to a society in transition and coping with the new agenda of youth issues, students are bringing dramatically changed and changing needs into each classroom every day.

Student fears and concerns have escalated significantly over those of previous generations and are acted out in different ways. Addressing the new agenda of student issues is the number one challenge to contemporary school leaders.

Today's students are different. Discipline is different too. The old ways don't work well anymore, but this doesn't mean that nothing will work. It's still possible to create an environment where kids can learn. We can take back our schools where they are out of control. We can provide a level playing field for all students.

Changing times call for innovative approaches. As a school leader, you may be called upon to be a "china breaker"—to crack the old mold and establish a new framework for learning and living together in school.

This guide will help by sharing what winning schools across the country are doing to rethink their philosophies on discipline, to retool their techniques, and to reinvent positive relationships within the school. It all begins and ends with the culture of the organization.

CHAPTER TWO

SHAPING A SCHOOL

CULTURE THAT WORKS

FOR LEARNING

(AND AGAINST DISCIPLINE PROBLEMS)

A school stands or falls on the effectiveness of its discipline. Without order, safety, and a sense of security and civility, schools can't work and learning will not occur.

What many educators, parents and others don't understand however, is that school discipline isn't about rules, regulations, regimentation, policies, or punishment. Healthy and productive student behavior is a by-product of the beliefs and values of the organization.

The roots of positive discipline lie in the way people (adults and students) think about themselves and others and the way they treat each other every day. It is the culture that drives the discipline of the school.

HOW THE CULTURE DRIVES THE SCHOOL'S DISCIPLINE

Every human entity develops its own unique character. Every school has its own personality. You can feel it when you first enter a building.

Some schools feel unfriendly, sterile, and "institutional." Others are welcoming and inviting like a busy kitchen where lots of good things seem to be happening all at once. The feeling tone is a reflection of the culture of the school. This culture determines, more than anything else, how people perform and act toward one another.

An organization's culture is made up of unwritten norms, mores, and expectations. It is the climate that shapes day-to-day relationships. This climate is developed and nurtured over time by history, habit, tradition, stories, heroes and celebrations which define and reinforce how people are supposed to behave.

7

In schools, the organizational culture can work for or against learning. A positive culture is the first condition of a successful school. Where a supportive environment has been established, students tend to behave because that's the "way people act here." The culture of the school:

1.   Sets standards (what's accepted and what's not);
2.   Defines quality and success;
3.   Creates a synergy that makes the whole greater than the sum of its individual components;
4.   Identifies which behaviors are valued and rewarded;
5.   Sends a powerful message about "how we do business here."

In schools where the culture supports learning and promotes productive behavior:

- Students and staff members feel good about themselves.
- Everyone has a say; people feel empowered because someone listens to them.
- A feeling of family is encouraged.
- Everyone knows why they are there and what they're supposed to do.
- The organization is organic and self-renewing. People accept change.
- Participation is encouraged.
- Helpfulness is a way of life.
- People have fun.

An effective school climate helps people produce, honors effort, and forgives mistakes. In schools where all students feel accepted, valued, recognized, and rewarded, good discipline is the norm.

A true "learning culture" is all-inclusive. There are no insiders or outsiders as illustrated below:

The Learning Culture

Effective administrators realize the power and importance of culture in molding and motivating behavior. Defining the dream and designing the culture of the organization are the most important jobs you have as a school leader. If you don't attend to the culture of the school, the rest of this book won't be enough to help you achieve positive discipline. The good news is that, once established, a learning culture tends to be self-perpetuating.

USING YOUR SCHOOL'S IMAGE AS A SELF-FULFILLING PROPHECY

Schools are like classrooms. If everyone has a purpose and goes about the business of achieving it while helping others in the process, discipline largely takes care of itself.

Once a school has established a reputation for positive discipline and respectful learning, the culture becomes a self-fulfilling prophecy. The internal and external image defines what the school stands for and students become predisposed to conform. Peer pressure and the Pygmalion effect go a long way to perpetuate a productive school climate.

People become what they believe. Expectations determine outcomes. It works for individuals; it works for groups; and it works for schools.

A positive "learning culture" pulls students to perform and behave at their best. Insiders take pride in upholding the school's standards and newcomers learn and accept how to act readily. "That's the way it is in this school."

Nurturing a positive school culture and using it as a self-fulfilling prophecy requires continues diagnosis of what's working and what's not. (A healthy culture listens to itself.)

There are lots of well-researched instruments available for measuring school climate (for example, *School Work Culture Profile*, University of South Florida, 1988; *Cooperative Learning School Environment Survey*, University of Minnesota, 1993), but it doesn't take a scientific analysis to gauge the status of a school's culture. The signs of a polluted climate are usually self-evident and easily detected just by paying attention to what's going on every day (see *Informal Audit of School Climate* that follows). Whenever these signs occur frequently and consistently, the school is in trouble and it's probably going to get worse.

Whatever the culture of the school is, it tends to be self-perpetuating. Vandalism breeds more vandalism. Violence triggers more violence. If the school is known as a "tough place," students will act tough and will poison an expectation of toughness to future generations of students. Likewise if the school has an image of business-like learning and respectful behavior, students will tend to uphold the tradition.

An Informal Audit of School Climate
(Symptoms of a Sick Culture)

1. Absenteeism is high (among both students and staff).
2. Lots of kids are failing.
3. Participation in school activities is declining.
4. It's hard to get parents to come to school.
5. There is an absence of laughter in the building.
6. It's hard to find anybody reading on their own for fun.
7. Lounge talk is mostly about problems, gripes, poor conditions, lack-luster administration and "bad kids."
8. Students and staff members look grim and tense on Monday mornings.
9. Union reps are frequent visitors to the school.
10. Students don't stay around after school for help.
11. Paper work takes precedence over people work.
12. The school uses lots of labels for kids.
13. The building is littered and dirty and no one seems to care.
14. Teachers don't know students' names.
15. Sexist and racist graffiti are commonplace.
16. The rule book is thicker than the curriculum guide.

There's nothing more important that you, as a leader, can do for discipline than to help build a strong learning culture within the school. Successful administrators do this by:

- Keeping the school's real purpose on everyone's agenda as a front-burner issue.
- Setting high standards and not backing off.
- Modeling respect, fairness, trust, and risk taking.
- Recognizing and rewarding effort and excellence.
- Honoring differences.
- Reinforcing positive behavior and performance.
- Celebrating mistakes as well as successes.

- Being open and accessible.
- Letting everyone have a piece of the action in decision making.
- Communicating/publicizing individual and group accomplishments. (Don't be afraid to brag; it helps realize the school's promise and prophecy.)

The place to start in creating an environment where all students can learn is with the way people in the school think about kids, behavior, control, and punishment. The cornerstone of the culture in any school is its philosophy of discipline.

HOW TO DRAG YOUR SCHOOL'S DISCIPLINE PHILOSOPHY INTO TODAY'S REAL WORLD

The school's discipline philosophy is simply the staff's commonly-held beliefs about what kids are like, what constitutes acceptable behavior, and what it takes to achieve it. This philosophy usually isn't written down; but it shapes expectations for behavior and guides every act of reward and punishment in the school.

Many discipline models and methods popular in the past are no longer effective because they are based on a set of beliefs that time has passed by. Certain beliefs about children and behavior no longer apply to contemporary society (the real world in which today's students live).

Examples of outdated beliefs about discipline include the following:

1. It's up to the school to determine what's right and wrong.
2. One rule covers all.
3. Respect is a given.
4. There is no gain without pain.
5. Students have to be quiet for learning to occur.
6. Students and parents shouldn't question authority: "Don't ask why—just do it."
7. Students who behave badly are "bad kids."
8. Most students learn "proper behavior" at home before they come to school.
9. Parents will stand behind the school rules.

Such beliefs may have had validity at one time; but they aren't true today. Any workable philosophy for maintaining school discipline must be based on "what is," not on "what was."

What Was and *What Is* in School Discipline

What Was	What Is
Kids were considered innocent.	Kids are street wise.
Physical punishment was condoned.	Corporal punishment is outlawed.
Schools were immune from most lawsuits.	School personnel are liable.
Leadership was autocratic.	Leadership is plural; participatory decision making is becoming the norm.
Drugs were used only by adults.	Drug use often starts at an early age.
Acts of violence were relatively uncommon.	Violence is part of everyday life for many children.
Schools were racially homogeneous.	Diversity is increasing in most schools.
Teachers were masters.	The teacher is servant and facilitator.
Problem kids were separated from the mainstream.	Inclusion is the accepted model.
Progress was based on age and "seat time."	Progress is based on mastery.
Most students remained in the same school.	Students are mobile.
Nuclear families were the norm.	There are all kinds of families.
Severe discipline problems were limited mostly to ghettos and inner cities.	The same problems exist everywhere. (There's no place left to run.)

The old beliefs often led to a philosophy based on obedience, fear and punishment, designed to catch kids being bad: "If we catch 'em off base, we'll put 'em out."

Many educators cling to yesterday's beliefs and continue to operate in a state of denial. They won't accept society's changes and refuse to update their discipline philosophy. Denial, wishful thinking, and a yearning for the past make up a sure-fire recipe for discipline disaster. It's hard to have a clear vision when your head is buried in the sand.

To drag your school's discipline philosophy (kicking and screaming if necessary) into today's real world, you must help your staff understand current trends in society, accept kids as they really are today, and set expectations that are realistic.

Five fundamental premises undergird a viable philosophy of discipline for schools today:

1. All kids can learn and can learn to behave appropriately.
2. There are no throw-away kids. (Society can't afford the loss.)
3. Discipline is more about teaching, learning, and problem solving, than about punishment.
4. The best discipline is self-discipline.
5. Everyone has responsibility for solving problems in the school.

If you can get your staff to begin to accept these beliefs, you're well on your way to better discipline.

A philosophy built around consequences and control is out of touch with today's reality. What will work is a philosophy that *emphasizes positive expectations* (the self-fulfilling prophecy again), *recognizes differences,* and *provides options.* Obviously, it's still important to set standards defining what citizens in the school can and cannot do. It's more important, however, to stress what the school will do to be ready for all learners and what everyone is expected to do to help each other succeed.

In the most effective schools, the staffs believe that discipline goes beyond blaming, shaming, and ineffectual rules to concentrate instead on forming a "partnership of empowerment" by:

- listening before setting standards;
- keeping rules simple;
- valuing diversity;
- working hard to guarantee that all students learn;
- never backing away until the job is done.

Of course, philosophy isn't enough. The best game plan in the world won't win ball games unless someone executes it. Beliefs don't change anything unless they are translated into action. But if the belief is strong enough, the action will follow.

The remainder of this chapter shows how some schools are putting the new beliefs about discipline to work in improving behavior and creating a healthy learning culture. The best place to start is by building trust.

TRUST-BUILDING PROGRAMS THAT CAN TURN YOUR SCHOOL AROUND

In any organization, cultural cohesiveness is maintained through either fear or trust. In schools, the fear-driven philosophy has failed. Trust remains as the only glue that can hold a learning culture together. Positive discipline depends on a high level of trust among students and staff. The greater the trust, the fewer the discipline problems.

Consequently, more and more schools are taking a page from the corporate book on leadership and management by initiating trust-building programs as part of their normal operation.

In the private sector, a broad range of organizations from professional sports teams such as the Minnesota Vikings to international companies such as *Investor's Diversified Services* (IDS) have attempted to revitalize their corporate culture by introducing trust-building/team-building training for key personnel.

The IDS model is typical of such programs. At IDS, the *Leadership and Team Development Program* (LTD), based on activities developed at the famous Pecos River Learning Center, has been implemented nationwide. The following are distinguishing features of the program:

- Participants are "invited," not required to attend.
- Only teams (not individuals) can participate.
- Experiential training sessions last up to 4 1/2 days.
- The stated purpose of the program is to provide personal (introspective) experiences and team (interactive) exercises to foster individual and group leadership, shared accountability, and team building.
- Specific goals are enhanced: *T*rust, *A*ccountability, *S*upport, *T*ruth, and *E*nergy (TASTE).

Each training session is organized around risk-taking activities designed to help individuals and teams break down barriers, let go of "excessive baggage," go to the edge and beyond, and gain a new vision of teamwork. Examples include:

1. **Electric Maze:** The team challenge is to move all members one at a time, across a programmed carpet without triggering a penalty buzzer.
2. **Trust Fall:** Participants are challenged to fall backward from off a wall, without looking, into the arms of teammates.
3. **Blind Trust Walk:** Participants are led blindfolded on a treacherous "walk" by an unknown partner.
4. **The Tower:** In order to reach the top of the tower (a simulated rock climb), participants must cooperate and plan strategy under pressure. No one can succeed alone.
5. **The Zipline:** Participants, who are harnessed to a cable, push themselves off the edge of a cliff and "zip" down the cable to waiting teammates.
6. **The Finger-Lift:** A team of participants hold up one member by using just two fingers each.

Every exercise in the LTD program drives as a metaphor for what happens and can happen in a culture where the trust level permits risk taking and teamwork spells success.

What works for the corporate community can work for schools. Any involvement in developing understanding and mutual trust within the school can pay big dividends in better discipline later on.

Schools have adapted trust-building and team-building programs in a variety of ways. Some have limited such programs exclusively to staff members in the belief that it is the adults who set the tone and model the culture for learners. Others have extended these programs to students where they feel it really counts.

Mt. Edgecumbe High School (Sitka, AK) brings in new students prior to the opening of school for intense trust-building training and induction into the school's continuous improvement culture.

St. Louis Park (MN) Senior High uses an overnight retreat environment to provide experiential sessions for both staff and students to increase understanding and awareness of the multicultural make-up of the school. Training sessions include incoming students and selected upper-class mentor leaders, as well as representatives of various ethnic groups. Participants run the gamut from student council members to gang leaders.

Although formats vary, a typical student training session looks like this:

Trust Development Agenda

Day 1

> Orientation/Overview (Why are we here?)
> Introduction and Ice-Breaking Activities
> Activities Explanation and Coaching
> Team Exercises
> Debriefing

Day 2

> Team Exercises
> Transfer of Learning Discussion
> Team Exercises
> Transfer Discussion
> Team Planning (What do we do when we get back to school?)
> Individual Sharing (What I've Learned)
> Closure

Before undertaking any extensive trust-building program, the school must be willing to live with the outcomes. Old mystique may be broken down; communication may be flattened out. A culture based on trust is scary for the untrusting. The rewards, however, can be a school that is more open, more problem-free, and more fun.

Whatever trust-building approach is used, it's worth the effort. Trust is a must and there's no better place to begin to improve discipline and create an environment for successful learning. It may also be a way to instill harmony in a school struggling with racial unrest.

CELEBRATING DIVERSITY AS A POSITIVE FORCE IN THE SCHOOL

Diversity has added a new dimension to discipline problems in many schools. Not very many years ago, racial tension and conflict were for the most part limited to metropolitan urban areas. Today, interracial relations among students have become an issue almost everywhere. There just aren't many all-white, all-black, or all-anything public schools anymore. In some places, minorities have now become the majority. By the year 2000, it is estimated that 42% of all public school students will come from minority groups. This emerging cultural pluralism poses a whole new set of problems for administrators concerned about discipline.

In schools, as in society, prejudice exists in many forms. Bigotry breeds problems and they won't go away on their own. Likewise, tension between races is often fed by the sense of frustration and rage felt by many minority students because of the barriers that society—including schools—have placed in their path.

In many schools that have experienced a large increase in the number and variety of minorities represented in the student body (often including a significant influx of immigrant students who don't speak the English language) teachers and administrators are simply unprepared to deal with the problems that may arise. They often equate diversity with discipline problems and succumb to an attitude of hopelessness. It doesn't have to be that way.

It is possible to manage diversity in ways which avoid clashes between racial and ethnic groups and which build an equitable and inclusive culture that is a positive force in the school. The best schools today do this by: (a) turning diversity into an asset, rather than a problem; (b) building bridges and sharing the strengths of all groups; and (c) providing opportunities for different groups to learn from each other and expand their multicultural understanding.

Where students are exposed to an inclusive environment that represents all races, ethnic backgrounds, and cultural heritages, plus celebrates differences, the school becomes more like the real world. This is education at its best.

It has to start with self-knowledge on the part of the adults in the school. If staff members can acknowledge their own blind spots, prejudices, and preconceptions, they will have gone a long way toward making diversity work for learning and toward preventing discipline problems. The goal should be to view the student body as a "human mosaic" of many colors which can achieve common goals through differences.

If diversity is to become a source of pride and a positive force in the school, you as a leader must consistently send four unflinching messages:

1. All students have value as human beings and deserve respect as worthwhile persons.
2. There is more than one way to be human, to learn and to contribute.
3. Despite differences, all students are more alike than different.
4. There is strength in diversity.

Once the message is out, the staff must "walk the talk" and demonstrate that the school means what it says. Every effort you make to promote intercultural and interracial acceptance/understanding can become a powerful strategy for dealing with discipline problems. Some of the techniques which have worked for many schools, include the following:

- Strictly enforce all antidiscrimination laws. (As administrator, you are always front-line compliance officer.)
- Implement a multicultural curriculum. Insist that teachers teach the truth about the treatment and contributions of minorities in history.
- Adopt a strict antidiscrimination policy.
- Review all policies and publications to assure fairness. Be sure that published photographs of students reflect the diversity of the student body.
- Consider diverse cultures when planning the school calendar. Honor the religious holidays of minority groups.
- Recruit minority staff and volunteers.
- Showcase role models representing all cultures.
- Launch a school-wide campaign to encourage students to take a stand against acts of discrimination based on race, religion, sex, age, culture, or physical and psychological limitations. An effective centerpiece for such a campaign is a personal pledge form to be signed by individual students (see the sample pledge for St. Louis Park).
- Have your school pair off with another school that has students of different racial or ethnic backgrounds—study together, exchange choirs, develop cooperative programs, and so on.
- Organize support for victims of hate crimes.

- Respect each person's or group's request for identification (such as "persons of color").
- Commemorate special events such as Black History Month.
- Hold a Multicultural Expo where all groups can spotlight their history or black heritage.
- Use inclusive language and avoid terms such as "pow wow" which may offend some students.
- Form a student-staff Human Mosaic Committee to plan ways to value and celebrate diversity.
- Break down stereotypes by providing accurate information and dispelling myths about cultural groups (for instance, "They all look alike").
- Recognize and understand the unique status of tribal sovereignty to American Indians.
- Don't permit a hostile environment (use of racial slurs, labels, inflammatory symbols, etc.) to exist in the school.

Diversity doesn't make learning and working together easier, but it can make your school better and stronger as illustrated below:

The Dynamics of Diversity in a Learning Culture

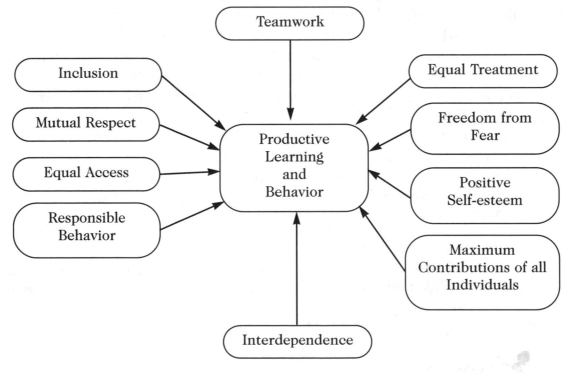

Antidiscrimination Pledge

St. Louis Park Senior High School

St. Louis Park Senior High School staff and students are committed to continually develop and maintain an atmosphere of respect for all individuals regardless of race, social class, sex, age, religion, physical/psychological conditions.

I will not tolerate racism, cultural/ethnic discrimination, religious intolerance or harrassment or "put down" remarks about a student or staff's race, religion, social class, ethnic background, age, sex or physical/psychological limitations.

The best and most effective learning for tomorrow's citizens and leaders takes place in a multi-cultural setting.

Every student is as unique as his/her fingerprints. Stereotypes and labels shouldn't be allowed to obscure this individuality. It's up to schools to value individual uniqueness and cultural differences. When this happens, behavior problems diminish. Celebrating diversity is just one of the new approaches to improving school discipline.

NEW WAYS TO WORK WITH TODAY'S STUDENTS FOR BETTER DISCIPLINE

When the old culture and the old methods don't work anymore, it's time to try something new. The traditional discipline models based on fear, punishment, obedience and "catching kids being bad" simply aren't successful with today's children and youth. We have to find some better strategies for creating a disciplined environment for successful learning.

There will always be a place for rules and consequences in schools, as in all organizations; but these aren't enough. Successful schools today are building a new paradigm for achieving productive student behavior based on support, acceptance and "tough love" as outlined below:

Today's Strategies for Positive Discipline and Effective Learning

1. Recognition (for effort as well as for achievement)
2. Respect for differences
3. Encouragement
4. Success experiences for all
5. Leadership opportunities for all
6. Equal access
7. Honest answers to honest questions
8. Flexibility
9. Responsibility for things that really matter
10. Options ("choice")
11. Self-discipline
12. Self-evaluation
13. Realistic expectations
14. Authentic feedback
15. Personalization and individual attention
16. "Elbow room" to learn, grow, and try new things
17. Praise (for little gains as well as for major accomplishments)
18. Alternative programs

19. Constructive criticism
20. Celebration of mistakes and successes
21. Being listened to
22. Somewhere to go with complaints
23. Second chances
24. Multiple ways to demonstrate learning and mastery
25. Zero anonymity
26. A school that "never walks away"

When you reduce fear and replace it with the action-principles above, discipline has got to get better. It's hard to cause trouble or show disrespect for a school that works hard to find out what you're good at, appreciates your contributions, respects your individuality, and gives you a chance to succeed and lead. That's what a learning culture is all about.

It's up to you to find new ways to provide opportunities for success and leadership for all students. The following ideas have worked and are working in many places:

- Let students conduct their own parent-teacher conferences.
- Route leadership positions frequently.
- Elevate academic, fine arts, and fitness awards to the status of athletic honors.
- Provide leadership training for all students.
- Publish a monthly list called "Look Who's Doing a Good Job."
- Spotlight students on faculty committees.
- Make it easy for students to initiate ideas for new courses and activities.
- Let students evaluate teachers.
- Use students as spokespersons for the school throughout the community.
- Build in ways for students to vent frustration and anger (forums, petitions, and so on).
- Arrange meetings between groups of students representing all facets of the student body with the School Board.
- Involve students in the "visioning" process of the school.
- Establish a user-friendly grievance procedure for students.
- Let a variety of students become "media celebrities" over the school owned/operated radio or cable TV station.
- Include informal student leaders, as well as positional leaders, in school planning.

- Let students teach teachers what they know better than the adults (electronics, computer graphics, and so forth).
- Create a Student Appeals Council regarding attendance and eligibility issues.

If you can guarantee respect and recognition for every student and provide everyone (young and old) in the school with some "glory" in their daily life, behavior will improve. The basis for successful discipline is helping all students experience a cycle of success:

Cycle of Success

When this happens, you've taken a lot of the mystery out of maintaining discipline.

In keeping with the ideas above, one of the most promising approaches to resolving discipline concerns is to use students as part of the solution instead of just part of the problem.

CONFLICT RESOLUTION: STUDENTS HELPING STUDENTS SOLVE PROBLEMS

Student-managed conflict resolution programs were introduced as early as 1982 in San Francisco. Now, the National Association of Mediation in Amherst, Massachusetts, reports that more than 2000 schools from the elementary to the collegiate level have such programs and the number is growing. Using the students themselves as mediators to settle student-to-student disputes is a prime example of the kind of "new" approach needed to achieve effective discipline today.

Based on the premise that students are often more willing to take problems to peers than to teachers or administrators, these programs empower students to solve problems on their own. Discipline becomes no longer just the job of adults. Students are trained to help each other handle common conflict situations.

The purpose of all Conflict Resolution programs is to teach students of all ages how not to hurt each other by showing them ways to end disputes without throwing punches or pulling a gun. Conflict managers try to get kids to "talk it out" or "work it out," instead of arguing or fighting. When students learn to deal with their conflicts in a positive way, they feel a sense of greater control over their own destiny.

The first step to setting up a conflict resolution program is to identify and train an adult coordinator, who, in turn, teaches the staff what conflict resolution is all about. When the teachers are comfortable with the approach, students are selected to serve as conflict managers (mediators). These students are usually nominated by their peers and/or recommended by teachers. The best mediators are students who are self-confident, caring (a "helping" attitude), not easily swayed, good listeners, and perceived as leaders. Other students often know who these individuals are as well as or better than the adults in the school.

Once chosen, student conflict managers normally receive from 6–20 hours of intensive training involving lecturers, observations, discussions and role-playing. In addition to learning the ground rules for mediation (see "Guidelines for Successful Conflict Resolution"), the students are taught a wide range of skills including:

- problem-solving
- compromising strategies
- negotiating approaches
- eye contact
- reading body language
- framing issues
- finding win-win solutions

- active listening
- questioning techniques
- empathy exercises
- anger management
- interpreting "I" messages
- brainstorming alternatives

Guidelines for Successful Conflict Resolution

1. The process must be entirely voluntary.
2. The party may "withdraw" at any stage of the process.
3. Once a mediation has begun, no interruptions are allowed.
4. All disputing parties are allowed full opportunity to present their sides of the conflict.
5. The process is as confidential as the parties want it to be.
6. The goal is to help the parties reach agreements that allow them to continue their relationships.
7. Both parties must agree to any settlement.

Once training is completed, the mediators are ready to go to work on a full spectrum of common student-to-student conflict situations such as:

- Name calling;
- Bullying;
- Invasion of privacy;
- Harassment;
- Rumor spreading;
- Racial incidents;
- Fighting;
- Playground arguments;
- Snatching or hiding personal property;
- "Bugging" one another.

Working in teams of two, mediators try to develop trust between the parties, get to the bottom of the problem, facilitate open discussion, and identify options. Some schools have found it helpful to provide a simple outline or worksheet for mediators to follow during each session (see Conflict Resolution Worksheet). To get the system up and running quickly, many schools identify conflict managers by special caps or T-shirts, set aside a specific room for mediation sessions, and post a regular schedule when mediators are available.

Mediators are not expected or allowed to find fault, punish, tattle, scold, or arbitrarily decide outcomes. If a conflict remains unresolved, mediators may refer the issue to an adult staff member. The adult coordinator is also always available to support and counsel the student conflict managers at any point in the process. As with all systems, there are potential pitfalls in any conflict resolution model. Some students may refuse to participate. Some mediators may become too cocky. Some sessions may end in confrontations that only make matters worse. Conflict resolution isn't appropriate for all problem situations and student mediators can't replace the adults in the school. Despite the limitations, however, the rewards can be significant.

Many schools, with established conflict resolution programs, report striking results and multiple benefits such as:

- Reduced discipline problems requiring adult attention
- Fewer injuries and referrals to school nurses
- More open communication
- More time for teaching

Conflict Resolution Worksheet

1. What is the problem/conflict?
2. Where did the incident occur?
3. Why did each party behave the way they did?
4. What are some possible solutions (What if ...)?
5. What solution seems best to the parties?
6. Why is this a good solution?
7. Are there any problems with the solution?
8. Who is going to do what? When?
9. How will we know when it's done?
10. Do both parties agree?

- Improved morale
- Reduced tension
- More prompt resolution of conflicts
- Greater cooperation among all students
- Heightened self-esteem
- More self-discipline
- Improved leadership and language skills
- Increased "prosocial" attitudes toward conflict
- Acquisition of life-long problem-solving techniques
- A ripple effect spills over into the home as parents report students using conflict resolution strategies in handling family disputes.

Conflict resolution provides another option for dealing with today's discipline. It can help solve present problems and prevent future ones. It's one specific way you can start to improve behavior and create a better learning environment in your school.

The next question is, "If students can help students resolve conflicts, can students help each other solve other kinds of problems?" More and more schools are finding that the answer is "Yes!"

GUIDELINES FOR A SUCCESSFUL PEER COUNSELING PROGRAM

Kids love to talk to kids. Students tend to listen to and accept what other kids tell them, often ignoring what parents and teachers have to say. For many students, peers are the most important influence in their lives. These are all good reasons to think about introducing "peer counseling" into your school.

Growing in popularity over the past 2 1/2 decades, peer counseling programs take the Conflict Resolution mode one step further by training and enabling students to help their peers to cope with and resolve on their own a full array of youth issues such as:

- Peer relationships
- Death
- Divorce
- Gangs
- Academic problems
- Pregnancy
- Incest
- Loneliness

- Drugs
- School attendance
- Depression
- Sex
- Running away from home
- Family abuse
- Weight concerns
- Stress

Unlike Conflict Resolution programs, however, peer counseling arrangements are limited to middle, junior high, and high schools.

Obviously, peer counselors cannot serve as therapists or pseudopsychologists. They must be aware of their limitations and know when to refer students who are in danger or need professional help. Nevertheless, they can be an untapped resource for diffusing many individual and group issues that could escalate into major discipline problems.

Simply defined, peer counseling is a multifaceted student assistance program where kids help kids and act as resources to one another. These programs are designed to be preventive by promoting responsible behavior using peers as role models for other students. The students selected as peer counselors are trained to provide aid to age mates and younger children in solving personal, social, family and school problems. In some situations, peer counselors extend their help to nursing home residents, needy adults, and the homeless, as well as present informational programs throughout the community.

The basic role of the peer counselor is to serve as a friend, confidant, tutor, trouble-shooter, advocate (sponsor), ombudsman, and liaison with adults in authority for students with problems.

Most such programs follow objectives and guidelines similar to those promulgated by the Harrisburg (PA) Public Schools:

Guidelines for Peer Counselors
(Harrisburg, PA)

- Develop positive feelings about one's self
- Learn to deal with everyday problems effectively
- Learn to share feelings openly and honestly
- Use academic skills and strengths to help others achieve
- Respect others' right of privacy by maintaining strict confidentiality
- Display a nonjudgmental attitude when listening to others
- Accept differences in feelings and opinions of others
- Demonstrate an understanding of and interest in others
- Avoid giving advice by encouraging others to explore their own alternatives
- Avoid pushing others to respond when they appear unwilling
- Maintaining a "C" average and regular attendance
- Know when to refer students to their own counselor
- Support school policies while working toward the improvement of the school climate

Peer counselors are known by many names across the country, such as Natural Helpers, Peer Tutors, Peer Helpers, Peer Assistance Leaders (PALS), Peer Leaders, Peer Facilitators or Peer Partners. Likewise, peer counseling programs can take many forms, as illustrated below:

Portland, OR

The Portland Peers Project focuses on grades 6–8 and emphasizes problem solving, student empowerment, referrals and drug information. During 1989–90, approximately 400 middle school students received training as peer assistants. Care is taken to draw peer counselors from every strata of the student body.

Setauket, NY

At Ward Melville High School, students selected for the S.H.A.R.P. Program (Students Helping and Reaching Peers) enroll in a full-credit course on leadership and problem solving. Students successfully completing the course may enroll in an advanced class and serve actively as peer counselors in the school.

Glenwood, MD

The Glenwood Middle School program is organized around 5–Teams ("Esteem") through which peers support each others' efforts toward improvement in several areas.

Other variations include matching a peer counselor with each new incoming student, using secondary students as peer tutors/counselors for elementary pupils who are at-risk, and pairing gifted students with special education students to provide new friendships and experiences on a different level.

Whatever the format, the credibility and effectiveness of any program rests squarely on the quality of those selected as peer counselors. Some schools initiate their program by polling the entire student body to identify student leaders who are perceived as "natural helpers" (students who other students seek out to talk about problems and issues). In this way, the nominees represent the natural support system which already exists in the school.

Other commonly used selection procedures include requiring a formal application from perspective peer counselors, which is then reviewed by a staff committee (see the *Peer Counselor Application Form* that follows); limiting selection to a cadre of upper class students; and using veteran peer counselors to select new additions to the program. As in Portland, many schools take care to assure that all ethnic groups and subcultures in the school are represented among the peer counselors selected. In the right circumstances, even gang members and former troublemakers can emerge as effective peer counselors.

Some of the mechanics that have proved helpful in operating a successful peer counseling program include:

1. assigning an adult leader to provide training, support, and follow-up (including debriefings) for peer counselors;
2. providing adequate training in communication, helping skills, coping techniques, and reflective listening;
3. gaining parent permission for students to serve as peer counselors; and
4. making student counselors visible by posting the names or using an identifying badge or logo.

Most schools using some form of peer counseling program report substantial success (although for some unresearched reason girls tend to use peer counselors more frequently than boys do). These programs work for a variety of reasons including those outlined here:

- Peer counseling is spontaneous and nonthreatening.
- Peers are often perceived as being more understanding, accessible, and easy to approach than adult authority figures.

Peer Counselor Application Form

Name:_____ Grade: _____

Address: _____

Phone: _____ Homeroom: _____

I.   Explain why you think the Peer Counseling Program is important to the school.

II. Describe why you want to be a Peer Counselor.

III. Give an example of how you have helped another student solve a problem.

IV. List your grade average: _____

V.   List your extra-curricular activities:

VI. List three teachers who will recommend you.

VII. Do your parents support your desire to become a peer counselor?

_____Yes _____No _____Haven't Discussed

Student Signature: _____

Return this form to your homeroom teacher.

- Peer counseling can provide faster, more efficient, and ongoing support.
- The nature of the program tends to bolster student self-esteem and self-confidence.
- The program can encourage multicultural peer networking.
- Students are often very sensitive and wise in dealing with other students.
- Students feel ownership for the program.

- Peer counseling involves students in their own growth and development.
- Awareness of student issues is heightened throughout the school.
- Leadership opportunities are provided for many students.
- The program enriches the entire climate (culture) of the school.

The power and relevance of peer counseling is, perhaps, best revealed in the following comments from real-life students involved in such programs:

> "…a student came to me because she had done some things at a party and felt bad about it. We talked for several days, then periodically after that."
>
> "…helped someone to keep from beating up their mom."
>
> "…helped my best friend because her parents were going through a divorce and since my parents went through one, I was able to understand."
>
> "…someone I admired as having their life together came to talk to me about stress—it seemed to help her put things in perspective to talk to me."
>
> "…a classmate's chemical use was out of control and I organized an intervention.
>
> "…a girl came to me worried that she had a sexually transmitted disease. I was able to refer her to a clinic for testing."
>
> "…a student was hospitalized for attempted suicide and it seemed like she was all alone in the hospital. Another Natural Helper and I went to visit."
>
> "…a student talked to me about an abusive father and I was able to listen and comfort her."
>
> As one teacher summed up, "These programs aren't to be judged by a win-loss record, but rather by the fact that they are there."

Peer counseling provides a unique way to capitalize on the fact that students not only have problems, but also, often have solutions. Using students to help peers address and resolve problems makes them part of a caring school community, supports an encouraging culture in the school, and builds better discipline. Of course, students can't do it all on their own.

How to Match Students with "Caring Adults"

One of the assets which distinguishes "winners from losers" among students is the presence of a caring adult in their lives. With an increasing number of divided, dysfunctional, and diminished families in our society, this is an asset denied many students. It's hard for little children, or even older ones, to do right when no adult knows or cares. We need to take steps to ensure that this doesn't happen.

There's no excuse for any children going through school without some grown-up knowing a little about what's going on in their lives and taking an interest in them.

Good schools are figuring out systems for matching a caring adult with every student. This can be done through effective mentoring, adult tutoring, advisor-advisee or grandparenting programs (see the sample proposal titled *Male Minority Mentor Proposal*). Some schools simply assign adult staff members with the responsibility for tracking individual students (particularly at-risk students) and paying attention to their progress. The caring adult doesn't always have to be a teacher. Custodians, secretaries, aides and hall monitors can also play the role of adult sponsor.

The important thing is that there is a personal adult presence in the school life of every child. This is an integral part of a culture which drives good discipline.

Schools are more than rooms, books, computers, lessons, and ball games. Schools are human organizations bound together by history, tradition, relationships, dreams, and expectations. These intangible influences constitute the culture of the school, which largely determines how people behave. As a school leader, if you don't pay attention to the culture of the organization at the onset, you'll end up paying a lot of attention to discipline disorders and damage control later on.

Male Minority Mentor Proposal
(Hopkins, MN)

Purpose:

To assist in training and educating minority children in how to be successful and responsible adults; especially targeting young black males of single parent households.

To introduce young minority males to professional, successful, and talented minority men with the goal of inculcating and cultivating positive self-image, discipline, and responsibility.

To assist single parent households...with encouragement, support, and guidance with parenting of minority children.

Implementation:

Families are targeted through school personnel.

Contacts begin as soon as possible in the school year and at an early age in order to have the greatest impact on the student.

A board of directors made up of successful, responsible African-American adults recruit and screen possible mentors.

Suggested Mentor Responsibilities:

Meet with student's counselor and teacher to evaluate the student behavioral and educational needs.

Meet with parent and student and go over the plan.

Attend the first school conference of the year with the parent.

Is available by phone to confer with the student, teacher, parent, and counselor as needed.

Personal contact is made with the student about once a month (social activities).

Lead by example.

How Changing School Programs Can Promote Positive Discipline

When trying to prevent or resolve school discipline problems, most of us look first at changing things like policies, rules, regulations or security measures. Too often, we don't look at the programs we offer as a possible source of discipline difficulty. What we offer and how we offer it has a lot to do with whether or not "kids are buying what we're selling."

In many schools, the program is a big part of the problem. It's hard for students to commit, strive, or behave when faced with programs in which they have little interest or in which they are destined to fail. It is possible, however, to have programs in which all students can succeed.

What it Takes to Have a Curriculum Where All Students Succeed

A good deal of the traditional curriculum and instructional program has been based on the premise that not all kids can learn what we teach in schools. Historically, we have reserved the richest and most challenging learning experiences for some students, while providing others with dull, dead-end programs and a "soft" curriculum. Too often, we've settled for really teaching only certain students and merely babysitting the rest. This isn't good enough any more.

Not too many years ago, it would have been heresy to suggest that students of all ability levels can benefit from being taught higher level thinking skills. Through most of our history in schools, we've saved the "good stuff" only for the best students. Today, this kind of "haves and have nots" approach has backfired and has helped create many of our worst discipline nightmares.

The truth is that all students can learn and succeed. If street kids" are smart enough to learn how to be part of the marketing system in the drug culture, they're smart enough to learn almost anything the school has to teach. Our job is to design, package and deliver programs in which every child wins at the learning game. When this happens, many of today's discipline problems will become things of the past.

A real-world curriculum which can engage and empower all learners focuses on legitimate "customer" needs and concerns, emphasizes the immediate use/application of learning, and provides multiple passages to desired goals. It resembles a road map that shows a variety of divergent routes all leading to a common destination. Students may choose different paths for different reasons. Many will follow the mainstream freeways from where they are to where they want to go; while others may choose to take the "blue highways" which are less traveled and take longer, but end up at the same place. In short, students are viewed as explorers, teachers as guides, and the curriculum as a journey.

The centerpiece for any elementary or secondary school program in which every student wins is an *Outcome-Based Curriculum* driven by *Authentic Assessment.*

A growing number of schools, school systems, and even states are scrapping time-honored requirements for "seat time" and course offerings and replacing them with specific competencies (exit outcomes) which should be mastered by all students. Known by many names (Outcome-Based Education, Objective-Based Environment, Learner Success Model, and so on), these programs are rooted in a new set of beliefs about students and learning as shown below:

Foundations for Successful Learning

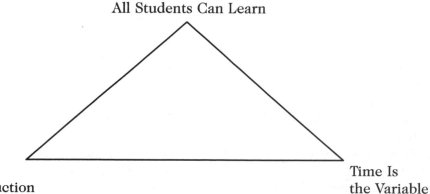

All Students Can Learn

Assessment
Drives Instruction

Time Is
the Variable

In simplest terms, Outcome-Based Education (OBE) is committed to the fact that all students can learn what they need to know given appropriate instruction and adequate time. If students are slow to catch on to essential skills or knowledge, the school doesn't move on without them; rather, they are retaught using different approaches for as long as it takes. All students succeed!

The sequential steps common to most OBE programs include the following:

1. Establish and communicate essential learner outcomes.
2. Measure where each student is in relation to each outcome.
3. Provide relevant instruction including multiple ways for students to learn and to demonstrate learning.
4. Align what is taught and what is tested with stated outcomes.
5. Use continuous assessment to verify progress and determine where to go next with each student.
6. Provide reteaching (correctives) for students who need them.
7. Provide expanded opportunities (enrichment) for students who are ready.
8. Celebrate successes of all students.

Under this approach, the school never gives up on or walks away from any child. (The outcome-based school is a patient school.) When the entire curriculum is thus designed as a success model for all students, there is less failure, less frustration, less anger, and discipline improves.

The anchor of any OBE curriculum is accurate and authentic assessment. Traditionally, teachers have designed tests largely to find out what students don't know and to sort out winners and losers.

Under OBE, the purpose of assessment isn't to penalize, label or sort students. Instead, measurement is used to identify individual student needs, to make decisions about what to do next, and to determine when it's time to move on.

As used in implementing OBE, authentic assessment reaches beyond traditional pencil and paper tests and includes any legitimate means for finding out what students know and can do and for giving them the most favorable opportunity for demonstrating competency. In addition to the customary normed-referenced and criterion-referenced tests, authentic assessment relies on a variety of learning projects and products such as:

- Written/oral reports
- Demonstrations
- Presentations
- Exhibits
- Displays
- Performances
- Dramatizations

- Debates
- Panel discussions
- Art work
- Portfolios
- Original experiments
- "Thinking" journals
- Photo and/or video albums

Using multiple measures of learning progress offers many advantages for both students and teachers:

1. Provides students with options for proving what they know.
2. Plays to students' strengths by allowing them to demonstrate all they know.
3. Emphasizes producing, rather than reproducing knowledge.
4. Showcases the student's best accomplishments, rather than spotlighting weaknesses.
5. Measures progress when the student is ready, not just when the teacher is ready.
6. Accommodates all learning styles.
7. Demonstrates breadth and depth of learning.
8. Measures understanding as well as recall.
9. Emphasizes meaningful practice (rehearsal) over cramming.
10. Allows for collaboration and cooperative learning.
11. Takes the mystery out of tests.
12. Minimizes unfair or unhealthy comparisons.
13. Avoids fear of trick questions.
14. Removes unrealistic, artificial time limits.
15. Fosters an environment in which everyone can pass.

When students are allowed to do "whatever works" to show what they know, assessment is seen as nonthreatening, fair, and sometimes, even as fun.

Implementing Outcome-Based Education grounded in Authentic Assessment is one way to create a curriculum that promotes better learning and discipline. Other features of a modern success-oriented curriculum include the following:

Early Intervention

One of the problems with many school programs is that too many students fail too soon, especially in poor urban areas with high minority populations. In some areas, over one-half of the student population has failed one or more grades by the end of elementary school. Early failure leads to hopelessness, fear, and frustration which spawn a host of behavior problems later on. When little children, usually eager and excited about attending school, fail early-on, there's something wrong with the program. It doesn't have to be that way.

Failure in the early years is preventable. The answer is to "front-load" the program through an early-intervention approach which concentrates the school's best resources, materials, and teaching strategies on the crucial preschool, kindergarten, and primary grades. Where one-on-one tutoring is needed, it is provided by whatever means possible, including volunteers. The goal of every school should be a zero-tolerance curriculum which refuses to permit five- and six-year-olds to fail, especially in reading. Early intervention is a far better investment than remediation in later years.

Numerous programs throughout the country, such as the widely recognized *Success For All* system developed at Johns Hopkins University, have demonstrated the power of early intervention. Success For All schools have spread from the Baltimore area where they were founded to districts in at least 15 states. Other programs, with names such as *Reading Recovery, Kindergarten Plus,* and *Success By Six,* have made significant progress toward assuring that every little child "makes it" in school, no matter what it takes. If every school had a curriculum featuring heavy doses of early intervention, many more students would succeed throughout school and many of our worst discipline problems would virtually disappear.

Resource-Based Instruction

In the modern age of technology, the entire universe can become the classroom. If the school is doing its job today, students can assess information from literally everywhere on and off this planet. This is why successful schools are moving toward Resource-Based Instruction (RBI).

Resource-Based Instruction is simply the use of multiple resources in a variety of formats and technologies to achieve curriculum goals. The focus is on information, not on the package it comes in. This is the antithesis of the traditional textbook-driven curriculum. The underlying premise is that by using all available resources, more can be learned quicker and with better results.

Under RBI, students learn from the same real-world resources that they increasingly encounter in their outside-of-school lives such as:

- Print material
- Video discs
- Interactive TV
- CD ROM Systems

- Teleconferencing
- Satellite Transmissions
- Microfilm/Microfiche
- Hypermedia

One of the most powerful things you can do to engage and excite students about learning and divert energy and attention from negative behavior is to build your curriculum around Resource-Based Instruction.

Multicultural, Gender-fair Content

If the school program is prejudiced, students spot it, resent it, and reject it in a hurry. Pluralism within the student body requires a curriculum that is multicultural, gender-fair and bias-free. Today's students expect and deserve to learn fully and fairly about their respective cultural heritages and about real-world role models with whom they can relate. Some schools have tried to compromise this issue by merely eliminating negative references to certain minority groups. That's not enough.

Likewise, tokenism falls short of the mark. Commemorating special events such as Women's History Month once a year or honoring the legacy of Martin Luther King on one special day isn't enough. What it takes to reach all students is across-the-board integration of multicultural, bias-free content and materials throughout the curriculum.

No school can get by telling only one side of the story anymore. All cultures must be represented and respected across the curriculum. The experience and contributions of all groups and both sexes must be acknowledged and documented. When this happens, all groups are validated and all students can find something to be proud about and to strive for.

The future of our society depends upon intercultural respect and cross-cultural cooperation. It should start in school. A multicultural gender-fair curriculum is a good beginning which can lay a foundation for harmonious relationships within the school and beyond.

Zero-Tracking

The long-standing practice of pigeon-holing students into different lock-step tracks of learning doesn't fit today's schools. Siphoning off groups of learners for a low-grade curriculum stigmatizes some students, stifles learning, and generates rebellious behavior. Many leading schools are now abandoning tracking based on a growing body of research which shows that all students learn well together when tackling the same curriculum. If the curriculum is viewed as a journey, everyone should have equal access, be allowed to progress at their own speed, and be permitted to change lanes when it suits their purpose.

Japanese schools, touted for their excellence, have traditionally offered a single curriculum for all students. If some pupils take longer or have to work harder, at least they still have a crack at the best the school has to offer. This is one lesson we should learn from eastern education.

Where trouble exists, the curriculum may be part of the problem. Changing it as outlined above can help turn a deteriorating discipline situation around by increasing the odds for the success of all students. Of course, the curriculum isn't the only program in the school that may need to be changed to foster effective learning and better behavior.

HOW TO PERSONALIZE EDUCATION THROUGH SCHOOLS-WITHIN-A-SCHOOL

Size is not the friend of good discipline. For many years, school planners have believed that bigger is better. Large elementary schools are cost-effective, permit greater flexibility in scheduling and assigning students, and provide more opportunities for parent choice of teachers. Likewise, mega-secondary schools make possible a much broader range of course offerings. Unfortunately, big schools also promote anonymity, isolation, and depersonalization which can contribute to negative attitudes and antisocial behavior. Students in large schools lose the sense of "family," connectedness, and belonging found in smaller ones. As a result, many schools today are seeking to achieve the best of both worlds by building their programs around the concept of schools-within-a-school.

For at least four decades, lighthouse schools such as Evanston Township (IL) High School, Newton (MA) High School and Topeka (KS) West High School have operated on a "house-plan" of organization. Now, more and more elementary, middle, junior high, and senior high schools across the country are adopting the schools-within-a-school format.

Proponents of the "little school" organization explain the concept in many ways:

- Subdividing a large student body into smaller groups for purposes of instruction and guidance;
- Creating families, clusters, or neighborhoods of students who work with a stable team of teachers over an extended period of time;
- Subdividing a large institution into units comprehensible to the student;
- Forming little schools within a larger one.

Whatever the description, the purpose is to break up big schools into smaller units in order to personalize the learning experience for every child.

Advantages of the schools-within-a-school organization include the following:

1. Students can no longer hide behind a mask of anonymity.
2. Every student is "known" by the teachers with whom he/she works.
3. There are greater opportunities for all students to participate.
4. Instruction can become more individualized.

5. Students have easier access to teachers.

6. The school can take on a feeling of intimacy.

7. Closer relationships develop between students and faculty (people really know each other).

8. All students can feel they belong.

9. The individual identity of each pupil is preserved and individual differences can be accommodated.

10. The school loses its "assembly-line" feeling.

11. Staff members can focus on the worth of the individual.

12. Every student can feel like they are a part of the school.

All of these pluses are vividly conveyed by students at the new Champlin Park High School in Brooklyn Park, MN, who describe their school-within-a-school as "our territory," "someplace we can call our own," and even "warm, cozy place to learn." Champlin Park is divided into three "houses." Each house has its own office, team of teachers, classrooms, and assistant principal. Students work with the same teachers for 2–3 years.

This same learning format can be applied to elementary or middle schools by forming multiage groups (MAG programs) within the larger school which stay together and learn together with the same teachers for more than one year.

As school size increases, the capacity to relate to individual students diminishes proportionately. In large schools, the only way for some students to be recognized or attract attention is to get into trouble. The need to act out frustration is reduced under a schools-within-a-school organization which provides a personal education for every student. This is another way you can enhance learning and improve discipline in your school.

Earmarks of Successful Alternative Programs

No matter how much the curriculum and/or the school organization are changed, there are certain students (mostly at the secondary level) who can't make it. They aren't stupid and they're not outlaws. For these kids, the trauma of adolescence or other forces in their lives makes it difficult for them to cope with the structures and expectations of the regular school program. As long as these students are required to remain in the mainstream, the school will be a problem for them and they will be a problem for the school.

Too often, schools focus on forcing every student to fit into the established program, rather than creating programs which fit all students. Education isn't a one-size-fits-all proposition. Instead of trying to hammer round kids into square holes, why not make more holes for all shapes of learners? In today's schools, some form of alternative program is needed to assure success for all students.

Alternative programs, schools or minischools, originated in urban areas and were initially aimed at drop-outs. Now such programs serve thousands of students and are found in or associated with leading schools in all corners of the country. In Minnesota alone, over 15,000 pupils attend some kind of public or private alternative program each year. For many, it is the only means of staying out of trouble and staying in school.

Whether housed on-site or at a separate location, the goals of most alternative programs are threefold:

1. To provide an alternative choice to the "system;"
2. To offer a different path to graduation;
3. To facilitate the transition to adulthood.

Students served by alternative programs represent all classes and ability levels. Many have had problems with drugs or abuse. Some are pregnant, homeless, or living on their own. Others have failed, dropped out, or been expelled. Still others have simply fallen behind or are "burned out" in regular education. What they have in common is that they are struggling with the mainstream program, feel out of place, unhappy, and hopeless in the regular classroom and they're probably not going to make it without some kind of fresh start. For these students, an alternative program offers a much-needed second chance.

Although alternative programs assume a variety of formats, the most successful ones share certain key components such as:

- Programs designed around learner outcomes (OBE). Usually these outcomes are the same as those required in the regular curriculum.
- Personalized instruction.
- Expectations that all students can and will succeed.
- Interdisciplinary content.
- User-friendly entry and exit procedures, including opportunities for self-referral.
- Small classes.
- Close linkage with all of the support services of the school.
- Diagnostic evaluation of individual students.
- Expanded opportunities to work in small groups.
- Special atmosphere of trust and respect.
- Variations in the length of the student day from part-time to full-time.

- Customized packages of learning services.
- Regular feed-back to each student.
- Emphasis on self-evaluation.
- Team teaching.
- Informality in the classroom (first-name relationships).
- Reliance on learning projects and products to demonstrate competence.
- Available day care.
- A work-study component.
- A well-defined space (often an off-site location is desirable because many students associate bad experiences, trouble, and failure with the regular school facilities).
- Modified attendance policies.
- Increased site-based decision making.
- Opportunity to receive a regular diploma from the home school. (Being able to graduate with "their class" is a sensitive and emotional issue for many students in alternative programs.)
- Teachers willing to "be there" for students to listen and assist with all kinds of problems.

Where alternative programs with these features exist, graduation rates go up and discipline problems decrease. Many administrators argue that regular education would benefit by incorporating these same elements into the mainstream program.

Advisor-Advisee Programs Revisited and Revitalized

The positive influence on discipline demonstrated by the personalized atmospheres of schools-within-a-school and alternative schools has caused many school officials to revisit once-popular homeroom and advisor-advisee programs. Until recently, such programs had been widely abandoned because, without proper planning, they frequently deteriorated into wasted periods of downtime used only for paper-shuffling, announcements, and administrivia.

The rebirth of the advisor-advisee movement represents a revitalized effort to make school programs more intimate and less institutional. Second generation advisor-advisee programs emphasize closer long-term relationships between students and adults in order to make the educational experience up close and personal for all learners.

The most successful "reborn" homeroom/advisor-advisee approaches feature: (a) small groups of students (15–20); (b) relating to the same adult (teacher, coun-

---

Role of Advisors
(sample)

1. To monitor each advisee's academic, extracurricular and social progress throughout the duration of the program.
2. To build a relationship of trust, confidentiality, support, and open communication with each advisee.
3. To foster trust, friendship and team building within the advisee group.
4. To serve as a liaison and ombudsman for each advisee with the rest of the school staff.
5. To foster and facilitate formal and informal communication between parents and the school, including conducting parent-teacher conferences.
6. To "signal" appropriate school personnel of any problems-in-the-making affecting any advisee.
7. To assist students in solving school-related problems, including mediation of conflicts between students.
8. To follow the prescribed "curriculum" of advisor-advisee learning activities.
9. To recognize every advisee's successes (large and small).
10. To maintain a portfolio record of each advisee's progress and experience in school.

---

selor, administrator, paraprofessional, aide, secretary, custodian); (c) meeting on a daily basis (15–25 minutes); (d) implemented over a 2–4 year period; (e) working with a well-planned program of experiential activities; (f) emphasizing social development, self-esteem building, study skills enhancement, and fun.

Many schools now favor advisor-advisee units that are cross-graded and selected randomly. Whatever the make-up of the group, advisors attempt to create a supportive, personal, and positive relationship with each student (see *Role of Advisors*, which follows).

While earlier homeroom-type programs often lacked direction and left responsible adults pretty much on their own, today's updated versions focus on specifically defined goals such as those outlined below:

Goals of a Successful Advisor-Advisee Program

- Establish a home-base for every student.

- Provide a safe and supportive environment designed to bolster students' sense of belonging.
- Develop a meaningful, long-term personal relationship between each student and one caring adult.
- Serve as a vehicle for helping students engage in self-evaluation, set goals, learn problem-solving techniques, build lasting relationships with other students, and develop values of respect for others.
- Find ways to help every child experience recognition and success in school.
- Serve as the first-line of communication between the home and the school.

The greatest difference between old-style and modern advisor-advisee programs is the existence of a well-developed, systematic plan (curriculum) of themes and activities to be followed in achieving the intended outcomes. Where such programs really work, every advisor is supported by a comprehensive, step-by-step handbook containing materials, ideas, suggestions, techniques, and activities (see examples that follow).

Successful advisor-advisee programs are activity-oriented in order to engage student interest and participation. Types of activities commonly used include the following:

- Get-acquainted Activities
- Contests
- Sing-a-longs
- School Improvement Projects
- Aerobics
- Charades
- Community Service
- Pantomimes
- Cartoon Days
- Group Games
- Pen Pal Projects
- Tournaments
- Trivial Pursuit
- Trust-building Activities
- Scavenger Hunts
- Room Decorating
- Mural Making or Graffiti Wall
- Book Sharing
- Magic Tricks
- Puzzles
- Resource Speakers
- Hobby Sharing

To maintain relevance and vitality, activities should be evaluated and updated continuously (see *Sample Evaluation Form*). The goal is to keep the program meaningful, alive and fun for all students.

Changing your program to include a vibrant advisor-advisee component can give you one more tool for humanizing the school promoting student success, and heading off discipline problems.

Themes for the School Year
(Sandburg Middle School, Anoka, MN)

SEPTEMBER	Getting Acquainted
	National Hispanic Month
OCTOBER	Handicapped Awareness
	Stereotypes
NOVEMBER	Drug Awareness
	Citizenship
DECEMBER	Ethnic Month
	Respect, Responsibility, and Manners
JANUARY	Folk Tales and Storytellers
FEBRUARY	Afro-American Month
	Wellness
MARCH	Women's History Month
APRIL	Asian-Pacific American Month
	Conflict Resolution
MAY	Native American Month
	Decision Making
JUNE	Closure

Taking the School to Students Who Won't Come to School

Despite everyone's best efforts, there are always a few students who can't or won't come to school, even an alternative school. In extreme cases, it may be better that they don't. Years of failure, broken dreams, and run-ins with school discipline policies make the chances for success extremely remote. Too much negative history stands in the way.

Rather than expending enormous efforts to run-down chronic absentees, and engaging in protracted truancy hearings only to return the students to face further failure and cause more trouble for themselves and for the school, it may be better to take the school to the students. Sometimes, the best interests of both the student and the school are served by providing instruction on neutral turf. If it proves to be a win-win situation, that's what education is all about. A few schools are exploring ways to export educational programs to wherever the hard-to-reach students are. Some of the most promising approaches include the following:

Guidelines for the Week
(Sandburg Middle School, Anoka, MN)

MONDAY

Leisure Reading: All students must spend the period reading. The atmosphere should be one of absolute quiet. Students should be reading for their enjoyment. Do not allow them to read textbooks or assignments, except for novels. Each child is responsible for coming to A2 with a book in hand. During the time, the advisor should "model" silent reading.

TUESDAY/WEDNESDAY

Activity Days: Group activities will be conducted according to lessons in the manual. Students will not be allowed to leave the group. Advisors may use or adapt these activities for their group.

THURSDAY

Study/Individual Conferencing: Students use this time for quiet study or reading. Students are responsible for coming to A2 with all the materials they will need for the time. Advisors will use the time to conduct individual student contacts.

FRIDAY

STAR Day (Student-Teacher ARranged): Teachers and/or students choose the activity for the day.

BIRTHDAY TREATS

Once per month advisors will need to pick up enough birthday treat coupons (for special cake) for those students having a birthday in that month . . . Please note that September and May include summer months.

Learner-centered Education Centers

Using federal and state literacy funds, coupled with community education dollars, a few districts have established decentralized education centers. Typically, these centers offer learning opportunities for adults and other students who have not graduated from high school, including fifth year seniors, immigrants, and refugees.

Programs usually include survival skills, G.E.D. preparation, credit courses for an adult diploma, English-as-a-Second Language (ESL), and adult brush-up courses. Instruction is self-paced and learner-centered, rather than teacher-directed. Students work independently or with teachers and trained tutors. Sometimes,

---

Sample Evaluation Form
Sandburg Middle School, Anoka, MN

JUST WANTED YOU TO KNOW THAT . . .

*Activity Name:*_____

    Worked Well_____

    Needs Improvement _____

    Bombed_____

Reasons:

    Too long _____

    Too short _____

    Materials not appropriate _____

    Too mature_____

    Too childish _____

    Other_____

Recommendations:

If the activity did not work well, how would you like to see it changed?

Comments:

Name _____

Date _____

---

transportation and day care are available and both daytime and evening courses are offered.

Neighborhood Centers

In some of the nation's most crime-ridden areas where truancy and dropping out of school are the norm, some success has been achieved by creating neighborhood after-school centers. The goal is to save as many students as possible and eventually get them back into regular school.

    One of the best examples is the Petworth Neighborhood Center in Washington, D. C. The mission of the center is to "hold out hope" for kids on the street. Through the use of support groups and older children serving as role models, these centers strive to keep learning alive in even the most disadvantageous circumstances.

Mall of America School

In Minnesota, five urban and suburban districts have joined forces to try to bring the school to the nation's largest shopping mall. With the support of private funding and business partnerships, they hope to provide preschool and regular elementary programs for the children of employees at the mall, as well as work-study and transitional programs for secondary-age students who work full time.

Outreach Programs for Homeless Students

For the nation's over 700,000 homeless school-age children, getting to any school is incredibly difficult. Across the country, a number of shelters and transitional housing programs are beginning to provide on-site educational, tutoring, and guidance services for both children and their parents. These efforts are noteworthy first steps toward reclaiming the thousands of throw-away kids of our society.

Homebound Instruction for Chronic Absentees

Once reserved for pupils with an illness, injury, or disability, a growing number of schools are using one-on-one homebound instruction as a last ditch effort to reach and teach students who refuse to come to school and/or can't function in any school setting.

Many traditional educators reject these efforts to bring the school to hard-to-reach students. They still believe that education is a privilege and students who don't or won't conform to historic standards should lose their entitlement. More and more school leaders, however, are convinced that education is a necessity and schools must do whatever it takes to help all children succeed.

SUCCESS SECRETS FOR EFFECTIVE AFTER-SCHOOL PROGRAMS

Efforts to change school programs to boost student success and foster positive behavior shouldn't be limited to the regular school day. What the school has to offer before and after the normal day of instruction may be more important for some students than the regular curriculum itself. Some students find a "home" at school only after school.

Extracurricular activities have always been a powerful and positive force in the lives of some students. Unfortunately, however, such programs have often failed to reach many troubled, troubling, and at-risk kids. The time has come to revamp before and after-school programs in order to reach more students starting as early as the elementary years. Schools with the best activity programs have the best discipline.

In simpler times, students not involved in extracurricular activities went home after school where mothers or sitters provided a snack and supervised their homework, TV viewing, or play in the neighborhood. Today, such students often merely spill out into the streets, congregate at malls or arcades or spend hours at home unattended. The best thing schools can do for these students is to provide a well-rounded program of meaningful after-school activities for all ages that engages their interests, develops their potential, expands their horizons, and offers opportunities for success and recognition.

In today's "home alone" society, good schools don't open in the morning and lock up at midafternoon. Instead, they "are there" for the students whenever the students need them, day or night. Where communities provide a robust program of before and after-school activities, students take greater pride and ownership in the school and are less inclined to be disruptive or disobedient.

The trouble with many traditional activity programs is that they:

- Start too late in the student's school life;
- Cost too much;
- Reach primarily the "good kids" (eligibility requirements rule out many marginal students);
- Are limited almost exclusively to athletics;
- Are set up as just another place for many kids to fail (students who are cut from the squad or never get to play may be hurt more than they are helped by the activity program);
- Don't offer much for the students who need them most (too many programs miss some populations of students who do not feel involved, connected or a part of the school, including girls, minorities, at-risk students, ESL students, and special education students).

The best before- and after-school programs are user-friendly and offer something for every segment of the student body. Earmarks of a quality activity program include the following:

- *Covers all age groups starting in the elementary grades.* (See *Sample List of Elementary and Secondary Activities.*)
- *Are low cost and open to all students.* (Fees should be waived when necessary.)
- *Based on a well-defined Mission Statement and outcome-based goals just like the regular curriculum.* (See *Sample Mission, "Givens," and Goals.*)

- *Offers balance and diversity;* students need more than a choice between sports and detention after school. Diverse student populations require diverse outlets. Whatever is good for kids is a potential activity.

- *Are student-centered and student-driven.* Activities shouldn't be designed primarily as entertainment for adults.

- *Are flexible, fluid, and changed easily.* It shouldn't be difficult for students to suggest or initiate new activities.

- *Are widely publicized.* Some schools hold an Activity Fair at the beginning of school to inform all students about activity opportunities.

- *Stresses gender equity.* There needs to be a balance between activities for girls and boys. Activities for boys shouldn't receive a malproportion of funding, publicity or glory.

- *Undergoes continuous evaluation.* (See *Sample Activity Survey Form.*)

- *Has someone in charge.* Most large high schools have an Athletic Director; but how many have an Activities Director? Someone needs to be assigned responsibility for nurturing and coordinating the total activity program in order to meet the needs of all students. (See *Sample Activity Director Job Description*)

- *Respects all cultures.* (For instance, schools that schedule Friday contests only may be excluding Jewish students from participation.)

- *Experiments with nontraditional programs.* In some schools, the annual Battle of the Bands is one of the year's most popular events.

- *Provides recognition for participation in all activities.* Awards shouldn't be limited to athletics. Letters, banquets, and trophies should be associated with academic and artistic activities as well. Some schools even sponsor a *Caring Youth Recognition* program to honor students who render volunteer service in the community.

- *Emphasizes broad participation and success for all.* Some of the best athletic programs feature "no cut" and "everyone plays" policies. Too often, the "stars" get the most attention and need it the least.

- *Involves competent and motivated adult advisors.* Usually, programs work best when coaches and advisors are part of the regular staff accessible to students throughout the school day. Activity advisors should be as carefully selected and fully supported as coaches. (See *Sample Expectations for Advisors.*)

- *Stresses learning and having fun over winning.*

- *Features a flexible and humane eligibility policy.* Participation requirements should permit a "second chance" for kids who are bouncing back and putting their lives back together. (See *Sample Eligibility Policy.*)

- *Provides a system of due process for students and parents* with complaints or who feel unjustly treated.

Sample List of Elementary and Secondary Activities

Elementary

Before School:
Math Tutoring
Reading Tutoring
Private Piano Lessons

Released Days:
Equestrian Camp
Martial Arts Day
Rock Climbing
Open Roller Skating

Saturday Classes:
Radio/Electronics
Model Building
Clown Club
In-Line Dancing
Beginning Acting

After School:
Swim School
Cricket Gymnastics
Foreign Languages
Drama Club
Computer Fun
Baby-sitting Training
Children's Choir
Sketchbook Drawing
Jazz Dance
Instrument Lessons
Karate
Beginning Wrestling
Group Piano
Keyboarding
Fencing Club
Chess Club

Secondary

Athletics:
Cross-country Running
Football
Soccer
Swimming
Diving
Tennis
Volleyball
Basketball
Hockey
Slalom Skiing
Cross-country Skiing
Gymnastics
Baseball
Golf
Track and Field
Softball
Synchronized Swimming
Cheerleading
Dance Line

Nonathletic Activities:
Students for Drug Awareness
Band/Orchestra
Chess Club
Chorus
Debate
Drama
Earth Club
Publications
International Club
Intramurals
SADD
Math Team
Mock Trial
Odyssey of the Mind
Natural Helpers
Save Our Planet
Science Challenge Team
Radio D.J.s
Video Yearbook

Sample Mission, "Givens," and Goals
of the Student Activity Program

Mission Statement

To develop healthy personal relationships, appreciate leisure activities, and enjoy personal accomplishment and self worth.

"Givens"	Goals
Student activities should be voluntary.	Develop interests and provide alternative uses of discretionary time.
The activity program is a vital part of the school and has positive value for many students.	Promote a positive attitude toward self and others.
	Develop leadership.
There are different levels of motivation and students are motivated in different ways.	Develop healthy interpersonal relationships.
Students are motivated by both competition and cooperation.	Develop commitment.
The activity program does not and, probably, never will reach 100% of the student population.	Provide opportunities for socializing and making new friends.
	Have fun.
	Experience success.
	Stimulate student involvement in the school.

Sample Activity Survey

1. Have you participated in school activities?
    Yes
   _____ No

2. If not, why haven't you been involved?
   _____a.) Outside activities.
   _____b.) Job.
   _____c.) I don't like the activities offered.
   _____d.) My friends aren't involved.
   _____e.) Other.

3. If you are involved in activities outside of school, are they:
   _____a.) Job.
   _____b.) Church-related.
   _____c.) Volunteer work.
   _____d.) City recreation programs.
   _____e.) Other.

4. If you work, how many hours per week do you work?
   _____a.) 10
   _____b.) 20
   _____c.) 30
   _____d.) 40

5. Were you aware of all activities offered by the school?
   _____ Yes
   _____ No

6. If so, how did you find out about the activities?
   _____a.) Friends.
   _____b.) Involved previously.
   _____c.) Orientation Program.
   _____d.) Announcements.
   _____e.) Other.

7. Would you have joined if a friend asked you?
   _____ Yes
   _____ No

8. Would you have joined if an advisor actively recruited you?
   _____ Yes
   _____ No

9. Would you have joined if the activities weren't so competitive?

   _____ Yes

   _____ No

10. If you've been involved, in how many activities did you participate?

    _____a.) 1

    _____b.) 2

    _____c.) 3

    _____d.) 4

    _____e.) More than 4

11. What was your primary reason for joining an activity?

    _____a.) Friends were involved.

    _____b.) Liked the advisor.

    _____c.) Like the activity.

    _____d.) I'm good at the activity.

    _____e.) For my resume (college application).

    _____f.) N.A. (not applicable).

12. Did your involvement in the activity increase your enjoyment of it?

    _____ Yes

    _____ No

13. Was the activity:

    _____a.) Too competitive.

    _____b.) Not competitive enough.

    _____c.) Just right.

    _____d.) Wasn't a competitive activity.

    _____e.) N.A.

14. Did the activity help you feel good about yourself?

    _____ Yes

    _____ No

15. Did you develop leadership because of your involvement?

    _____ Yes

    _____ No

16. Did you make new friends in the activity?

    _____ Yes

    _____ No

17. Did you have success in the activity?

_____ Yes

_____ No

18. Did you have fun in the activity?

_____ Yes

_____ No

19. Were you treated fairly by the advisors?

_____ Yes

_____ No

20. Were you ever in an activity and dropped out before it was over?

_____ Yes

_____ No

21. If so, why did you drop the activity?

_____a.) Too time consuming.

_____b.) Too competitive.

_____c.) Problems with advisor.

_____d.) My friends left the activity.

_____e.) It wasn't fun anymore.

_____f.) N.A.

22. Were you ever in an activity one year, but did not participate the next year?

_____ Yes

_____ No

23. If so, why didn't you continue in the activity?

_____a.) Too competitive.

_____b.) Didn't like it that much.

_____c.) Didn't like advisor.

_____d.) Didn't think I could make the team.

_____e.) N.A.

24. Did your involvement in an activity ever cause you to think less of yourself?

_____ Yes

_____ No

25. What suggestions do you have for improving the school's activity program?

Sample Activity Director Job Description

Position:

Activity Director

Responsible to:

Principal

Duties/Responsibilities:

1. Provide vision, leadership, and coordination of the student activity program.
2. Assist in recruiting, selecting and evaluating qualified activity advisors.
3. Evaluate the overall activity program and recommend changes as needed.
4. Promote and provide staff development programs for activity advisors.
5. Assist in developing and allocating the school's activity program budget.
6. Assist in scheduling school activities.
7. Publicize school-sponsored activities.
8. Serve as spokesperson for the activity program throughout the community.
9. Process complaints regarding student activities.
10. Keep the principal informed of all matters related to the student activity program.

Sample Expectations for Activity Advisors

To implement the goals of the Student Activity Program, the following standards and expectations have been established for all advisors:

- Enthusiasm for the activity is expected of all advisors.
- Appropriate discipline is the responsibility of all advisors.
- Advisors should continually seek self-improvement.
- Sound principles of teaching and learning should be used in advising all activities.
- Advisors should be fair and unprejudiced with all activity participants.
- Students have a right to expect advisors to have genuine interest in and an up-to-date knowledge of the specific activity involved.
- The safety and welfare of all participants should be uppermost in the advisor's mind.
- The advisor's primary responsibility is to each individual student participant.
- The advisor's actions and statements should always reflect respect for the school.
- The advisor has a responsibility to promote the specific activity throughout the school and community as appropriate.
- Each advisor is responsible for protecting and maintaining the physical plant of the school.

Sample Eligibility Policy

Students must be making satisfactory progress toward graduation to participate in activities.

Students must also have passed all but one class the previous quarter. Students receiving more than one failing course grade will be placed on academic probation and their work will be monitored by the appropriate supervisor. If a pattern of poor performance continues, they may be declared ineligible. While on probation, students may continue to participate as long as they have good attendance, assignments completed, and satisfactory performance on tests.

Students who fall below the requirements above, but who are making significant progress in performance and accountability may seek provisional eligibility from a 3-member review panel comprised of the principal (or designee), the advisor, and a counselor.

In redesigning before- and after-school programs, you should keep in mind that not all activities have to be "fun and games." The school can also use this time to provide students with much-needed individual tutorial attention and assistance with academic problems. Many elementary and secondary schools are replacing traditional "detention" sessions with voluntary "3rd Base" (the place to go before you go home) or "ASK" (After School Kids) programs which offer help with homework, reteaching opportunities, and supervised quiet study and catch-up time.

For many students, the activity program is a "second curriculum." It may be the one place where they find their niche and experience success. When students gain a sense of accomplishment and belonging through one or more activities, they feel better about themselves and about the school and they're less likely to be involved in discipline problems.

TEN WAYS TO USE TECHNOLOGY TO TURN STUDENTS ON

If you could make only one change to infuse excitement into your school's programs, turn kids on to learning and turn off bad behavior, that change should be to adopt as much state-of-the-art technology as possible. Today's kids are computer literate and technologically savvy. They love it, learn it, and learn from it quickly and readily.

If your programs don't include up-to-date technology, you're out of step with your students and they're not going to buy what you're selling. Using the latest technological tools to enhance instruction will go a long way to energize learning and exorcise discipline problems.

The following are ten specific examples of the many ways schools can use contemporary technology to get students excited about what the school has to offer. (Each of these practices is currently in use in one or more places across the country.):

1. Provide a conference telephone for student use in interviewing and communicating with a variety of resources within the community and beyond.

2. Develop a school-operated FM radio station to serve as an awareness and training station for students interested in broadcasting.

3. Establish remote communication with a local senator or representative using interactive TV and cellular telephone contact to allow students to follow a favorite bill through the legislative process first-hand.

4. Arrange for students to access the Internet worldwide database network. (The federally subsidized Internet collection of computer networks already has an estimated 15 million users in 40 different countries.)

5. Use a "virtual reality" physics laboratory with specially designed helmets ("eyephones") to enable students to test the effect of gravity on a bouncing ball.

6. Make lap-top computers available for student and/or family checkout and use.

7. Equip student homes with Community Link terminals that allow students (and parents) to access school information (homework assignments, attendance records, activity schedules, lunch menus), use an on-line computer encyclopedia for research projects, or "chat" one-on-one with users across the nation. (Originating in France, such programs are now being introduced in schools in California and Minnesota.)

8. Open up computer labs and media centers for student and community use during after-school and evening hours.

9. Develop cooperative programs with other schools throughout the world using computer networks and fax exchanges.

10. Use camcorder TV documentaries as an alternative to traditional term papers or research reports.

Integrating cutting-edge technology into curriculum and instruction brings the school's programs into the real world for students. The result is more enthusiasm for learning, more success for more students, and better discipline.

Some schools become their own worst enemies by perpetuating outdated programs and activities that are detrimental to both learning and student behavior. Good programs don't guarantee positive discipline but bad programs almost certainly lead to boredom, rebellion, and negative student conduct.

Assistant Principals Can't Do It All Anymore—Staffing for Effective Discipline

Rules don't create positive discipline. People do. Visible adult presence and active staff engagement with students at all times is the key to orderly, businesslike behavior. With more kids and more problems in schools, it takes more hands than ever before to maintain a disciplined climate where effective learning can occur.

In past years, many schools vested the primary responsibility for schoolwide discipline in a single position—the dreaded Assistant Principal. (There was a certain irony in the commonly used title, "Vice" Principal.) The job was too much for one person to handle then, and it is even more so now. In today's schools, discipline is everybody's job.

What It Takes to Get the Job Done Today

Good discipline cannot be achieved in any school until all staff members (licensed and classified) accept it as part of their personal responsibility. Teachers can no longer enjoy the luxury of leaving the discipline outside their classroom to the administration. Each teacher's span of responsibility extends to all students in the school. Likewise, custodians, secretaries, aides, and cooks must do their bit for better discipline.

Looking the other way is no longer acceptable. Walking away from trouble is an act of professional cowardice. Assuring student safety and civility throughout the school is every adult's business. Positive discipline requires a unified team effort involving everyone on the payroll.

What it takes today are teachers and staff members standing in the halls between classes, eating with students in the cafeteria, taking their turn on the playground, showing up at extracurricular activities, and being visible wherever students congregate before and after school. Teaching is no longer just about helping students learn in the classroom. It's also about showing you care and dare enough to teach kids how to behave wherever and whenever you encounter them in the school. Staff members don't have to become humorless prison guards, but they do have to uniformly insist on responsible behavior by all students all day every day.

In addition to making discipline part of everyone's job description, leading schools are finding creative ways to reallocate human resources in order to assign specialized personnel to deal with special types of discipline problems. It's not uncommon for modern elementary and secondary school staffs to include a variety of specialized discipline-related positions such as the following:

- Police liaison officers
- Hall and security monitors
- Discipline aides
- Social workers
- Management aides
- Teacher-deans

Not every school needs to have all of these positions, but it's certainly going to take more than an Assistant Principal to get the job done today. It's your responsibility, as school leader, to figure out what positions will work best in your environment and to find the right person for each job. The following sections describe the specific roles which can be played by different types of specialized discipline personnel.

HOW TO MAKE EFFECTIVE USE OF POLICE LIAISON OFFICERS

Many people, including educators, are resistant and reluctant to accept the idea of having a full-time police presence at school. They feel it validates threats and dangers they would rather deny, and fear the creation or perception of a police state in the school.

Practice has proved the fears unfounded. A growing number of urban and suburban schools have initiated police liaison programs and, almost universally, report success and satisfaction with them.

In actuality, integrating a professional police officer into the school team enhances everyone's sense of safety and security, expedites the reporting and investigation of crimes by and against students, and promotes better understanding between the student body and law officials.

A large school is like any other community. The presence of on-site police protection makes sense. Students in school deserve the same level of service and protection that their parents demand in the community at large.

Police liaison programs work best where school and law enforcement officials agree in advance upon a common philosophy (see example) and follow the simple guidelines below:

1. A full-time patrol officer is assigned to the school during the student school year.

2. Cost of the program is shared between the school and the local police department.

3. Officers are carefully selected and assigned on a rotating basis, with no officer serving more than three consecutive years.

4. Liaison officers work in plain clothes.

5. If possible, minority officers are assigned where the school has a significant minority population.

The roles and responsibilities of a Police Liaison Officer can be many and varied as illustrated in the list of functions that follow:

Police Liaison Officer Functions

- To serve as a resource to teachers and administrators in the prevention and diversion of juvenile delinquency behavior.

- To consult with the school staff in maintaining maximum safety.

- To work with the Juvenile Court System and other agencies concerned with juvenile crime prevention and control.

- To make public appearances and give information, assistance and guidance to the PTA, service clubs, church groups, and so forth.

- To assist the school in large crowd control situations.

- To investigate incidents involving juveniles such as trespassing, theft, vandalism, truancy, weapons violations, and illegal drug use.

- To provide safety lectures and other classroom presentations when appropriate.

- To advise the school on matters of security and policy.

Police-School Liaison Program Philosophy
(example)

Responsibility for law enforcement involves the interaction by law enforcement officers and juveniles. Too often the very nature of police contacts with young people lead to misunderstanding and mutual animosity between the juvenile and the law officer. The School Liaison Officer Program is designed to foster contact between the officer and students in both a structured experience and various informal interaction settings. It is anticipated that the program will be instrumental in improving understanding between the Police Department and the juvenile clientele of the community.

The schools and the police share a mutual responsibility for the welfare of our youth. The shared responsibility makes delinquency prevention and treatment a joint objective. Thus, it is important that both schools and the law enforcement community work together in the best interest of our youth even though the education and social development remain the primary duty of the school, while delinquency identification and control continues to be the major concern of the police.

The School Liaison Officer will be available to advise, assist, and counsel the school staff in matters relating to delinquency prevention and other areas of mutual concern to both police and the school system.

- To assist with the supervision of field trips, extracurricular events, and so on.
- To participate in case conferences involving students with a history of violations.
- To maintain high-profile visibility throughout the school as an example and deterrent to crime.
- To help organize safety and anticrime campaigns and programs in the school.
- To serve as the first call for help in reporting incidents of child abuse, sexual harassment, or other illegal acts, and to make referrals as appropriate.
- To improve communication, trust, and rapport between students, school officials, and the police department.
- To create respect and understanding for law and the role of law enforcement by bringing together police, school, and student representatives in a positive climate.

- To develop early identification of delinquent and predelinquent behavior and facilitate early intervention and referral.
- To be available to counsel students and parents regarding law violations.
- To make primary and follow-up investigations of students at the request of school administrators.
- To keep the school administration informed concerning police apprehension of students during and outside of school.

Police liaison officers can bring different expertise and a new perspective to the school team and can help cut red tape in the process. Both the school and the police department reap benefits from a closer relationship.

The presence of a police officer in the school is not an ominous threat to the school's culture. In many cases, it's just what it takes to help everyone breathe a sigh of relief, feel better and safer, and work more harmoniously together to keep discipline on track.

DEFINING THE ROLE OF SECURITY MONITORS

In addition to (or in lieu of) Police Liaison Officers, many schools are adding nonlicensed Security Monitors to their discipline staff. Known by many different titles, including *Hall Monitor, Security Aide* and *Discipline Aide*, these low-cost personnel (usually hourly employees with no fringe benefits) can serve as extensions of the professional staff in enforcing discipline throughout the school. Sometimes, college students majoring in criminology or police science can fill the bill. Wherever possible, it's always advisable to hire Security Monitors of both sexes.

Armed only with walkie-talkies, Security Monitors can be in places which can't be covered by teachers or other professional staff members while classes are in session. Their primary role is to move throughout the building and grounds checking security, reporting any suspicious circumstances or activities, spotting problems-in-the-making and stopping trouble before it starts. In addition, they can provide supervision for time out, in-school suspension, and detention sessions. Often, they also serve as positive role models for many students. The following are examples of typical job descriptions for nonlicensed discipline personnel:

Security Monitor—Job Description
(example)

Responsible to: Principal

Responsibilities:

1. Exercise preventative measures to reduce the possibility of delinquent acts or violations of school rules.
2. Provide supervision and protective security for the school buildings and grounds.
3. Assist in the enforcement of specific student regulations and be cognizant of the legal rights of students.
4. Assist at school functions when assigned.
5. Assist in the investigation of thefts, vandalism, violations, and emergency situations as directed by the Principal.
6. Regulate traffic and parking on school property.
7. Be knowledgeable of juvenile law enforcement, traffic control, alcohol and drug regulations, investigative procedures, human relations, and be trained in First Aid procedures.

Security Monitors aren't professionals, but they can provide an additional adult presence in the right place at the right time. When it comes to discipline, you can't have too many eyes, ears, or hands at work to keep the total school running smoothly.

STEP-BY-STEP PROCEDURES FOR CONDUCTING BACKGROUND CHECKS ON SECURITY PERSONNEL

It pays to dig deeply when screening and selecting discipline personnel, including running formal criminal background checks on final candidates. Security Aides, Hall Monitors, and other discipline staff members work with students in sensitive situations, have easy access to vulnerable parts of the building and deal with highly confidential information. You can't afford to have anyone with questionable background or character in these positions.

Many school systems now routinely conduct criminal record background checks on all new hires, especially teachers, custodians, and aides who work privately with students. If this is not your practice, it is essential that you run such

---

Hall Monitor—Job Description
(example)

Responsible to: Principal

Responsibilities:

1. Become familiar with the school, students, and staff, and maintain positive rapport and communications.
2. Provide supervision and security within the building as directed.
3. Provide appropriate direction and assistance to students.
4. Exercise surveillance of unauthorized persons on school property.
5. Assist in the investigation of rule violations as directed.
6. Be knowledgeable of school guidelines and regulations, and assist in the enforcement of all school rules.

---

checks on discipline personnel to validate your trust in the employee and to reduce your risk and liability should something go wrong later on.

The first step in background checking is to contact all references and previous employers. These checks have limited value today, however, because employers are increasingly reluctant to divulge much information, particularly negative information, about former employees. Many personnel offices will now only verify dates of employment and disclose nothing else for fear of violating data privacy requirements and/or other legal repercussions.

Personal contact via a visitation or phone call is the best way to conduct reference checks. Sometimes, previous employers will tell you things about a candidate that they won't put in writing. It's even better if you can find someone on your staff who personally knows someone working for the previous employer and have them check with their contact on the candidate's background.

Traditional reference checks aren't enough in today's risky society. Some schools have hired an employee with good references only to find out later that the person has a felony background of child molestation or criminal sexual conduct. If this happens in your school, you and your students may be at risk and you will have little defense if a problem arises. Student safety and prudent risk management necessitate conducting a formal criminal record background check before hiring any discipline personnel.

Most states now permit authorized school officials to request criminal record checks from their chief law enforcement agency (Department of Public Safety, State Bureau of Investigation, Bureau of Criminal Apprehension). Although exact procedures will vary from state to state, the typical steps involved are as follows:

Disciplinary Aide—Job Description
(example)

Responsible to: Principal

Responsibilities:

1. Provide supervision for time-out and in-school suspension during the school day.

2. Provide supervision and give direction and assistance to students assigned to detention.

3. Supervise students in the halls and lavatories, and assist with bus loading and unloading.

4. Review bus violations with students and parents when necessary.

5. Arrange conferences regarding discipline with staff, students, and parents as needed.

6. Assist in the enforcement of student regulations and in the investigation of rule violations as directed by the Principal.

---

1. Obtain a signed/notarized release of information and authorization from the candidate in question (see *Sample Release Form*).

2. Offer employment to the selected candidate contingent upon a satisfactory report from the appropriate state records check department.

3. Submit a formal request for a felony record background check to the appropriate state agency (see *Sample Records Request Letter*). The request should include the subject's complete name (no middle initial), date of birth, and signed/notarized release form. Most states will also require a small fee for each individual record check.

Unfortunately, most agencies will report only felony violations committed and recorded within the state involved. If desired, a more thorough nationwide records check may be obtained from the FBI. This will usually involve finger-printing the candidate and paying a substantially higher fee. At this time, most school districts are not pursuing criminal record background checks to this level, except in special circumstances.

In addition to checking with state and federal law enforcement agencies, there may be specific occasions when school officials will want to verify or seek further information from other sources such as:

• County Courthouse (Some counties will do free civil records searches.)

• State Department of Motor Vehicles

Sample Release Form

I, _____, hereby authorize and grant my informed consent to permit _____ School District and/or its agents to collect data that concerns me, as identified below, which is classified as private data pursuant to state statute. I understand that the purpose of permitting_____ District to have access to this information is to determine my suitability for employment.

This authorization shall be valid for a period of twelve months from date of signature, but may be canceled at any time upon written notice to the District.

Employment Records

_____

name and address of current and past employers (use back if more space is needed)

Educational Records

_____

name and address of educational institution(s)

Criminal History and Record

_____

Driving Record (for positions requiring driving)

_____

Name _____
       first   middle   last   other names known by

Date of Birth _____

Social Security Number _____

Drivers License Number_____

Signature_____ Date _____

Notary Stamp of Seal:

Subscribed and sworn to before me this _____ day of _____,

_____.

Notary Signature _____

My commission expires _____

Sample Records Request Letter
(school letterhead)

Date: _____

State Criminal Apprehension Bureau

_____

_____

To Whom It May Concern:

This letter constitutes a formal request for your agency to conduct a criminal history and record background check on the prospective employee(s) named below:

Name	Date of Birth
Joseph Lyle Smith	11–21–69
William Scott Jones	8–2–71

Enclosed you will find the required fee payment and signed authorization for release of criminal records for the subject(s).

Your prompt attention to this request is appreciated.

Sincerely,

_____

Authorized School Representative

- State Department of Education
- State Licensing Boards
- Professional Associations
- Credit Bureaus

Today's schools must have sufficient staff to ensure student safety and enforce school rules at all times. It's equally important, however, that all discipline personnel be completely honest, trustworthy, and reliable. Hiring the right people is critical. Scrupulous background checking can help you make the right choices.

WHY SOCIAL WORKERS ARE MORE IMPORTANT THAN EVER

In the battle for better discipline, effective leaders can't rely solely on adding specialized personnel. They must also find new ways to use established positions. School social workers are a case in point.

Historically, social workers have been merely the welfare arm of the school. Now, as more and more problems at school are rooted in problems at home, they are frequently the school's point person in dealing with a variety of sticky discipline problems. Many administrators will admit privately today that they would gladly trade off some other traditional positions (for instance, psychologists, counselors, and so on) for more social workers.

Because of their unique training and expertise, social workers can do things other school professionals can't or won't do. Often, social workers have more "street smarts" than many teachers and administrators and are willing to tackle situations that most of the staff feel are beyond their area of responsibility or competence.

The lack of cooperative corrective measures undertaken by the home and the school acting in concert has created and exacerbated much of our current discipline difficulty. The social worker is often the school's best bet for reinventing a coordinated home-school approach to solving behavior problems.

Many teachers and administrators don't understand the dynamics of today's nontraditional families and don't know how to work with them. Social workers do! If you don't have a part- or full-time social worker, you may want to rethink your staffing pattern.

Among the unique discipline-related services which frequently can best be performed by social workers are the following:

- Get in the middle of dysfunctional family situations and help parties sort out solutions.
- Help teachers understand unusual family emergencies or problems.
- Track down and establish contact with hard-to-reach parents.
- Find out what families really need and help them get it.
- Make home visits.
- Monitor the progress of both individual students and families.
- Intervene at the first sign of trouble at home or at school.
- Serve as an advocate for needy families in securing appropriate social services.
- Represent the school in court cases involving truancy and other violations.
- Gather evidence regarding suspected child abuse or neglect.
- Spearhead family outreach programs.
- Develop family profiles and case studies.
- Be a resource for families and school personnel on where to go for help.
- Serve as a classroom resource for teaching conflict resolution skills.
- Conduct group sessions for chronic offenders and at-risk students.
- Serve as a liaison between custodial and noncustodial parents.
- Help identify, report, and follow-up on cases of sexual harassment or abuse.

- Participate in case conferences.
- Mediate conflict situations between the home and the school.
- Provide staff development programs on dealing with nontraditional families.
- Make referrals to a full range of social service agencies.
- Interpret stressful family and individual situations to the rest of the staff.
- Facilitate sensitive parent-teacher conferences.
- Assist in the transition of immigrant families, including obtaining appropriate interpreters when necessary.
- Help make newcomer families feel more comfortable in dealing with the school.
- Serve as a liaison to other youth agencies in the community.
- Be a friend to students and families who need one badly.

As one social worker summed up his special role in the school, "We take the orders, we do the shopping and we deliver the goods."

Social workers are typically more action-oriented than theory-based. As such, they can be key actors and valuable allies in dealing with all kinds of discipline problems. If, as predicted, schools of the future become the hub of one-stop social service centers, social workers will become even more singularly important to the operation of the school.

USING MANAGEMENT AIDES FOR ONE-ON-ONE SUPERVISION

In some schools across the country, management aides are also playing an expanded role in maintaining school discipline. As in the case of social workers, the role of these aides (sometimes identified as Support Aides, Behavior Aides or by other titles) has been broadened to include greater responsibility for helping handle behavior problems.

As more medically fragile and physically disabled students have been mainstreamed into the regular classroom, some have needed to be attended by full-time support personnel. Frequently, management aides have been assigned to provide physical support (such as lifting, handling wheel chairs, and so on) and any other assistance needed by the child in order to work alongside mainstream students.

In some schools, the use of such aides has been extended to students with emotional or behavior problems requiring occasional physical restraint or forcible removal from the classroom (see *Sample Job Description*). This expensive full-time, one-on-one service has usually been supported by Federal and/or state special education funds.

Management/Behavior Aide—Job Description
(sample)

Responsible to: Principal and Supervising Teacher

Responsibilities:

1. Assist in developing and maintaining behavior management programs.
2. Maintain a system of day-to-day data collection for assigned students.
3. Maintain a complete file on all referrals.
4. Implement behavior management strategies as directed by the teacher.
5. Be involved in crisis interventions when a student is out of control.
6. Contact and involve parents directly as authorized by the supervising teacher.
7. Perform such other duties as assigned by the Principal or teacher.

A few risk-taking administrators have stretched the concept even further by assigning management aides to out-of-control students who do not qualify for special education support. The rationale for such extreme action is that it's unacceptable to allow one unmanageable or violent student to wreck havoc on an entire classroom or school, intimidate staff members, and disrupt the learning of large numbers of students.

If it takes one-on-one supervision to control such students, the school had better be prepared to provide it until another remedy is found. This is a costly, last-resort approach, but it may be the best immediate, short-range slution in extreme cases.

BLUEPRINT FOR USING TEACHER-DEANS TO IMPROVE DISCIPLINE

Like social workers and management aides, all teachers must get more involved in schoolwide discipline. Behavior and school climate won't improve until everyone gets into the act. One way to begin to involve teachers more directly in the overall discipline management of the school is to create teacher-dean positions.

Typically, teacher-deans are veteran teachers reassigned for part of the school day to assist in general administration and discipline. The number of such positions will vary depending upon the size of the school. Assignments are usually rotated annually in order to involve more staff members. Close to full-day coverage can be achieved by staggering assignments as shown:

Teacher-Dean Daily Schedule
(example)

Period	Teacher A	Teacher B
1	Classroom Assignment	Dean Assignment
2	"	"
3	"	"
4	Dean Assignment	Prep Time
5	"	Classroom Assignment
6	"	"
7	Prep Time	"

The best candidates for this hybrid role as teacher and quasiadministrator are seasoned professionals with a broad background of experience dealing with a variety of students, a keen interest in overall school improvement, and a commitment to high standards of performance and behavior. Although the exact duties of teacher-deans will vary from school to school, they normally include the following:

1. Monitor attendance for an assigned segment of the student population and follow-up in cases of unexcused or excessive absences.
2. Process all discipline problems involving the assigned group of students.
3. Advise the Principal on matters of discipline and school policy.
4. Serve as a liaison between the teaching staff and the Principal.
5. Undertake special projects such as revising the policy manual, developing an Activity Advisor's Handbook, and designing an alternative program model.
6. Serve as acting administrator in the absence of the Principal.

Schools that use the teacher-dean model cite a number of advantages such as:

• Entails less cost than adding licensed administrators.
• Introduces fresh viewpoints and different perspectives to the administration of the school.
• Involves more people in discipline management and evens the workload.
• Provides opportunities to introduce more women into an administrative role.
• Facilitates flexibility in assigning staff.
• Frees the Principal for more instructional leadership activities.
• Provides professional growth opportunities for teachers.
• Brings discipline closer to the classroom.

- Enhances communication between the teaching and administrative staff.
- Gives teachers greater insights into the complexities of schoolwide discipline.
- Keeps the Principal and other administrators in touch with the realities of the classroom.
- Promotes consistency of expectations and enforcement among staff members.
- Strengthens unity of purpose throughout the entire staff.
- Causes teachers to feel they are represented and "heard" by the leadership of the school.
- Helps to humanize disciplinary action (teacher-deans often know students and parents better and can adjust disciplinary action to fit unique, individual circumstances).
- Strengthens accountability as students must relate to teachers at more than one level (students know who they are dealing with.).
- Helps prevent teacher burn-out.
- Builds a residue of rapport between the staff and the administration.

Using teacher-deans can be a win-win situation for any school:

- The Principal gets more help;
- Teachers feel more involved;
- Students benefit from more consistent discipline;
- The entire school enjoys better behavior.

The teacher-dean model can be a good first step toward marshaling all the forces of the school to support positive discipline.

MAKING EVERYONE PART OF THE SCHOOL'S DISCIPLINE TEAM

There's a difference between a bowling team and an orchestra. A bowling team consists of separate players, each striving for their personal best, who add up their individual scores when they're done to see how they came out as a team. An orchestra, on the other hand, is made up of individual talents all playing in unison from the same score to produce a collective effect. A good school is like a fine orchestra.

Throughout this chapter, the need for teamwork in creating a disciplined learning environment has been stressed. It takes more than an Assistant Principal to maintain school discipline. It takes more than Police Liaison Officers, Security Monitors, social workers and teacher-deans. It takes everyone working together.

All adults on the school staff share an interest in the success and welfare of all learners, in the general school climate, and in the total health of the organization. (Anyone lacking this interest should get out of the business.) Consequently, everyone should be involved in the disciplinary process and overall student management. Every staff member has an obligation to be visible in the building, attentive to what's going on around them, and willing to stop bad things whenever they see them anywhere in the school. When this happens:

- Early intervention is facilitated.
- Congruence of philosophy and expectations is enhanced.
- Sanctions are applied consistently.
- Problems are solved in their early stages.

Unfortunately, effective teamwork is not the norm in most schools. Many teachers feel that their responsibility for discipline ends at the classroom door, unless they're paid an extra stipend for a specific after-school or evening supervisory assignment. Likewise, most classified personnel (custodians, secretaries, cooks) believe that discipline is someone else's job. These attitudes can set up any school for failure.

Winning schools aren't the result of adding up individual score sheets. They're the product of an orchestrated effort involving all players all the time. As school leader, it's your job to make everyone an active part of the discipline team. The foundations for making positive discipline a group effort are outlined below:

Four Foundations of Schoolwide Discipline Teamwork

Schoolwide Discipline Plan	Schoolwide Support System
Staff Development for Everyone	Special Teams for Special Problems and Projects

1. Schoolwide Discipline Plan

Every school should have a comprehensive discipline plan containing expectations and consequences (interventions) hammered out and agreed upon through participation by all staff members.

Regardless of their respective assignment in the building, each employee should have a thorough working knowledge of the accepted plan and an understanding of their obligation to carry it out. The plan should also be communicated carefully to all students and parents annually. A sample schoolwide discipline plan appears in the following:

Behavior Intervention Program
Aquila Primary Center
(A National School of Excellence)

Behavior Goals:

C—Cooperate.
A—Act responsibly.
R—Respect yourself and others.
E—Encourage and enjoy each other.

Behavior Expectations for All Students:

Throughout the Day (Schoolwide):

- Show respect and courtesy to all people.
- Behave safely.
- Walk quietly in and around the school.
- Use appropriate language.
- Leave your gum at home.

Classroom Guidelines:

- Be respectful of other students and your teacher.
- Treat others as you would like to be treated.
- Follow directions of your teacher.

Hallway Guidelines:

- Walk at all times.
- Always speak in a low voice so other students will not be disturbed.
- Stay on the right side.
- Stay in line when you are with your class.
- Always have permission to go to the bathroom and return to your room quickly.

Lunchroom Guidelines:

- Be nice to other people.
- Always talk in a moderate voice.
- If you need help, raise your hand.
- Stay in your seat until dismissed.
- Eat your own lunch only.
- Clean up your area.

Playground Guidelines:

- Be kind to others, reach out and make new friends.
- Play only in designated areas.
- Share equipment with others.
- Return equipment to an adult.
- Follow directions of the playground aide.
- Stay outside unless an adult gives you permission to enter the building.

- Line up quickly when the bell rings.
- Act—don't react—and play without pushing and shoving, kicking and karate movements, tackling or touching others, throwing things, inappropriate language, fighting, throwing snow or snowballs.

Intervention Strategies/Levels:

Level 1 (Cooperative Discipline):

This level represents minor behavior that needs correction (for instance, running in hallway). Staff members will use verbal redirection, or other cooperative discipline strategies.

Level 2 (Repeated Offenses):

At this level, the adult leader or teacher has determined that verbal redirection or other cooperative discipline strategies are not working. The staff calls for an I-Team (Intervention Team). After consultation, it will be determined whether the student is given a one-to-one redirection (coaching) by the I-Team or removed from the classroom. A note will be mailed to the parents.

Level 3 (Crisis Level Concerns):

This category of behavior necessitates the student's removal from a given area as a result of overt disruption in the classroom, physically dangerous acts, assault of another student, illegal acts, blatant sexual behavior, overt defiance, and so on. The student will be removed from the classroom or other area and referred to the "Time Out" room. A behavioral improvement form will be sent home and a conference will be scheduled with the parents and the student in attendance.

Level 4 (Crisis Level Concerns Are Continuing):

Level 3 behaviors are continuing. Staff interventions have not been effective. Level 4 will result in an "In School Suspension" wherein the student is required to be out of the classroom or other area where the problem occurred, for a major part or all of a day. A behavioral improvement form will be sent home and a parent conference scheduled with the student present along with members of the staff and the Intervention Team.

Level 5 (Student is Out of Our Control):

Level 5 represents behavior so severe that it threatens the safety of other students while the I-Team has continued to intervene, but has been unsuccessful. This will result in an "Out of School Suspension." This suspension could be for 1–3 days. Legal documents will be sent home via mail to the parents and a parent conference will be required for admission back to school.

Level 6 (Protection Level Concerns):

At this level, school personnel have detected signals which might indicate neglect or abuse. Concerns are raised as a result of absence, fatigue, unexplained hunger, stress characteristics, or dirty appearance. A referral may also be made when it appears that the student is depressed and distracted, which warrants investigation. All Level 6 concerns will be reported to the police or child protection agency as required by law.

---

2. Schoolwide Support System

Teachers and other staff members are more willing to accept an active role in all-school discipline if they know that others are doing their share and that they will be supported by co-workers. It's up to administrators to set up a schoolwide support system to undergird unified staff efforts and to let each individual know that he/she is not operating in isolation.

Support comes from frequent opportunities to ask questions, clear up gray areas, and discuss solutions to individual and collective discipline concerns.

A support system can be implemented through existing department heads or grade level chairs or by forming Assistance Teams throughout the school. Nonlicensed staff members should be included in the loop of whatever support system is created.

3. Staff Development for Everyone

You can't expect the staff to tackle schoolwide discipline unless it knows exactly what to do and how to do it. Any total school discipline plan needs to be buttressed by appropriate staff development programs involving all categories of employees. Inservice training should focus on positive reinforcement strategies, conflict resolution techniques, intervention skills, or whatever is needed. Chapter 12 spells out details of effective staff development programs aimed at improving discipline.

4. Special Committees for Special Problems and Projects

Every school has its own set of special discipline problems which seem to escalate from time to time. When this happens, the best approach is to form an ad hoc task force of representative staff members to plan and implement an all-school response until the problem is once again under control. All such special committees should include nonteaching staff, as well as faculty members. Examples of specific ad hoc discipline committees include the following:

- School Climate Committee
- Vandalism Prevention Committee
- School Security Committee

- Peer Counseling Committee
- Bus Safety Committee
- Discipline Philosophy Committee
- Student Involvement Committee
- Student Handbook Committee
- Drug Awareness/Prevention Committee
- Emergency Procedures Committee
- Attendance Improvement Committee
- Antitheft Action Committee
- Parking Lot Safety Committee
- Weapons Control Committee
- Student Security Advisory Committee
- Ethnic Pride/School Pride Committee
- Sexual Harassment Information Committee

Individual teachers and administrators can't enforce positive discipline, but an entire staff, acting as one, can. When all staff members are charged and empowered to handle schoolwide behavior problems, things change. Empowerment multiplies power. If you can get everyone on your staff to be part of the discipline team, you will have taken a giant step toward establishing an orderly academic environment where all kids can learn.

CREATIVE USE OF ADVOCATES AND OMBUDSMEN

If you try everything and nothing works, it's time to think of something new. When you've done all you can do to utilize specialized discipline personnel and involve everyone in the disciplinary process and student behavior is still unsatisfactory, you need to come up with a different approach. One new idea, as yet untested but widely discussed among educators, is the use of individual advocates or ombudsmen for difficult students. This may be an idea whose time has come in your school.

Most administrators are familiar with outside advocates for special education students who represent the child and parent in seeking the highest level of service possible. These advocates aren't always popular with school officials, but they do get results.

A few schools have also tried adding an advocate to their staff to serve gifted and talented students. These advocates help high potential students break down stereotypes, deal with prejudice, find out about educational and career possibilities and get the most out of the system.

The same approach might work for students who are severe discipline problems by using paid or volunteer advocates/ombudsmen to champion their rights, negotiate workable individual behavior contracts, and help the student learn how to live with and within the system.

Typically at discipline conferences, the viewpoints of the school and the parents are represented, but those of the student may not be. An advocate could be the voice of the child in dealing with adults in difficult situations.

Like a good probation officer, the advocate could serve as:

- Sponsor;
- Mentor;
- Cheerleader;
- Broker of services;
- Personal advisor;
- Substitute parent;
- Friendly task master;
- Reality checker;
- Adult confidant.

The job of the advocate would be to see that the student gets a fair shake; but also to show the student how to get along with the school and society.

When all other approaches fail with an extremely difficult student, the use of a personal advocate might work. It's worth a try. If every child had an advocate in their corner at all times throughout the educational process, we probably wouldn't have many of the discipline problems we have today.

The bottom line in assuring proper discipline is that it takes sufficient people to get the job done in today's schools. All schools feel understaffed and they probably are. Nevertheless, it's your responsibility to use whatever staff you have efficiently and effectively to maximize order, safety, and security and to make good discipline a front-burner issue for every adult working in your school. Anything less is unacceptable.

How to Deal
with Gangs
in School

Most educators and parents don't understand gangs and are scared to death of them. When most adults hear about gangs, they think of drugs, violence, and law-breaking. To some young people, however, gangs are exciting, rewarding, and even "romantic." The truth is today's gangs may be all of these. Most importantly, they are antisocial, dangerous, and destructive. The good news is that no school or community has to be controlled by gangs.

The term "street gang" is a misnomer in contemporary society. Gangs are everywhere. Nothing has made teachers and administrators more nervous and alarmed than the relentless migration of gangs from urban to semi-urban, suburban, and even rural areas throughout the country.

Although gangs and gang activity seem to be stabilizing and perhaps decreasing in hard core areas such as New York, Chicago, and Philadelphia, their presence is increasing elsewhere. Pressure from sophisticated police units and rivalry from more established gangs are driving some gang leaders from the inner city to outlying areas. Rural communities are often attractive because they are unexpecting, unprepared, and easier to intimidate and terrorize. Many successful inner city gangs are now setting up "franchise gangs" in rural areas.

Wherever they are found, most gang members are school-age kids. This makes gangs and gang violence a high priority concern for school leaders. Like most antisocial behavior problems, however, there are ways to deal with gangs, to keep them out of the school, and to prevent them from holding any school hostage and disrupting discipline. It starts with understanding today's gang culture.

83

WHAT GANGS ARE ALL ABOUT

Gangs are the catch-all for throw-away kids. They encompass all ethnic and cultural groups. There are Asian, Black, Hispanic, American Indian, and White (Skinheads) gangs.

They may vary in composition and activities and have multiple agendas, but gangs share one common overriding principle: Making money!

Gangs are big business in today's society. They make incredible profits trafficking in drugs, prostitution, robbery, theft, and extortion. Drug deals are at the root of 80% of all gang activity. Illicit profits are what drives today's gangs and what attracts many young people to their ranks. Although some have quasireligious ties (the Vice Lords preach a hybrid of Islamic teachings and urban black street psychology), what gangs worship most are ill-gotten dollars.

Today's gangs aren't loose-knit groups of like-minded young people. They are highly sophisticated, well-organized institutions. Many feature a well-defined, militaristic hierarchy of rank, power and privilege and may have several branches (the well-known Vice Lords organization includes many subgroups such as the Insanes, the Travelers, and the Conservatives).

Examples of Gang Hierarchy
(Vice Lords)

Five-star Universal Elites
Three-star Universal Elites
King of a Branch
Minister of Justice
Branch Elites
Foot Soldiers

Although most members are 9–18 years of age, many gangs are run by adults (some operating out of prison) who make the rules, plan the criminal activities, and skim off most of the profits. The average age of members across the country is dropping as gangs seek out younger and younger recruits. New members are recruited through word-of-mouth advertising, peer pressure, harassment, threats, and force. Some grow up in families of multigenerational gang members and learn the trade by emulating older brothers or sisters.

Elementary age children are often recruited to run errands because they are subject to more lenient legal penalties if apprehended. Likewise, white kids with nice cars are valuable recruits because they can make drug deliveries with less chance of being stopped on suspicion.

In addition to regular members, gangs may touch the lives of many other young people who are referred to as "Associates" (kids who hang around gangs, but aren't actively involved) and "Wannabes" (kids who would like to become gang members). A typical span of gang influence is illustrated in the following:

SPAN OF GANG INFLUENCE

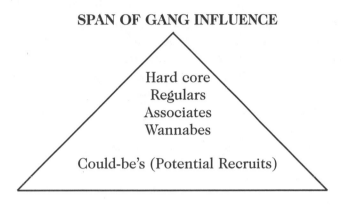

Hard core
Regulars
Associates
Wannabes

Could-be's (Potential Recruits)

"There are no good gangs," according to most police officials. Today's gangs are distinguished from youth groups of previous generations by their violence and illegal activity. They are armed, dangerous, and becoming more daring all the time. Members are sworn to die to defend the honor of the gang. A "warrior mentality" characterizes most gangs and most gang members, regardless of age. The gang culture tends to desensitize children to violence and to normalize criminal activity.

Turf is central to the operation of most gangs. Turf may refer to a geographical area or to a line of criminal pursuit. Any invasion of turf requires violent retribution.

Gangs are easy to get into and hard to get out of and most are dead-end. It's hard for many adults to understand why children and teenagers are so willing to get involved.

WHY GANGS APPEAL TO TODAY'S YOUTH

For many kids, gangs are a place to go when no one else seems to care or pay attention. Experts agree that the main reason young people gravitate toward gangs is to fulfill self esteem needs not met by dysfunctional families or society in general. Students, who feel they don't fit in, lack support at home or suffer repeated failure in school and elsewhere, sometimes find a "home" in the gang culture.

The middle school years constitute the primary age for gang recruitment. Students who are bullies, rebels, or attention-seekers are likely candidates for gang membership. Likewise, girls lacking a sense of self worth and special education students with various disabilities are especially vulnerable to the attractions of gang life.

Gangs are popular because they fill a void in the lives of many children and teens. They offer identification, recognition, status and security which are not forthcoming from any other source in the child's life.

Gangs also possess a mystique often appealing to impressionable young people. Gangs are perceived to have power and are frequently run by charismatic leaders. Gang members are viewed as folk heroes in some communities. They seem to enjoy a glamorous life style, travel in the fast lane, and appear to be above the law.

Economics also drive many young people into the gang fold. Gangs offer easy money quickly. Even little children can earn sizable sums of money serving as lookouts or errand-runners. Working at a monotonous job for minimum wage appears foolish to potential members who learn they can earn up to $500 a day performing menial tasks for the gang.

Other powerful incentives that draw kids to gangs include:

- Immediate protection and safety
- Drugs
- Easy sex
- Companionship
- Excitement/escape from boredom
- Rites of passage
- "Herd instinct"
- Ego trip (A chance to be a big shot)
- Purpose/reason for living

For many young people from impoverished backgrounds, gangs offer much, but deliver little. Living in the gang culture is a life of broken promises and shattered dreams. For many, the ultimate rewards are hard jail time or death.

The way to beat gangs is to offer children and youth better things to do and other chances to succeed and be recognized. Schools can do this better than most other agencies. Where schools are strong, gangs are weakest. High school graduates don't join gangs.

Special Concerns About Girls in Gangs

Although most gang members are male, girls and young women are being attracted in increasing numbers. There are a few all-girl gangs in the country, but in most situations females play an auxiliary role in gang life.

Girls join gangs for the same reasons that boys do. Fear and low self-esteem drive many girls into gangs. A few seem to be attracted by the macho "outlaw" image of male gang members. No matter what their reason for joining, gang life is hard on females. Like males, they age quickly in the gang culture.

The feminist movement hasn't reached street gangs yet. There is no equal treatment among male and female members. Females usually play a subservient role and are frequently used, abused, and subjected to physical and emotional degradation. They serve primarily as possessions, ornaments, and sex objects for male gang members. Girls are often used to advertise the gang and to attract new members. Promiscuity and rape are commonplace. Initiation for females often involves gang rape.

Jobs assigned to female members are usually low-level tasks such as:

- Acting as spies, lookouts, or decoys.
- Serving as drug runners.
- Holding weapons or stolen goods for male members because they are less likely to be searched.
- Allowing their address, house or apartment to be used for drug deals.

Throughout their gang life, females are exploited. Upon initiation, they are often marked by tattoos on their hands, wrists, ankles, thighs, or buttocks. Thereafter, they are treated as merchandise and required to witness crime, carnage, and bloodshed firsthand on a daily basis.

The consequences of gang membership for many young girls include:

- Financial dependency
- Beatings
- Pregnancy
- Sexually transmitted disease
- Addiction
- Incarceration (being busted is the cost of doing business)
- Mental illness
- Depression
- Early death

All gang members start out and end up as victims; but females are more brutally victimized than males. Because of the unique concerns about girls in gangs, some schools have provided special counselors and support groups for female students who are former gang members or who are trying to get out of a gang.

HOW TO SPOT GANG PRESENCE IN YOUR SCHOOL

Some schools end up with serious gang problems because they are caught by surprise and don't spot the early warning signs of gang encroachment into the school's culture. Too often, school officials are not "gang literate." They don't recognize the early indications of gang presence and activity. Naiveté and denial often prevent administrators and school boards from taking action until gangs already have a strong foothold within the student population. An attitude of "it can't happen here" is unrealistic and stupid in today's society.

Most gangs don't operate in secret. They advertise their presence. They stake out turf and want to be known and feared. Most gangs rely on their image of power to attract new members and to intimidate those who might stand in their way.

At the first hint of a radical increase in major school discipline problems, you shouldn't ignore the possibility that gangs might be behind it. An increase in vandalism, drug use, and locker theft often accompanies the introduction of gang members into the school. Another signal for caution may be sudden unexplained wealth among middle or lower socioeconomic students or families.

As a school leader, your best defense is to know what's going on with young people in your community. This requires staying closely connected with all youth-serving agencies. Social workers and probation officers often know that a gang has infiltrated the community long before school officials pick up on the clues. The police can be the school's best source of information on what's going on with kids in the street.

Graffiti is often the first calling card of a new gang in town. Many gangs use graffiti as a billboard to announce their presence and for "tagging" (staking out turf). The symbols and emblems used in graffiti are often the signature of a particular gang (see examples of gang symbolism in graffiti).

It pays to have someone on your staff learn to read the language and understand the hidden meaning of gang-inspired graffiti (any graffiti portrayed backwards or upside down is intended as a put down to the gang represented). The use of graffiti is such an integral part of gang communication and activity that the Los Angeles Public Schools have launched an antigraffiti campaign by hiring specialists to teach young children about the danger and meaning of gang symbolism.

In addition to graffiti, gangs employ a variety of articles and clothing (worn in a certain manner) to signal their existence and to identify their members such as:

- Handsigns
- Secret handshakes
- Nicknames (Street names within the gang culture frequently refer to strength, force, or violence)
- Hats or caps
- Handkerchiefs
- Shoelaces
- Scarves
- Gloves
- Belts/buckles

- Buttons
- Vests
- Jackets
- Jewelry
- Pacifiers
- Haircuts
- Slogans
- Jargons
- Colors (See *Traditional Gang Colors*)

Traditional Gang Colors*

Disciples	Black and Blue
Vice Lords	Black and Gold or Red
L.A. Bloods	Red
L.A. Crips	Blue

---

* Colors may change as gangs evolve and spread into new territories.

Of course, the appearance of gang signs and symbols doesn't always mean a gang invasion. Some wannabes and copycat students may use gang emblems and insignias innocently or to show off. It's important not to overact.

It's equally important, however, to know what to look for to spot any real gang presence in the school and/or the community. Once the existence of gang activity is verified, you must take action. Gangs won't go away by themselves and they won't stay out of the school if left alone.

HOW TO MAKE YOUR SCHOOL A SAFE-ZONE FROM GANGS

Gangs pose a serious threat to schools and communities; but threats can be diffused. There's no reason that any school has to be under siege because of gangs.

It's easier to keep gangs out in the first place, than it is to "ungang" a school once their presence has been established. In either case, however, it is possible to make your school "out of bounds" for gang activity and to assure that members leave their gang affiliation behind when they enter your building.

Most gang members are kids. Kids can be taught and retaught. That's what schools do best. Even in the most gang-ridden areas, administrators and school staffs can keep control, get control, regain control, and/or stay in control. Young people join gangs for a reason. If you take away the reasons for joining, you can neuter even the toughest gangs.

Examples of Gang Symbolism in Graffiti*

Gang	Common Symbols
Disciples	Six-pointed Star
	Pitchfork
	Heart with Wings of Flame
	"BGDN" (Black Gangster Disciple Nation)
Vice Lords	Five-Pointed Star
	Playboy Bunny
	Dollar Sign (It's all about making money)
	Allah's Eye
	Pyramid
	Champagne Glass (Connected with the playboy lifestyle)
	Crescent Moon
	Cane or Hook (Sign of strength)
	Top Hat (Another playboy reference)
	Crown with Three Points
	"V.C." (Vice Lords)
	"AMVLN" (Almighty Vice Lord Nation)
LA Bloods and Crips	L.A. Raiders Hats and Jackets

* Like most groups in society, gangs are in a constant state of evolution and may modify or change symbols periodically.

Successful schools which have prevented gang intrusion, suppressed gang activity, or turned around a gang-infested environment, have applied the following eight principles:

8 Principles of Gang Control

1. Safety First
2. Build In Success
3. Stay Tuned In
4. Know Your Enemy
5. 'Fess Up
6. Get Help
7. Take a Stand
8. Avoid Complacency

Safety First

Safety is the first order of business in any school. Scared kids can't learn. If students don't feel safe under the supervision of the school staff, they may join a gang to get the protection they need. Every school must do whatever it takes to assure that students are safe from:

- Intimidation
- Threats
- Extortion (shakedowns)
- Drug dealing
- Solicitation for sex or prostitution
- Harassment
- Demeaning or dangerous hazings and initiations
- Vicious ridicule
- Physical beatings
- Witnessing violence
- Life-threatening situations

Wherever gangs go, so do weapons and violence. If you eliminate these elements, you dramatically reduce the chances of gang control or influence at school.

Chapter 4 suggests ways to use the school staff to provide maximum safety for all students. Likewise, Chapter 6 details specific measures to curb weapons and violence on school property. The strategies presented have worked in many schools and will help make your school a "safe zone" from gangs.

One of the most important steps administrators can take to protect students is to stay open longer in order to provide a "safe haven" for children during after-school hours.

If your school is safe, you send a powerful message that the "good guys" remain in control and gangs will have to do business elsewhere.

Build in Success

If young people feel accepted and respected, get excited about learning, experience success and have fun at school, they won't need what gangs have to offer. The stronger the bond between the student and the school, the less likely the student is to become interested or involved in the gang culture. Good schools eliminate fear, remove obstacles, and build in success opportunities for all students. As discussed-previously, this may mean:

- Developing a supportive, self-actualizing school culture (Chapter 2);
- Creating a success-oriented curriculum through such programs as Outcome-Based Education (OBE), Authentic Assessment, and Resource-Based Instruction (Chapter 3);
- Offering multicultural, gender-fair content and materials (Chapter 3);
- Making state-of-the-art technology available to all students (Chapter 3);
- Personalizing the school experience through schools-within-a-school and advisor-advisee programs (Chapter 3);
- Revamping the activity program to meet the needs of all students (Chapter 3).

Anything the school can do to bolster student self-esteem and teach prosocial skills helps defeat gangs.

In many areas, particularly inner cities, the most critical need of students is jobs. School leaders should actively recruit potential employers and seek out worthwhile jobs for students who need them. Gangs flourish where poverty prevails. Solid work-study, on-the-job-training and career counseling programs provide an alternative to getting money from gangs illegally. Many schools are now hiring Transition Coordinators to help students cross over from school to meaningful employment. If you can help students succeed at school and at work, you've gone a long way toward loosening the hold gangs have over many students.

Another important way to help young people become unfettered from gangs is to provide them with alternative, nongang success models. To succeed, students need positive role models to offset the charismatic attraction of many gang leaders. If you want to win kids away from gangs, you should saturate the school with successful role models representing every race, culture, and career category. Effective role models don't have to be limited to professional athletes, rock stars, and entertainment celebrities. They can also include men and women who have achieved success as:

Teachers	Environmentalists
Computer Technicians	Psychologists
Police Officers	Parents
Scientists	Military Personnel
Lawyers	Pilots
Physicians	Business Owners
Ministers	Tradespeople
Artists	Politicians

Ex-gang members often make the best role models. They have a credibility that many others don't have and kids listen to them. The important thing is to show students that there are ways to "make it" besides consigning their lives to a gang!

Stay Tuned In

School leaders need to maintain an antenna attuned to what's happening with young people throughout the community. It's no longer enough to know what's going on in your classrooms and hallways; you must keep in touch with what's happening in the streets as well.

To avoid being blind-sided by unexpected gang activity and to plan appropriate responses, school personnel must stay in touch with:

- which gangs are present in the community;
- who the leaders are;
- what rivalries exist between gangs;
- which turf has been staked out by various gangs;
- what criminal activities community gangs are pursuing.

The best ways to stay tuned into gang-related developments are to be visible in the community, talk to kids, parents, and patrons, and maintain close contact with all youth-serving agencies. A citywide council of leaders representing the school, the police, church groups, boys' and girls' clubs, scouting organizations, probation officers, and the medical community can facilitate the exchange of up-to-date information among all parties involved. In some communities, a computerized gang tracking system is utilized to identify and track the whereabouts and activities of gang members. In others, school personnel hold weekly briefings with police representatives to review any warning signs of pending trouble.

Schools can't operate in isolation. What happens in the streets spills over into the school. You can't know too much about what's going on in the lives of the students you serve. Staying tuned in to what gangs are doing outside of school is the only way you can be proactive, rather than reactive in dealing with them in school.

Know Your Enemy

Gangs understand schools and know how the system works. They know how to plant members in a school to solicit new recruits and to open up untapped markets for drug dealing. It only makes sense that school personnel learn everything they can about gangs in return.

There's no excuse today for any school administrator not being knowledgeable about gang cultures, how gangs work, what gang signs look like, and how gangs gain control over students. Knowledge is power. The more you know about gangs, the better prepared you'll be to contain their influence in school.

Most local police departments have gang experts ready and available to teach school staffs all they need to know about gangs. Other valuable resources for information on gangs include:

> State Police and Peace Officers Associations
>
> State Attorney General's Offices
>
> State Departments of Education
>
> National Elementary School Principals Association
>
> National Association of Secondary School Principals
>
> American Association of School Administrators
>
> National Education Association
>
> Federal Bureau of Investigation
>
> U.S. Department of Education
>
> National School Safety Center, Wash., D. C.
>
> Office of Juvenile Justice and Delinquency Prevention, Wash., D. C.
>
> Center to Prevent Handgun Violence, Wash., D. C.

In addition to learning about gangs in general, school leaders are well served by getting to know individual gang members. By developing a one-on-one relationship with student gang members, administrators may gain access to inside information and may be in a position to negotiate or use personal diplomacy to ease tense situations.

Military strategists have always understood the value of "knowing your enemy." The same principle can give you an edge in handling gangs in school.

'Fess Up

Denial isn't a problem-solving technique. If you have a gang presence or problem in your school, the worst thing you can do is to try to cover up or downplay the situation. If there's trouble, the world's going to find out anyway and your image will be tarnished if you've tried to hide it.

It's always best to openly acknowledge the problem. This establishes your honesty, gives you a chance to provide a realistic perspective of what's going on and puts you in a position to get the help you need to deal with the situation.

If you report the situation first, you will be perceived as the primary source of information and you won't have to react continually to others' versions of what's going on.

You never go wrong going public with the truth. It's important that accurate information be shared with all of the audiences involved, including students, parents, the school board, the police, and the general public. Not everyone needs to know everything that's going on, but each audience deserves to know any developments that affect them.

In telling your story to the public, the media may be your best friend or your worst nightmare. Your attitude and demeanor will largely determine how the media handles the story. If you're honest, the media will probably report the facts fairly and without undue sensationalism. Some administrators falsely believe they should try to deny any gang activity in order to preserve the image of the school and avoid alarming the public. It never works. Effective leaders aren't afraid to admit problems facing the school. Telling the truth and taking the heat up front beats making lame excuses and looking like a liar later on.

Get Help

If gangs strike your school, you don't need to feel like the Lone Ranger. Police can't control gangs by themselves and neither can schools. You don't have to do it alone. Gangs are a community problem and it takes a communitywide effort to get rid of them. *Gangs are only as strong as schools and communities allow them to be.*

Collaboration and information-sharing are the keys to mounting a communitywide campaign against gangs. When gang members and gang signs start appearing in the school, you need to call on every ally you have to eliminate the threat. (Most schools have many more potential antigang allies than they realize at first.)

Of course, the police can help, but often parents are the school's most powerful partners in suppressing gang influence. Parents can help by:

- Talking to their kids about the dangers of gang life;
- Keeping track of where their kids are and what they're doing;

Tips for Releasing Information
About Gangs to the Media

- Report facts, not rumors.
- Don't play games with the media.
- Don't invent or embellish details.
- Avoid being defensive or angry.
- Be aware of your body language.
- Don't grandstand or try to come off as either a hero or a martyr.
- Don't be afraid to say, "I don't know," but avoid using the phrase, "No comment." (It always comes off sounding like you're hiding something.)
- Be brief. Explain the problem, why it happened, and what you're doing to resolve it.
- Don't obscure facts or use professional jargon. (Reporters hate it and so does the public.)
- Don't expect to have time to develop a prepared statement or to have an opportunity to see the story before it's printed.
- Return calls to the media promptly.
- Always assume you're "on the record."

- Reporting gang signs and activities;
- Assisting with security and peace keeping. (Parent Patrols are often effective in suppressing gang activities merely by maintaining a visible presence in areas where gang members hang out.)

From the first hint of gang encroachment into the school, parents should be fully informed and involved (see *Sample Parent Letter*). Some schools have also had success by establishing a gang hotline for parents or by holding neighborhood workshops to inform parents about gangs. The goal is to have parents stop asking, "What are *you* going to do about it?" and start asking, "What can *we* do to assist?"

In addition to parents and the police, there are many other sources of help in every community (some may surprise you.) The local Chamber of Commerce, Small Business Owners Association, and Realtors Association have vital stakes in the quality of life within the community and can often assist by providing jobs and funding gang prevention programs. Many civic clubs, fraternal orders, and veterans'

Sample Parent Letter
(school letterhead)

Dear Parents:

Our school and community are beginning to see signs of unwelcome gang activity. As we all know, gangs can pose a threat to student and community safety. It is clearly our intention to keep gang influences out of the school and to assure a safe and productive learning environment for all students.

Gangs can be strong, but a united community can be stronger. We need your support and help in eliminating this new threat.

Please join us at a Parent Information Meeting to be held at 7:30 p.m. on Wednesday, October 15, in the school auditorium. At this meeting, police and school officials will explain the current status of gang activity in our school and community and how we can work together to stop the spread of gang influence among our students.

We look forward to seeing you on October 15. If you have any questions, please call the school office at 777–4321.

Sincerely,

Principal

---

organizations have financial reserves which they may willingly tap to combat gangs in the community. The city's Park and Recreation Department, YMCA, YWCA, and Boys' and Girls' Clubs can offer recreational and leisure time programs which may attract students away from gangs. Other sources of help (funding, training, consultation, and people power) available in most communities include the following:

- Booster Clubs
- PTA
- United Way Organizations
- Alumni Associations
- City Government
- Employee Unions

- 4–H Clubs
- Political Parties
- Colleges and Universities (Many sociology, psychology, and criminology departments have gang experts available to help schools.)
- Local Bar Association
- Probation Officers
- County Sheriff's Office
- Highway Patrol
- State Bureau of Investigation
- Juvenile Court Judges
- Federal and State Gang Task Forces
- Churches (Many have chaplains and special ministries that serve street people, including gangs.)
- City Government
- Family Counseling Services
- Guardian Angels (A trained, volunteer youth peace-keeping corps)
- Public Health Department
- Community Action Groups
- Neighborhood Watch Organizations
- Private Security Firms
- Local Media (Public Service Announcements can be a powerful deterrent to joining gangs.)

No community has to be terrorized by gangs. Schools can and should be the catalyst for galvanizing community support and action to be rid of them.

When gangs become uncomfortable enough, they move on. Often, the children and teenagers of the community are the most relieved to see them go.

Take A Stand

In today's society, every school should take an unflinching public stand against gangs. There should be no mistake in anyone's mind that the school is determined to remain a neutral, safe-zone from gangs. The first step is to adopt a no-nonsense policy outlawing gang activities and banning gang regalia from all school premises and functions (see *Sample Policies*).

Some administrators have been overly cautious about legal issues related to eliminating gang signs and symbols. They cite fear of being held liable for violating students' rights to freedom of speech. In actuality, school officials are more apt to

(Sample Policy #1)
Highline Public Schools
Seattle, WA

GANG ACTIVITY OR ASSOCIATION

Gangs which initiate, advocate, or promote activities which threaten the safety or well-being of persons or property on school grounds or which disrupt the school environment are harmful to the educational process. The use of hand signals, graffiti, or the presence of any apparel, jewelry, accessory, or manner of grooming which, by virtue of its color, arrangement, trademark, symbol, or any other attribute that indicates or implies membership or affiliation with such a group, presents a clear and present danger. This is contrary to the school environment and educational objectives and creates an atmosphere where unlawful acts or violations of school regulations may occur.

Incidents involving initiations, hazings, intimidations, and/or related activities of such group affiliations which are likely to cause bodily harm, or personal degradation or disgrace resulting in physical or mental harm to students are prohibited.

The superintendent will establish procedures and regulations to ensure that any student wearing, carrying or displaying gang paraphernalia, or exhibiting behavior or gestures that symbolize gang membership, or causing and/or participating in activities which intimidate or affect the attendance of another student shall be subject to disciplinary action.

The superintendent will provide in-service training in gang behavior and characteristics to facilitate staff identification of students-at-risk and promote membership in authorized school groups and/or activities as an alternative.

---

be held liable if they fail to protect students from gangs. Schools may be found legally negligent if they fail to preserve every student's right to be protected against:

1. Foreseeable criminal activity;
2. Crime or violence that could be prevented through supervision;
3. Identifiable dangerous situations;
4. Dangerous individuals negligently placed or allowed in school.

(Sample Policy #2)
Highline Public Schools
Seattle, WA

GANG ACTIVITY OR ASSOCIATION

The type of dress, apparel, activities, acts, behavior, or manner of grooming displayed, reflected, or participated in by the student shall not:

- Lead school officials to reasonably believe that such behavior, apparel, activities, acts, or other attributes are gang related and would disrupt or interfere with the school environment or activity and/or educational objectives;
- Present a physical safety hazard to self, students, staff, and other employees;
- Create an atmosphere in which a student, staff, or other person's well-being is hindered by undue pressure, behavior, intimidation, overt gesture, or threat of violence;
- Imply gang membership or affiliation by written communication, masks, drawing, painting, design, emblem upon any school or personal property or on one's person.

If the student's behavior or other attribute is in violation of these provisions, the principal or designee will request the student to make appropriate correction. If the student refuses, the parent/guardian may be notified and asked to make the necessary correction. The principal will take appropriate corrective and disciplinary action.

Students identified as being gang involved, influenced, or affiliated will be provided assistance, and/or programs that discourage gang involvement or affiliation, enhance self-esteem, encourage interest and participation in school or other positive activities, and promote membership in authorized school organizations.

School policy should make it perfectly clear that gangs aren't to be tolerated. Once such antigang policies have been enacted, they should be publicized widely and enforced rigorously.

To reinforce their position, school leaders should go one step further by actively lobbying for tougher laws and stiffer penalties for gang-related crimes. Some cities and/or states have adopted ordinances/statutes imposing heavy fines and jail sentences (up to 40 years for repeat offenders) for gang crimes committed in a "school zone" (usually defined as one city block or 300 feet from the school and including school buses). Such laws also often allow for treating minors, 14 years and older, as adults for gang-related violations on school property.

Schools and gangs don't mix. It's your job as a school leader to do whatever it takes to get this message across to everyone in the community, especially to the gang members themselves.

Avoid Complacency

When things are calm, it's easy to become complacent and complacency breeds vulnerability. Once gang influence has been suppressed, school staffs should continue to take steps to assure that new outbreaks don't occur. The following measures have aided many schools in maintaining control over gang activity:

1. Remove or cover up any gang-oriented graffiti as promptly as possible.
2. Implement a *Gang Awareness Curriculum* to teach basic information on gangs as early as the elementary grades. (The Portland, OR, schools have employed such a program since 1988 with positive results.)
3. If necessary, block any new gang members from enrolling in the school.
4. Separate rival gang members whenever possible.
5. Transfer particularly troublesome or dangerous gang members to another school with fewer gang affiliates.
6. Offer alternative programs for hard-core gang members.
7. Extend conflict resolution and mediation programs to include gang-related disputes.
8. Try to involve gang chiefs (who are usually natural leaders) in legitimate roles of responsibility in the school.
9. Provide support groups for gang members who are trying to "get out."
10. Accept gang members from other schools who want to get a "fresh start."
11. Pay special attention to the student parking lot where the first signs of gang regalia often appear and many drug deals go down.
12. Monitor outsiders closely and don't be afraid to enforce trespassing laws when necessary.

Gangs don't belong in school and don't have to be tolerated. It's your job to keep them out. The action steps outlined previously can help; so can the tested techniques for reducing weapons and violence which follow.

C H A P T E R   S I X

WHAT TO DO
TO CURB VIOLENCE
IN SCHOOL

Readers didn't know how to react when a midwestern pawn broker recently advertised a "back-to-school special" on hand guns. As it turned out, the advertised special was supposed to be for musical instruments; but the original ad might have been true. Guns are rapidly becoming essential school supplies in some areas and violence is part of the daily lesson plan for many students.

Kids don't invent violence. They learn it. In contemporary society, children of all ages are mastering the subject better than ever. Ten children under the age of 19 die every day as a result of gun injuries (National Center for Health Statistics) and on a typical day, 100,000 pupils carry guns to school (Center for Disease Control).

Violence is deeply ingrained in today's culture, where many children and teenagers are being raised in an arsenal. Violence in schools only mirrors violence seen at home, in the media, and on the streets.

Not so long ago, the only violent act in most schools was an occasional schoolyard scuffle. Today, incidents of beating, mugging, fighting, rape, assault, stabbing, and shooting are everyday occurrences in inner city schools and are becoming more common in smaller schools, suburbs, and rural areas. In many places, violence has become the accepted means of settling disagreements among school children.

Experts agree that there are many reasons for the escalation of school violence such as:

- Bad role models
- Child abuse

- Media hype
- Parental apathy
- Gang rivalries
- Sexual abuse
- Drug disputes
- Racial clashes
- Vendettas
- Name-calling incidents
- "Romantic" disagreements
- Jealousy over possessions
- "Weaponization" of society

Whatever the cause, there's too much violence in schools and it's getting worse. Students can't learn and teachers can't teach in an atmosphere of fear, danger, and intimidation. There is a bright spot, however; many schools are finding ways to end the violence and to restore the school as a safe haven for students and adults. The first and most important step is to wipe out weapons in school.

NEW WAYS TO KEEP WEAPONS OUT OF YOUR SCHOOL

An armed camp is not a learning culture where all kids can succeed. Weapons have no place in the school. It's your responsibility to get them out and keep them out.

This isn't easy when weapons are readily available and more powerful than ever. Guns, and other weapons, are easy to get for students of all ages. They often get them from home or from friends. Sometimes, they steal them or buy them from surplus stores or from underground sources.

The growing influence of gangs worsens the situation. The credo of many gangs is, "The bigger the gun, the bigger the person." Many gangs are engaged in an arms race of automatic weapons.

Of course, guns aren't the only weapons to worry about in school. A weapon can be any instrument or device that can be used to threaten, attack, hurt or kill another person. Weapons frequently seized in schools across the country include:

- Firearms
- Knives
- Razors
- Blackjacks
- Chuckka sticks
- BB Guns
- Air Guns
- Acid

- Brass Knuckles
- Loaded Cartridges
- Explosive Devices (pipe guns)

- Wire
- Chains
- Broken Glass

Children may bring these weapons to school for protection, to show off, or to hold for an older gang member. For many of them, carrying a gun or a blade is a way of life.

Since weapons are plentiful, it takes a comprehensive program of education, screening, and removal to eliminate them from school premises. The following weapon-prevention strategies have worked in many elementary and secondary schools:

- Adopt and enforce a tough, "zero-tolerance" policy banning guns and other weapons (including toy guns and imitation weapons) from all school property and functions with stiff penalties, including immediate suspension and expulsion (See *Sample Policies* later in this chapter.)

- Establish separate, specific procedures for dealing with special education students involved with weapons. Such procedures must comply with the requirements of all applicable federal statutes such as the *Education Handicapped Act* (EHA), the *Free Appropriate Public Education Act* (FAPE), and the *Individual with Disabilities Act* (see *Sample Procedures*).

- Launch a schoolwide antigun campaign featuring posters, buttons, bumper stickers, and telephone stickers, with a strong message, "GUNS KILL—KEEP THEM OUT OF SCHOOL."

- Train all staff members to recognize and identify different types of firearms and other instruments which can be used as a weapon.

- Teach students to report all weapons to an adult. The message should be, "It's O.K. to report guns in school to protect everyone's safety."

- Establish an intelligence hotline for reporting weapons or suspicion of weapons on the school campus.

- Notify parents of school incidents involving guns and other dangerous weapons and elicit their support in keeping the school gun-free (see *Sample Parent Letter*).

- Make any incident involving the use of a weapon at school a permanent part of the student's record.

- Require students expelled for violence or use of a weapon to provide evidence of rehabilitation before readmission.

- Conduct unannounced "sweeps and searches" of school premises to uncover concealed weapons. The Prince Georges County (MD) Schools use a SAFE

(Schools Against a Fearful Environment) team to conduct random searches of district schools. Students should understand in advance that lockers are owned by the school and can be searched with probable cause.

- Encourage students and parents to enter into nonviolence contracts, similar to the pledge to avoid alcohol use made popular by SADD (Students Against Drunk Driving).

- Urge parents and community members to use "gun safes" to keep firearms under lock and out of the hands of children.

- Install metal detectors and other security devices as outlined in the next section of this chapter.

- Monitor student backpacks, bookbags, and sports bags where weapons can be concealed, or require students to keep them in their lockers. Montgomery (AL) Schools require the use of see-through plastic or mesh book bags.

- Lobby for tougher standards of gun control, including a waiting period and proof of age before purchase.

- Cooperate with local police to implement a gun buy-back program using donated funds to purchase guns from minors with no questions asked.

School leaders don't like to be intractable; but bringing weapons to school is one place where the line must be drawn. Guns and other weapons are unacceptable in schools. You should use every legal means possible to make the school weapons-free. If you can't keep guns out of school, close the doors. Learning and lethal weapons are incompatible.

SECURITY MEASURES THAT REDUCE VIOLENCE

School security is serious business today. The better the security and surveillance within the building, the safer students and staff members are from external intrusions and internal eruptions of violence. Good security goes hand-in-hand with better discipline and reduced violence. Good security today requires both human and technological supervision. Security is just another name for *Vigilance*.

When school is in session, the best security is provided by the people who work there. Chapter 3 tells you how to allocate and deploy staff to guarantee maximum security and safety throughout the school. In addition, all teachers and support staff members should be trained in how to spot trouble-just-waiting-to-happen, to stop volatile situations from escalating into violence and to intervene and break up fights. (See the following tips.)

Many incidents of violence in schools are precipitated by persons who don't belong there in the first place (gang members, students from rival schools, dropouts,

(Sample Procedures)

TSES PROCEDURE: WEAPONS
Anoka-Hennepin (MN) Schools

Philosophy

Students with disabilities who engage in behaviors which create or have the potential to create unsafe situations will be disciplined as determined appropriate by the placement planning team, including special education building consultant and principal, or designee. Disciplinary action and/or changes in school building educational program or placement will take the student's disability into account and will be in compliance with procedural safeguards of federal and state law and regulation.

When a student with a disability is involved in a situation which creates or has the potential to create an unsafe condition, implement the following procedure:

Immediate Action

1. Suspend student for up to five days.
2. Thoroughly document incident. (It may be necessary to interview witnesses to acquire the information.)
3. Include the following data.
   A. Describe physical site.
   B. What occurred immediately prior to the incident?
   C. Describe the incident:
      1) Who was present when the situation occurred?
      2) What was said?
      3) Describe the actions of all involved.
   D. Describe the intervention.
   E. Photograph any property damage or evidence of student injury, when possible.
4. Make appropriate report to police.
5. Schedule a team meeting. which must be held within 5 school days of a suspension.

Possible Recommendations of the Team

1. Suspend an additional five days to provide time to assess and identify an alternative program if the student continues to create an immediate and substantial danger to surrounding persons or property.

2. Return to a school upon completion of suspension. This must occur.

3. Return to same school with modified I.E.P.

4. Place student on homebound (a temporary solution only).

5. Placement at another building, same level of service.

6. Placement at another building, increase in special education service.

7. Seek injunctive relief while seeking alternative placement if the student is "truly dangerous." (Must seek attorney's opinion prior to making recommendation.)

Conditions for Expulsion

1. Expulsion can be considered only in the event that the student's behavior is unrelated to their handicapping condition;

2. The student's behavior is related to illegal use of drugs or alcohol;

3. Homebound is provided until another appropriate placement is available. The homebound program constitutes a change of placement and requires a homebound I.E.P. and parental approval.

---

suspended students, noncustodial parents). Vigilance means keeping track of who's in the building at all times.

There's a difference between maintaining a welcoming climate for legitimate visitors and patrons and leaving the school wide open for anyone to wander in off the streets undetected. Some schools have adopted a compromise solution by:

1. Limiting the number of unlocked entrances (check with fire marshal first).

2. Using aides, volunteers, or older students to staff a reception area, meet all visitors, and to escort them to their destination in the building.

3. Posting notices that all visitors must report to the designated receiving area or the office directly.

4. Issuing name tags to identify visitors, volunteers, and substitute teachers.

5. Inviting neighbors to assist with security awareness by reporting any suspicious individuals entering the school area.

Supervision can also be extended beyond the regular school day by scheduling community education classes in the school during evening hours, providing escorts to the parking lot after nighttime activities, and/or hiring private security guards to patrol the building and grounds after hours.

Sample Parent Letter
(school letterhead)

Dear Parents and Guardians:

I want to share with you the facts about an incident at school earlier this week, so that you will know what happened and how the school dealt with it.

On Tuesday, the Assistant Principal was informed by a student that another student had brought a gun to school. When called, the student admitted that he had a gun in his locker. The student was suspended immediately and the expulsion process has begun.

Incidents like this are rare, but three points about this event bear emphasis:

1. No student who brings a weapon into the school will be allowed to continue to attend. Steps to expel the student will be taken immediately.
2. We will communicate promptly and openly with students and parents about any incident involving a firearm at school.
3. The great majority of our students are responsible citizens. They care about their school community, as evidenced by the student who reported this incident.

In every community, young people are confronted with tough choices. Teamwork and vigilance are required of parents, educators, and responsible students to maintain a healthy learning environment to support good choices on the part of our students.

I appreciate the level of support families have given in the past and believe that our strict enforcement policy reflects community values. If you have questions or comments about the handling of this incident please call me.

Sincerely,

Principal

Where human supervision ends, technological surveillance can take over. Modern technology has added a new dimension to school security. It pays to re-examine your school's safety devices periodically by having professionals conduct a security audit of the entire building.

One of the most controversial applications of technology for security purposes is the use of metal detectors to seek out concealed weapons in schools. With weapon-use on the rise, more and more schools are employing hand-held wands

Tips for Handling Fights in School

1. Use your best authoritative voice to get combatant's attention.
2. Remind the parties of school policy and consequences for fighting.
3. Elicit help from other staff members or students to subdue the parties.
4. Try to separate the combatants as quickly as possible.
5. Watch out for weapons; don't take chances. (If necessary, use Mace or a fire hose to stop the fighting.)
6. Once separated, try to "talk the parties down."
7. Send someone for medical help if needed.
8. Disperse all onlookers and clear the area.
9. Get someone to record the names of witnesses.
10. Inform/alert administrators, the police liaison officer, security monitors or other authorities as appropriate.
11. Preserve the fight scene until cleared by someone in authority.
12. Write up the incident in as much detail as possible. (See *Sample Incident Report Form*.)

or walk-through metal detectors to screen students and check lockers for guns and other metal weapons. The National School Safety Center estimates that 1/4 of the largest school systems in the country now use metal detectors in one way or another.

Some schools use the devices to randomly search students at periodic intervals. Others use them only to check out rumors and follow-up on tips. They also have been utilized widely at school parties and special events where many outsiders are in attendance.

Opponents argue that subjecting large numbers of students to metal detector screenings is demeaning, constitutes an invasion of privacy, and violates student civil rights. Users of metal detectors, on the other hand, maintain that desperate times call for desperate measures. Safety is more important than minor inconvenience and loss of privacy.

Additional means which can improve security and reduce the risk of violence include the installation of:

- Magnetic locks on all doors;
- Closed circuit TV cameras and monitors inside and outside the building (even the presence of an unloaded camera can be an effective deterrent to violence and unlawful acts);

Sample Incident Report Form

Type of Incident: _____

Date of Incident: _____

Time and Location of Incident:_____

Students Involved: _____

_____

_____

Names of Witnesses:_____

_____

Injuries (if any): _____

What seemed to cause the incident?:_____

_____

Describe the circumstances and what happened: _____

_____

_____

_____

To whom was the incident reported?: _____

_____   _____
Signature   Date
                                       (Must be completed within 24 hours)

- Electronic audio or movement sensor alarm systems;
- Improved lighting throughout the building and grounds, especially in parking lot areas;
- Mirrors to provide surveillance of hard-to-see areas (redesigning certain parts of the physical plant and relandscaping to eliminate areas obscured from view can also improve security);
- Panic buttons in particularly hazardous sections of the building.

Security-conscious administrators are always looking for ways to improve supervision, surveillance, and safety measures throughout the building and grounds. It's better to have too much security than too little in today's schools. Investments in better security now are less costly than paying for damage control and liability claims later on.

HOW TO PLAN AN ANTIVIOLENCE EDUCATION PROGRAM

Preventing violence through education is better and easier than stopping it once it has become commonplace in the school. Students of all ages, even tough kids, can be taught to be nonviolent.

Teaching nonviolence should start as early as possible (preschool) and be reinforced continually through all levels of schooling. The goals of an effective antiviolence education program are simple:

1. To help individuals think more of themselves;
2. To develop prosocial skills;
3. To teach about the dangers of violence;
4. To take away the "romance" of violence;
5. To teach students how to avoid and evade violence and to protect themselves;
6. To train students to alert an adult when violence occurs;
7. To teach better ways than physical force to settle problems between individuals and groups.

In the beginning, teaching against violence can be very basic. Following years of experience in dealing with juvenile offenders, Judge Isabel Gomez of the Hennepin County Court (MN) maintains that if schools would teach only one simple rule, "No hitting," violence and other disciplinary problems would be curtailed drastically at all levels. Psychologist John Rosemond advocates giving young children a daily dose of "Vitamin N" (saying "No") as a means of equipping them to stay away from violence.

At all levels, schools can model and teach nonviolent behaviors indirectly by:

• Demonstrating moral, ethical, and humane leadership from the top;
• Following a discipline plan which promotes and upholds values of dignity and support for all students;
• Developing student government and decision-making processes that truly involve students and foster a sense of "this is our school;"
• Designing a learning culture of respect throughout the school.

In today's world, however, indirect instruction and subtlety won't suffice. With lessons of violence presented vividly in the media and on the streets every day, someone has to proactively teach ways of nonviolence. As more faltering families fail to teach nonviolent values, it looks like it's up to the schools. Every school should have some form of program of direct instruction against violence.

The explosion of violent acts involving children and youth has sent educators scrambling to develop meaningful antiviolence curriculums and materials. Programs of antiviolence education take many forms including drama, role-playing, media presentations, and traditional teaching strategies. The best combine a variety of formats in order to reach the greatest number of students.

It is possible to build your own antiviolence curriculum based on your school's and community's unique needs. In many cases, a tailor-made program can be most effective. There are lots of resources available to assist staffs in shaping a home-grown curriculum against violence such as those that follow.

Teaching Tools for Antiviolence Education

1. *A Family That Fights* (S. C. Bernstein, Albert Whitman & Co.)
2. *Every Kid's Guide To Handling Feelings* (J. Berry, Children's Press)
3. *Don't Feed the Monster on Tuesday: The Children's Self-Esteem Book* (A. Moser, Landmark Editions)
4. *Don't Pop Your Cork on Monday: The Children's Antistress Book* (A. Moser, Landmark Editions)
5. *I Have Feelings Too* (T. Bergen, Human Sciences Press)
6. *It's O.K. to be Different* (M. Golant, Tom Doherty Associates)
7. *Liking Myself* (P. Palmer, Impart Publishers)
8. *Mommy and Daddy are Fighting* (S. Paris, Seal Press)
9. *Something is Wrong at My House: A Book About Parents Fighting* (D. Davis, Parenting Press)
10. "Sooper Puppy" (video on self-esteem, MTI Film)
11. *Stick Up for Yourself: Every Kid's Guide to Personal Power and Positive Self-Esteem* (G. Kaufman and L. Raphael, Free Spirit)
12. *This is Me and My Single Parent* (M. Evans, Bruner/Mazel)

There are enough good ready-made programs out there, however, that you don't have to reinvent the wheel. The following is a sampler of successful antiviolence programs and materials that can be adopted or adapted for any school:

1. *Ouch!* A violence-prevention play featuring multimedia drama, wide-screen TV and on-stage characters. The play addresses conflict in a variety of situations: between siblings, between parents, between parents and children, school bullying, and violence on TV. After viewing the play, students participate in follow-up activities over a 4–6 week period. (CLIMB Theatre Co., St. Paul, MN)

2. *The Eddie Eagle Gun Safety Program.* An accident prevention program for preschool through grade 6. The program consists of an animated video and

accompanying activity books. Teaches young children that guns aren't toys and what to do if they find a gun accessible to them. (National Rifle Association)

3. *Teaching Harmony in Schools.* An outcome-based education model and inservice course on implementing the teaching of nonviolence in the curriculum. Helps teachers develop lessons which stress self-control, conflict resolution and staying calm under fire. (Dennis Smith Self-Esteem Institute, St. Cloud, MN)

4. *FAST (Families and Schools Together).* Developed cooperatively by Vanderbilt, Duke University, Penn State University, and the University of Washington, this program aims to prevent chronic aggressive behavior through early intervention. Participants are selected children entering the first grade and parents, especially single mothers, who are paid to be partners in the program. FAST features skill training, tutoring, and parent education. (National Institute of Mental Health)

5. *Turn Off the Violence.* Sponsored by a grant from the Bureau of Justice Assistance, the program offers family guides and other information on topics such as alternatives to violent entertainment, dealing with bullies, nonviolent methods of conflict resolution, and building blocks to strengthen families. (Turn Off the Violence, Minn., MN)

6. *Kids and Company: Together for Safety.* An elementary school program designed to teach children how to avoid risks and dangerous situations. Now offered in 30 states involving more than 100,000 students. (National Center for Missing and Exploited Children)

Whether you develop your own program locally or purchase a commercially available program, the implementation steps are essentially the same:

1. Assess the status of violence in your school. Talk to kids and parents, review discipline referrals and school nurse records, and exchange information with local police to identify the greatest problems facing your students.

2. Target your intended audience (grade levels, gang members, minorities, at-risk students, and so on).

3. Define specific goals and objectives you want to accomplish with your students.

4. Develop an original program of content, materials, and activities or select a commercially prepared program which is age-appropriate.

5. Pilot the program on a limited basis (include some of the toughest kids in school in the pilot audience).

6. Evaluate and revise as needed.

7. Implement the program schoolwide.

Teaching kids to be nonviolent in today's culture is not easy, but if we can't teach them to get along and solve problems peacefully, we probably can't teach them anything else.

HANDLING THE WORST CASE SCENERIO: TERRORISM IN THE SCHOOL

Despite all the best educational, preventive, and security measures, schools, like other institutions, are vulnerable to unexpected, inexplicable acts of random violence and senseless brutality. In a violence-ridden society, the possibility of hostage-holding, childnapping, terrorism, and even massacre exists everywhere—even in schools.

You can't dismiss the remote chance that some crazed individual, armed and dangerous, might threaten to turn your school into a slaughter house for no apparent reason. It has happened in restaurants, public buildings, hospitals, and schools in a few instances around the country in recent years. It pays to be prepared for the nightmarish prospect of a maniac on the school grounds.

Obviously, school personnel have not been trained to handle a drugged or deranged individual menacing the safety of students. Should such a situation happen in your school, it's not the time for theatrics. Reasoned response, rather than reckless heroism, is called for. Although every situation will differ, experts offer the following sugestions for managing such unthinkable threats in a school:

1. Talk about such possibilities in advance. Have some general plan in mind.

2. Keep a list of emergency phone numbers readily available.

3. Call 911 for HELP immediately!

4. Leave negotiating with the threatening party to experts (police, psychologists).

5. Put your best person in charge of communicating/dealing with the dangerous party until police assume responsibility. This may be the police liason officer, counselor, or yourself.

6. Seal off the area of the school involved if possible.

7. Evacuate students not affected by the situation a safe distance from the school.

8. To the extent possible, follow the demands and requests of the dangerous party until an experienced negotiator takes over, but don't agree to anything that worsens the situation or endangers more people.

9. Keep the threatening party talking, if possible, until help arrives.

10. If known, try to contact someone (family member, friend, coworker) close to the treatening party to help calm him/her down.

11. Designate one person to handle communication with the media, parents, and so forth, during the episode.

12. Be prepared to provide debriefings and counseling to all affected students when the situation is over.

An emergency plan is like an insurance policy. You hope you never have to use it; but if trouble strikes, it may be a lifesaver. Expect the best, but prepare for the worst case scenario.

SAMPLE ANTIVIOLENCE POLICIES THAT WORK

Curbing violence in schools begins and ends with a rock-solid policy of banning guns and other weapons. Good policies serve both a symbolic and practical purpose. They send an unequivocal message about where the school stands and provide a clear-cut guide to action at the same time. Policies without enforcement are useless; but enforcement without a policy is random, irregular, and ineffective.

The following are four real-world policy statements that have worked for school districts across the country.

One of the scariest things about contemporary society is the increased incidence of random violence committed by children against children without remorse or regret. The current cycle of babies having babies who grow up to be violent teenagers who then have more babies, who grow up to be even *more violent,* has got to be broken.

On top of everything else they have to do, schools are going to have to be where it starts. Stopping violence in the schools is the first step. Schools can't be allowed to become shooting galleries.

Violence is not a given. It can be reversed and replaced by rational behavior. Many schools are already making it happen by following the direction set forth in this chapter. Just as unchecked discipline problems are a prelude to violence, positive discipline and a success-oriented learning environment are precursors of a tomorrow where we can all get along together inside and outside of school without violence.

(Sample Policy #1)
Weapons In School
Wichita (KS) Public Schools

Board Policy:

Possession or use of a weapon in a school building is prohibited. A pupil found to be in possession of a weapon on school premises before, during, or after school or at any school-sponsored activity is subject to administrative and/or legal action.

Administrative Implemental Procedures:

1. Weapons are identified in two categories:
   a. Articles commonly used or designed to inflict bodily harm and/or to intimidate other persons.
   b. Articles designed for other purposes but which could easily be used to inflict bodily harm and/or intimidate. Examples would be belts, combs, pencils, files, compasses, scissors, and so on.
2. A pupil acting in an aggressive or belligerent manner with any article will be administratively judged to be in possession of a weapon. Disciplinary action will be taken.
3. A pupil using a weapon in a fight or altercation will be administratively judged to be a danger to others and self and will be subjected to extended suspension or expulsion proceedings, or other appropriate disciplinary action.
4. Administrators or other designated school officials, employing their professional judgment, will confiscate any article previously identified as a weapon under 1(a) above. Such weapons will be submitted to the appropriate law enforcement agency.
5. A pupil who has caused injury to another person with a weapon, intended or unintended, will be subject to disciplinary and/or legal action.
6. A pupil in possession of a weapon is in violation of state statutes.

(Sample Policy #2)
Dangerous Weapons in the Schools
Horsehead, Central School District (NY)

Schools should be an example of observance and respect for law. Schools also must be highly conscious of the health and welfare of students, staff, and the public. In this regard, all dangerous and illegal weapons shall be taken from any person on school property. Dangerous weapons taken from pupils shall be reported to the pupil's parents. Confiscation of weapons may be reported to the police. Appropriate disciplinary and/or legal action shall be pursued by the building principal.

Weapons under the control of law enforcement personnel are permitted. The principal may authorize persons to display weapons that are registered and handled in a legal manner for purpose of education or the community use of school facilities. The principal may prescribe the special conditions or procedures to be followed before giving such authorization.

(Sample Policy #3)
Possession of Weapons and/or Ammunition
New Richmond (WI) Public Schools

No one shall possess a weapon and/or ammunition while on school premises, in any district vehicle or at any school event without written authorization from the building principal or his/her designee. Authorization may be given when a weapon and/or ammunition is handled in a legal manner for the purpose of education and in other cases when possession does not violate a state law.

The only exceptions to this policy are:

1. Weapons and/or ammunition under the control of law enforcement personnel;
2. Weapons and/or ammunition under the control of military personnel who go armed in the line of duty.

The board defines a weapon as, but not limited to, a gun, knife, razor, karate stick, metal knuckle, toy, or look-alike weapon or other object that by the manner in which it is used or is intended to be used, is capable of inflicting harm.

The building principal or his/her designee if present, or the person in charge of the school event or his/her designee, shall contact law enforcement officers as soon as possible when there is reason to believe a person is possessing a weapon and/or ammunition in violation of this policy. All weapons and/or ammunition known to be in possession in violation of this policy shall be confiscated by staff members or law enforcement officers. Any weapon and/or ammunition confiscated by staff members shall be turned over to law enforcement officers to be disposed of according to law enforcement or state guidelines.

When staff members or law enforcement officers confiscate a weapon and/or ammunition from a child under 18 years of age, the building principal or designee shall report the incident to the child's parent/guardian.

Any person who knowingly possesses or goes armed with a weapon while on school premises, in any district vehicle or at any school event is subject to the penalties outlined in state law. Disciplinary measures within the school shall be the responsibility of the building principal or his/her designee.

(Sample Policy #4)
Weapons
Howard County (MD) Public Schools

Policy Statement

The Board of Education believes that the presence on school property of weapons poses a serious threat to the safety and well-being of students and staff. It is unlawful for any person to carry or possess any rifle, gun, knife, or deadly weapon of any kind on any public school property. It is our belief, therefore, that the presence on school property of any weapon is strictly forbidden.

Implementation Procedures

1. The principal is directed to inform all students, parents/guardians, and staff of the weapons policy at the beginning of each school year, upon enrollment of a new student, and when deemed necessary by the principal.

2. If any student is suspected of being in violation of the weapons policy, the student must be referred to the principal who will determine if a violation has occurred.

3. If it is determined by the principal that a student is in possession of a weapon, the principal will, after securing the weapon, suspend the student, notify the respective Director, notify the police, and take steps to notify the PTA president of the incident. Care must be taken with respect to notification of the PTA president that confidentiality is maintained.

CHAPTER SEVEN

THE BEST
OF THE BEST IN DRUG
PREVENTION MEASURES

Experts estimate that babies born today will be exposed to more than 100,000 beer ads and commercials by age 21. That's a lot of "drug education." Maybe it's not surprising, then, that most students experiment with legal and/or illegal drugs by the time they graduate from high school.

The pervasive use of mind-altering chemicals is a major threat to our society. Unfortunately, kids are central to the drug culture worldwide. Kids buy drugs. Kids use drugs. Kids sell drugs. Kids rob, steal, and sometimes murder to get money for drugs. This makes drug prevention every school's business.

Where drug use prevails, education fails. The two cannot exist side by side. There is no question that drugs lie at the heart of many common behavior problems in and out of school. You can't successfully manage today's student population without meeting school drug problems head on.

The absence of drugs is a prerequisite to positive discipline and successful learning. When schools keep out or kick out drugs, gangs, and weapons, violent behavior usually goes with them. Schools have to be and can be drug-free.

There are signs that many schools are now winning the war against drugs. It starts with knowing what's happening with kids and drugs in your community.

CURRENT TRENDS IN STUDENT DRUG USE

The ebb and flow of student drug use varies over time and from place to place. The preferred "drug of the month" may change depending on price, availability, quality or crop conditions in different parts of the world. What doesn't change, however, is that nicotine and alcohol remain the most popular drugs among students everywhere and serve as the "gateway drugs" which open the way to experimentation with more lethal narcotics.

Through the 1980s and into the '90s, student use of illicit drugs began to level off and, in some areas, diminish. This long-term downward trend has led many to believe that school and community prevention programs are paying off. We're doing something right; but the news isn't all good:

- The United States still has the highest rate of illicit drug abuse and widespread trafficking in mind-altering drugs among industrialized nations of the world.
- Global production of heroin, cocaine, and marijuana continue to increase.
- The age of first exposure and use is steadily dropping.
- The use of inhalants is increasing among middle-level students in many parts of the country.
- In 1993, there was a resurgence (increase) in drug use by 8th graders.
- Student use of cocaine and crack is going up in some parts of the nation.
- "Crack babies" and students suffering from fetal alcohol syndrome are now reaching school age in substantial numbers.
- Incidents of drug-related crimes and violence involving youth are rising in most areas.
- The threat of AIDS has added a deadly dimension to all student drug use involving needles/syringes.

There is obviously a lot more work to be done. Too many students are still using too many drugs.

According to "Monitoring the Future," a continuing study of youth lifestyles and values funded by the National Institute on Drug Abuse:

- More than half of all teenagers have used some drug(s) at least once.
- More than one-half of teenagers have used marijuana at least once.
- Over 90% of teenagers have tried alcohol by their senior year in high school.

The top three on today's teen hit parade of drugs are:

1. Alcohol
2. Marijuana
3. Cocaine

As long as students are willing to waste their lives and their futures on drugs, schools must address the issue in every way possible. What schools do best is teach drug prevention and healthy life choices.

WHAT'S NEW IN DRUG EDUCATION

Since the 1970s, schools have learned a lot about what works and what doesn't in antidrug education. We've learned that scare tactics don't work, one-shot programs aren't effective, and teaching students to "Just say, 'No'" isn't enough.

Experience across the country has demonstrated repeatedly that effective drug education programs share the following characteristics:

- Programs are cumulative and integrated into the regular curriculum (not a separate add-on).
- Includes education about alcohol and tobacco (the gateway drugs) as well as illegal drugs.
- Starts in kindergarten (or earlier).
- Presents hazards and consequences without sensationalism or unsubstantiated threats.
- Addresses the broad range of motivation for drug use (see *Reasons Why Kids Use Drugs*).
- Includes education for the entire family.

Reasons Why Kids Use Drugs

1. Peer pressure/conformity
2. Fun/Get "high"
3. Escape pain (family and personal problems)
4. Low self-esteem
5. Thrill-seeking
6. Media and street models

- Teaches coping skills (positive affirmations, goal setting, reality checking, relaxation techniques, and so on).
- Bolsters individual student self-esteem.

- Teaches social skills (for instance, pressure-resisting skills).

Of all the approaches tried to date, research suggests that the best drug education systems are *Social Influence Programs,* which stress refusal and decision-making skills. Such programs cost little, require limited time (as little as 10 hours of direct instruction), and make a big difference. Two popular examples are:

1. D.A.R.E. (Drug Abuse Resistance Education). A program conceived by educators and taught by police officers that focuses on the "gateway drugs" and provides information and skills related to resisting peer pressure. By 1990, the program had been introduced into 49 of the 50 states.

2. "Project YES." A multimedia program designed to infuse antidrug content into regular subject area curriculum. Developed by the Orange County (CA) Department of Education.

As school leaders, you have an obligation to establish a sound, sequential drug education program based on the principles above. It makes little difference if the program is commercially developed or designed locally as long as the goals are clear and the facts are straight.

ROLE OF THE CHEMICAL HEALTH SPECIALIST

Preventive education programs work, but they take time and have to be repeated continually for new audiences. Some drug problems can't wait to be solved. They need action now, on the spot. That's why every school needs some staff member(s) specially trained to provide leadership in drug prevention, to help students with individual drug problems, and to assist entire families victimized by drugs.

Staffing needs evolve and change over time. At one point, many schools had need for vocational agriculture instructors. Today, such positions are almost nonexistent in public schools. The same fate has befallen driver's education teachers in many parts of the country where schools have gotten out of the driver training business. Today's needs are different. Now, *every school needs access to a chemical health specialist on staff, fulltime!*

There are too many problems too compelling to be handled as an add-on to the job description of an existing teacher, counselor, or administrator. Someday, chemical health specialists may work themselves out of a job in schools; for now, all schools need this kind of help. Establishing such a position on your staff isn't a frill. It's called survival.

Whatever title is used for this position (Drug Counselor, Chemical Health Coordinator, Chemical Dependency Worker, and so on), this person has to play an action role in the school. For some students and families, this will be the most important person on your staff.

Chemical Health Specialist
(sample job description)

Responsible to: Principal

Responsibilities:

1. Act as a resource on chemical health issues for students, staff, parents, and the public.
2. Collect and interpret data on student drug use in and out of school.
3. Conduct interventions with students and staff members as needed.
4. Conduct chemical dependency evaluations and make referrals as appropriate.
5. Assume leadership in developing parent/community education and awareness programs.
6. Provide leadership for Al-A-Teen and other support groups in the school.
7. Facilitate "second chance" opportunities and placements for students recovering from dependency problems and/or returning from treatment.
8. Work with law enforcement agencies to prevent, detect, and eliminate unlawful drug activities on the school campus.
9. Develop continuing in-service training for staff on chemical dependency and mental health issues.
10. Promote the teaching of healthy lifestyles throughout the curriculum.
11. Assist in developing and implementing preventive strategies.
12. Serve as liaison with community agencies involved in drug prevention.
13. Assist staff with the identification and referral of students who have other types of dependency, behavior, or abuse problems (for example, compulsive gambling, eating disorders, gang members, runaways, suicidal tendencies).
14. Perform other duties as assigned by the Principal or designee.

Drug problems are dirty, sticky, "tough love" situations. They don't get solved by theorists or bureaucrats. It takes an unflinching professional who takes risks, talks straight, and isn't afraid to tackle sensitive subjects head on (see *Sample Job Description*).

Handling personal, chemical health issues involving students or adults is often one-on-one work. *Reclaiming lives is labor intensive.* Even with severe budget limitations, no school can afford to shortchange itself or its students in providing drug counseling and chemical health staffing.

Sometimes, a single staff position isn't enough to handle all the drug problems in the school. Where the need is great, some schools have stretched tight dollars by adding low-cost Group Facilitator Aides to assist the licensed chemical health specialist (See *Sample Job Description*).

Group Facilitator Aide
(sample job description)

Responsible to: Chemical Health Specialist

Responsibilities:

1. Conduct student support groups within guidelines established by the chemical health specialist.
2. Provide support to regular classroom teachers in implementing the established drug education curriculum.
3. Confer with social workers, counselors, and administrators to discuss specific problems of group participants.
4. Assist with home activities when appropriate.
5. Perform other duties as assigned by the chemical health specialist.

Schools aren't treatment centers; but they are the only place some kids can go for help and get a second chance. Kids who are dependent on chemicals can't be independent learners. We owe them trained, professional staff to help get them back on track. That's part of what it takes to have good discipline and successful learning in schools today.

MAKING DRUG PREVENTION A COMMUNITY AFFAIR

When kids use drugs, it's not someone else's problem, but it's not the exclusive responsibility of the school either. Everyone in the community has a stake in drug-free schools. Where drug problems are under control, drug prevention is a community enterprise.

It's almost impossible for drug-dealers, gangs, or any other undesirable element to withstand the pressure of a cohesive community united behind a common purpose. Communities can be rid of drugs if they have the collective will to take collective action. Schools can and should be the catalyst for activating and galvanizing communitywide resources to drive out drugs. The usual steps for implementing a community antidrug action plan are:

(Sample Mission Statement)
Community Chemical Action Network
St. Louis Park, MN

The mission of the Chemical Action Network is to secure the cooperation and coordinate those formal and informal structures in the community that assist adolescents in making rational and responsible decisions about the use of mood-altering chemicals. The Chemical Action Network will unite the community resources in a program of education and awareness aimed at the concerns of young people in order to convert peer pressure to abuse chemicals into positive attitudes which enable individuals to create healthy lifestyles.

Goal 1: The Chemical Action Network will coordinate all formal and informal drug awareness efforts located in or impacting the St. Louis Park Community.

Goal 2: The Chemical Action Network will develop, recommend, promote, and coordinate the implementation of communitywide policies which lessen substance use by the youth of St. Louis Park.

Goal 3: The Chemical Action Network will encourage the positive involvement of youth in experiences to promote chemical health.

Goal 4: The Chemical Action Network will seek resources for programs and outreach efforts that alert parents and other concerned individuals to causes and symptoms of chemical abuse and provide information on alternatives and referrals for assistance.

1. Establish a community Drug Task Force or Chemical Health Advisory Committee.
2. Collect community data on drug use and abuse by all age groups.
3. Plan and execute communitywide prevention strategies.

Any communitywide task force on drug prevention should include representation from a cross-section of the population (schools, city government, law enforcement, parents, students, businesses, human service agencies, medicine, churches, synagogues, and the community at large) and have a clearly defined purpose (see *Sample Mission Statement*). The task force should mobilize the minority population within the community and should aim at changing adult behavior as well as student behavior.

Some citywide task forces have been successful in creating a full- or part-time position of Community Chemical Health Coordinator supported by a combination of city/school funding and private donation. Having someone in charge helps focus communitywide activities and gets things done by moving the committee's agenda from the board room to the streets where it will do some good.

Examples of activities that have contributed to successful antidrug campaigns in many communities include the following:

- Sponsor Red Ribbon activities to celebrate National Chemical Health Week. (Red ribbons are distributed to be attached to car antennas as a reminder of drug awareness and prevention. One community even tied a huge red ribbon around the city's water tower.)
- Produce drug prevention videos or public service announcements.
- Create a community Chemical Health Resource Library.
- Conduct community focus groups on drug problems and preventive measures.
- Compile a directory of self-help organizations and human services agencies in the community. Many community members are often surprised by the amount of help available close by (see *Sample List of 12-step Community Self-help Organizations*).
- Establish a speakers bureau and conduct community workshops on drug-related topics.
- Blanket the city with posters, billboards, and pamphlets with appropriate drug information.
- Lobby for reasonable statutory curfews for minors.
- Support strict enforcement of age requirements for purchase of beer and liquor.
- Arrange for local merchants to offer discounts to students with signed drug-free pledge cards.
- Harass street dealers, videotape drug deals in progress, picket "crack houses," and so on.
- Support positive youth activity programs.

An aroused community can take back its youth and wipe out drugs. When an entire community says, "No," even hard-core drug dealers listen. A strong school-community partnership is the best defense against student drug problems.

Next to a communitywide task force, the school's most powerful ally against drugs is usually a well-organized Parent Communication Network (PCN). In most places, PCNs are made up of parents committed to supporting each other in preventing alcohol and drug use among children through positive adult peer pressure.

The most common PCN activity is the compilation of a directory of parents who support drug-free activities for children and youth. Parents who agree to list their names in the PCN directory pledge to:

(Sample List)
12-Step Community Self-Help Organization

Adult Children of Sex Addicts

Adults Recovering from Incest

Alcoholics Anonymous

Al-A-Non

Al-A-Teen

Cocaine Anonymous

Coc-Anon

Codependents Anonymous

Co-survivors of Incest

Debtors Anonymous

Emotions Anonymous

Families Anonymous

Gamblers Anonymous

Self Abuse Anonymous

Sex Addicts Anonymous

Sex and Love Addicts Anonymous

Sexaholics Anonymous

Shoplifters Anonymous

Women with Multiple Addictions

Workaholics Anonymous

Gam-Anon

Jewish Recovery Network

Mental Illness Anonymous

Narcotics Anonymous

Nicotine Anonymous

Obsessive Compulsive Disorder Support Groups

Obsessive Compulsive Anonymous

Open Door (Agoraphobia and Panic Disorder Support)

Overeaters Anonymous

Parents Anonymous

Pills Anonymous

Recoveries Anonymous

Recovering Couples Anonymous

Spenders Anonymous

Tough Love Peer Support Groups

12 Steps for Kids Groups

Women for Sobriety

At the elementary age level

1. Always provide adequate supervision for your children and their guests.

2. Get to know the parents of your children's friends and communicate with them about where children are going, with whom, and if the event is supervised.

3. Communicate with other parents regarding videos and/or TV programs to be viewed by children when they have guests.

4. Attend parent education programs addressing basic parenting skills and drug abuse prevention information.

5. Work with the PCN groups and within the community to provide a unified approach to the prevention and reduction of alcohol and other drug use.

At the secondary age level

1. Sponsor drug-free and chaperoned events at home and/or in the community.
2. Educate yourself on parenting skills and other information related to drug prevention/intervention.
3. Communicate to children drug use prevention information and a strong no-use message on alcohol and other drugs.
4. Communicate with other parents about where your and their children are going, with whom, if an event is to be chaperoned and drug free, and set appropriate curfew.
5. Work with the Parent Network, the school, and the community whenever possible to promote a unified approach to preventing drug and alcohol use and abuse.

Other popular Parent Communication Network projects include providing parents with free information on drug prevention (see *Sample Tip Sheet*) and encouraging drug-free celebrations and events (see *Sample Parent Letter*).

Educators, parents, and community members can forge a powerful coalition to make the school safe from drugs. It's important that students not feel alone when dealing with the pressures and problems of drug use. It's equally important that the school not feel alone in combating drugs. There's plenty of help out there. It's your job to go get it.

(Sample Tip Sheet)
10 Steps to Help Your Child Say NO
(Supplied by OSAP—Office for Substance Abuse Prevention)

1. Talk with children about alcohol and drugs.
2. Learn to really listen.
3. Help your child feel good about himself/herself.
4. Help your child develop values.
5. Be a good role model.
6. Help your child deal with peer pressure.
7. Make family rules.
8. Encourage healthy creative activities.
9. Team up with other parents.
10. Know what to do if you suspect a problem.

(Sample PCN Parent Letter)

Dear Parents:

Every year young people begin to think about celebrations: Homecoming, prom, graduation, and spring break. Celebrations can be wonderful, but each year some celebrations end with drug (including alcohol) abuse, destruction of property, pregnancy, accidents, and sometimes death.

Can communities, parents, schools, law enforcement, and businesses working together discourage and eventually eliminate the student kegger, the motel/hotel scene, and limousine party? Can parents "just say no" to providing hotel/motel rooms and "just say no" when asked for permission to attend such an activity? The answer is "*YES*!"

Parents, you and your children should make plans for the spring celebrations and spring break. How about chemically free parties with adult chaperones? ... Talk to other parents, call a parent who is hosting a party to get the facts. Communicate with your student about your fears and values. Enforce reasonable curfews and support school policy regarding chemical use. Adults who care can make a difference. To make change happen, a lot of people must cooperate by supporting the same message, "You don't have to use chemicals to have a celebration and have fun!"

It has been our experience that the majority of students want parents to give them guidelines. We encourage you to help us help your son/daughter have chemically free social activities.

Sincerely,

Parent Communication Network Committee

HOW TO HAVE A DRUG-FREE SCHOOL

If you want kids to get high on learning, your school has to be out-of-bounds for drugs. Each year, the federal government recognizes hundreds of schools, representing every state in the union, for being drug-free. What works for these schools can work in yours. The keys to keeping any school free from drugs are:

1. *Prevention* (education);
2. *Intervention* (including support groups for recovering students);
3. *Promotion* (healthy life styles).

No school becomes drug-free until it says it is. That's what policies are for. Every elementary and secondary school today needs to have an unequivocal policy statement outlawing Tobacco, Alcohol, and Other Drugs (TAOD). These policies serve as blueprints for action which define the limits and spell out consequences. The better-written the policy, the clearer the message and the cleaner the application. Vague policies lead to fuzzy interpretations and sloppy enforcement. The following are examples of real-world anti-TAOD policies which have proved enforceable and effective in selected schools from different corners of the country. (Note one district even has a policy banning beepers, which are often used to contact students who serve as runners for drug deals.)

Once firm policies are in place, everyone has a responsibility to translate them into action. All staff members should be trained to spot students who may be having problems with drugs (see *Indicators of Possible Drug Use*). Emergency intervention guidelines should also be established to help staff deal with individual drug situations (see *Sample Guidelines*).

In many places, certain staff members are selected to serve as a Chemical Assessment Team (CAT) for the school. Members of the team work closely with the licensed chemical health specialist to evaluate referrals, take action when needed, and advise the administration on prevention and intervention strategies.

Make up of the CAT usually includes counselors, social workers, the school nurse, health instructors, special education personnel, coaches, and regular classroom teachers. The CAT review process may lead to several courses of action such as: case conferencing, continued "watch," parent contacts, referral to an outside agency, formal medical or chemical assessment, and/or special placement of the student.

Indicators of Possible Drug Use

- Physical changes such as marked weight loss or other changes in appearance.
- Signs of excessive fatigue or sleepiness.
- Uncharacteristic disruptive behavior (sudden outbursts, hyperactivity, use of obscenity, acting out).
- Sudden drop in grades.
- Change in social groups.
- Withdrawal/noninvolvement
- Appearance of drug-related paraphernalia (dark glasses, sandwich bags, thermos bottles, pipes).
- Unusually large amounts of spending money.

(Sample Policy #1)
Tobacco-free Environment
St. Louis Park (MN) Public Schools

...smoking and the use of tobacco products shall be prohibited on School District property including school buildings and grounds; in contracted and school-owned vehicles and other vehicles on School District property; and at school or District-sponsored events or activities. Possession of tobacco products by students on school property is prohibited and shall be considered a violation of this policy.

(Sample Policy #2)
Alcohol and Other Drugs Policy
Howard County (MD) Public Schools

The presence and use of alcoholic beverages and other drugs ... poses a serious threat to the health, safety, and well-being of students and staff. The ... system is committed to promoting and providing a drug-free academic environment for all students. Therefore, alcoholic beverages and other drugs are prohibited ... on school premises or at school-related activities in which a student participates (athletic event, field trip, prom) or in which the student does not directly participate but represents the school or student body simply by being there (for example, spectator at athletic event).

The Board of Education believes that a cooperative approach between the school system and the parents is necessary to eliminate alcoholic beverages and other drug use among our students through educational programs, counseling, and parent and peer leadership and support. Continuing efforts will be made to improve programs designed to educate students as to the physical, psychological, and social/legal consequences of alcohol and other drug use. Students are encouraged to seek counseling and will be reminded that there is a public law that provides confidentiality for students who seek counseling.

(Sample Policy #3)
Student Drug Abuse
Cheektowaga (NY) Central School District

It is the responsibility of every staff member to immediately report any indication of drug or alcohol abuse to the principal *and* the Health Office.

The procedures listed below will be followed when a student is found in possession or under the influence of drugs or alcohol while on school premises or at school-sponsored events:

1. If the student appears to be in physical distress, action will be taken immediately to obtain medical care as deemed appropriate by school officials. Parents will be notified *immediately*.

2. The student will be kept under the supervision of designated school personnel at all times.

3. Whenever possible, parents will be notified immediately and asked to come to school to take the student home.

4. The student will be suspended from school by the principal for a period of five days.

5. A conference with both parents will be held before the end of the five day period to discuss the student's behavior. Possible results of this conference can include:

   a. Readmission to school on a "probation-like" status, which would include barring the student from cocurricular activities.

   b. Transfer to another school for the remainder of the school year.

   c. Withdrawal from school.

6. In all cases where possession of the drug is in violation of the law, the school will file a complaint with the … police. The school also may refer the student to a recognized agency for counseling.

7. Any student who violates this policy two times will be subject to disciplinary action in accordance with the law. Such action could lead to the student being excluded from school permanently.

(Sample Policy #4)
Alcohol Use By Students
Grossman Union High School, La Mesa, CA

Possession or use of alcoholic beverages on school property is illegal. Any student who unlawfully uses, possesses, sells, or otherwise furnishes alcoholic beverages while on school grounds or during an activity off school grounds related to school attendance will be referred to the director of continuation education for administrative action....

...The options for action will include, but are not limited to, transfer to the continuation school program, transfer to another high school outside the district ... or appropriate disciplinary action at the local school ... A satisfactory record of achievement and behavior will be a condition of readmission to the regular high school.

(Sample Policy #5)
Student Discipline (Alcohol)
School District 25, Pocatello, ID

Use of, possession of, or being under the influence of alcohol by a student while on school grounds, in school buildings, in a school bus or at any school-sponsored function or activity is considered a major discipline problem....

First Offense

Disciplinary action will be initiated ... If the offense is deemed serious by the principal or designee, the case will be referred directly to the Board with a recommendation for expulsion....

Second Offense

In the event of a second violation of the alcohol policy, the student will be referred directly to the Board with a recommendation for expulsion. The parents/guardian and student will be advised of the expulsion procedure and their rights to a hearing at a meeting with the Board.

(Sample Policy #6)
Student Use of Beepers
New Richmond (WI) Public Schools

Student use or possession of "beepers" (electronic paging or two-way communication devices) is prohibited in school buildings, on school grounds, and in school vehicles. The building principal, however, is authorized to permit a student to use and/or carry a "beeper" for medical, school, educational, vocational, or other purpose where deemed appropriate.

Students violating this policy shall be disciplined in accordance with established procedures.

(Sample Guidelines)
Emergency Intervention Guidelines

The following procedures are intended as a process to follow if you *suspect* a student to be intoxicated or "high" on drugs. This intent, even for suspicions, will send a very important message that we want to promote a drug-free atmosphere. It is important to refer any student whom you suspect is using (drugs or alcohol) as soon as possible. You don't have to confront the student directly; but can instead follow these guidelines:

1. **DON'T PANIC.** Always be guided by what is best for the student.
2. Trust your instincts. It's O.K. if your suspicions turn out to be false. At least, the message of "no use" will be clear.
3. Respond immediately.
4. Try to separate the student quietly from the curiosity of onlookers.
5. Call the office to inform staff you need an escort *now* due to suspicions of a student's use.
6. The escort may be an administrator, aide, counselor, or social worker.
7. When the escort arrives, inform him/her of the specific behavior you are concerned about (even if it's only a "smell" of alcohol or marijuana).
8. The student will then be escorted to an administrator who will follow established procedures.
9. Do not retain any substance suspected to be nonprescribed drugs; such substance should be placed in a sealed envelope, labeled with the date and student's name and given to the Principal and/or the police for disposition.
10. Students who sell or attempt to sell unknown substances suspected to be nonprescribed drugs shall be reported for appropriate police action.

Much of the energy for an effective drug-free initiative often comes from the students themselves. The same peer pressure that drives some students to use drugs can be turned around to help keep kids straight, clean, and sober. Many schools have benefited from the leadership and positive role models provided by antidrug student groups such as:

1. **SAAD** (Students Against Drunk Driving). A nationwide organization with chapters in many secondary schools. The primary purpose of this activist organization is to eliminate underage drinking, drinking and driving, and drug abuse.
2. **AFDA** (Athletes for Drug Awareness or Activities for Drug Awareness). Many schools have such an organization designed for student leaders (for

example, athletic team captains and leaders of other extracurricular activities). Specific goals for these organizations usually include:

- Commitment to nonuse of mood-altering chemicals.
- Communication of this commitment to respective team/activity member.
- Creation of a team/activity process for handling drug violations by students.
- Formation of a speakers' bureau for elementary and junior high students providing a positive peer model.

3. **SWACA** (Students Who Are Chemically Aware). A club activity for middle and junior high school age students would like to remain chemically free. In most cases, the club has three main goals:

- To encourage students to commit to being alcohol, drug, and tobacco free.
- To plan and promote chemically free activities.
- To empower members to encourage others to make the same commitment to being chemically free.

One of the most powerful tools used by such student organizations is a no-use pledge/contract signed by both students and parents (see examples).

Contract
for
Chemical Nonuse

I pledge to make a personal commitment to a very important person—myself. I have chosen at this time in my life not to use mood-altering chemicals, particularly alcohol, marijuana, and other illegal drugs. I understand that if I want to feel good for whatever reason I might have, I will try to resort to natural highs to meet these temporary desires. If I find myself struggling to keep this contract, I will seek support to help me stay straight and sober.

_____   _____
Date   Student

                                     _____
                                     Parent

**Contract
for
Life***

A Contract for Life Between Parent and Teenager

Under this contract, we understand S.A.D.D. encourages all youth to adopt a *no use* policy and obey the laws of this state with regard to alcohol and illicit drugs.

Teenager: I agree to call you for advice and/or transportation at any time from any place if I am ever in a situation where a driver has been drinking or using illicit drugs. I have discussed with you and fully understand your attitude toward any incident with underage drinking or the use of illegal drugs.

_____
Signature

Parent: I agree to come and get you at any hour, any place, no questions asked, and no argument at that time or I will pay for a taxi to bring you home safely. I expect we would discuss this at a later time.

I agree to seek safe, sober transportation home if I am ever in a situation where I have had too much to drink or a friend who is driving me has had too much to drink.

_____
Signature

_____
Date

*Distributed by S.A.D.D., "Students Against Drunk Driving"

Other student and staff activities which have helped successful schools create a drug-free environment include:

- Holding joint parent-student forums to discuss the problems of drug use.
- Establishing an anonymous hot line for reporting illegal drug activities by students.
- Issuing wallet-size commitment cards for students willing to pledge abstinence from drugs.
- Including antidrug messages in the school's weekly bulletin of announcements to be read to all students (see examples).

Weekly Bulletin Messages
(sample to be read to all students)

Did You Know

Quick Facts
- Beverage alcohol is a central nervous system depressant.
- It is the most abused drug in our society.
- It can cause intoxication, unconsciousness, and even death.
- It is as potent as many illegal drugs.

Did You Know

Serious Side Effects of Inhalants
Judgment is often impaired. There is confusion, hyperactivity, irritation, tension, and often fright. Panic and physical aggression, even acute psychosis, have occurred with solvent abuse.

Did You Know

What Are the Physical Side Effects of Steroids?
Heart—Increased blood pressure and change in cholesterol levels associated with heart attacks and strokes.
Liver—Liver damage, tumors, and blood-filled cysts.

Did You Know

Children of Alcoholics
Many children of alcoholics develop common characteristics due to their parents' alcoholism. These include:
- fear of losing control;
- all or nothing, black and white behaviors;
- inability to relax or play;
- fear of feelings.

—Chemical Health Specialist

- Sponsoring chemically free dances and parties.
- Displaying healthy lifestyle posters throughout the building.
- Exchanging antidrug speakers with other schools.

- Holding vigils for victims of drunk drivers or other drug-related fatalities.
- Using a chemically free, overnight "lock-in" in the school gymnasium as a fund-raiser for antidrug programs.

The number of worthwhile prevention activities is limited only by the imagination and creativity of the staff and student body.

You don't have to put up with drugs in your school. A caring staff, informed students, concerned parents, and a supportive community make up the winning combination it takes to keep any school closed to drugs and open to successful learning by all pupils.

How to Handle
Sexual Harassment
in School

Just as educators felt that their plate was full, they've been handed another "hot potato." Sexual harassment, in and out of schools, has been a secret our society has kept too long. Most organizations have only recently and reluctantly begun to deal with it as a legitimate workplace issue. Now it has been catapulted to the forefront as a discipline concern involving student-to-student discrimination and misconduct. The issue has legal, moral, and economic ramifications for all school leaders and neither society nor the media will let us forget it.

Sexual harassment, in one form or another, touches all institutions, but schools are particularly vulnerable. No other entity deals with large numbers of volatile, energetic, and hormone-driven young people confined in limited space for long hours everyday. Incidents of harassing behavior among students occur daily in all schools regardless of size, level, or location.

The emergence of sexual harassment as an act of illegal discrimination must now change the way administrators look at and deal with such behavior. Sexual harassment among students won't go away by itself. School officials can no longer ignore it, deny it, or downplay it. The issue is now clearly defined as a test of mutual human respect and how people treat each other in schools.

What Is Sexual Harassment? What's Not?

Governmental agencies, as well as the nation's courts and conscience, have finally made it perfectly clear that sexual harassment is a form of discrimination and that students are legally protected from it. What once may have been passed off as a natural part of growing up and the inevitable testing and teasing between the sexes is now illegal. The old days of locker room, "boys will be boys" behavior are gone. It's not funny anymore!

In its simplest terms, harassment is any form of unwelcome sexual behavior imposed on one person by another. The operable word is "unwelcome." If any act of sexually oriented communication or behavior between two people makes one individual feel afraid, offended, or uncomfortable, it may constitute sexual harassment. Ultimately the definition of harassment lies in the eyes of the beholder. As one author has suggested, "sexual harassment is just a dignified term for disgusting behavior." In its most extreme manifestation, such harassment becomes sexual abuse and escalates to a much higher level of concern and potential penalty.

The laws of most states now recognize two kinds of sexual harassment: (1) *Quid Pro Quo Harassment*—the requiring or soliciting of sexual favors by the use of power (through threats or rewards) and (2) *Hostile Environment Harassment*—any unwelcome or unwanted communication of a sexual nature.

Obviously one or both forms of harassment happen frequently in schools across the nation. As a school official, you should also realize that harassing behavior can occur beyond the school, on school buses, at off-campus athletic or other extracurricular events, and so on. The responsibility of the school extends a "zone of protection" to students wherever they may be, as long as they are involved in school sponsored, authorized, or supervised activities.

Since harassment is largely a matter of perception on the part of the victim, it's risky to identify any specific sexual activity as being clearly outside the definition. Usually voluntary consential relationships do not qualify as harassment; but the picture can change quickly if the relationship sours and one party's behavior becomes "unwelcome" to the other. Likewise, a single incident would not ordinarily be classified as harassment. Sexual harassment normally requires a pattern of unwanted initiatives. Nevertheless, there are situations where one serious incident—even a single verbal infraction—can constitute harassment. Employees have been discharged for knowingly violating a policy that prohibits sexual harassment.

To help you distinguish between acceptable flirtation or innocent "horseplay" and unacceptable harassing behavior, experts suggest personalizing the situation by applying a simple three-point test such as the following:

Three-Point Test for Sexual Harassment

1. Would you want your son or daughter treating others this way?
2. Would you be comfortable if such behavior were directed toward your sister, wife, or daughter?
3. Would the behavior be offensive if it were videotaped and viewed by girls or women you respect?

One common mistake that administrators make is using *intent* as a criteria for judging harassment. A student or adult doesn't have to intend to harass in order to be guilty of unacceptable or illegal actions. Any sexual behavior that makes one party experience fear, embarrassment, or exploitation is against the law.

Unfortunately, some school personnel still take sexual harassment lightly. In reality, the effects on victims can be devastating including depression, diminished self-esteem, alienation from the school, and distrust of the opposite sex and the system as a whole. As a representative of the school system, it's your job to prevent any pattern of sexual interaction that creates an unhealthy physical or psychological atmosphere for any student.

EXAMPLES OF SEXUAL HARASSMENT IN SCHOOLS

Although the following list of infractions, which frequently take place in elementary and secondary schools, is not exhaustive, it can help heighten your awareness and sensitivity to the many faces of harassment. Any of the actions below can constitute acts of illegal sexual harassment:

- Whistling or making cat calls
- Sexual gestures
- Teasing and taunting
- Pulling down gym shorts
- Asking personal, sexually oriented questions
- Unwelcome touching
- Leering or staring
- Name calling
- Flipping up skirts
- Unwelcome requests for dates
- Propositioning
- Giving sexual gifts
- Stalking
- Snapping bras
- Personalized graffiti
- Off-color jokes
- Sexual or sexist language
- Suggestive or descriptive letters or notes

- Offensive T-shirts or caps
- Distributing nude pictures
- Unwelcome familiarities
- Grabbing or patting body parts
- Displaying pornographic materials
- Sexual innuendos
- Graphic descriptions of girls
- Rating students' sexual attributes
- Spreading rumors
- Intimidation
- Rape

When confronted with such a list, it's tempting for some school leaders to back off and give up saying, "There's nothing we can do to stamp out all these behaviors." Unfortunately, this isn't a choice. Eliminating illegal acts of harassment can be done and is being done in leading schools in all parts of the country. To correct long-standing practices takes courage and a willingness to undertake some bold initiatives; but timidity has always been the antithesis of leadership.

Turning around how students treat and act toward each other means turning around how everyone in the school thinks about communication, responsibility, relationships, and respect. The first step is to understand that student-to-student sexual harassment is different from most other discipline problems in the schools.

SPECIAL CONCERNS ABOUT STUDENT-TO-STUDENT HARASSMENT

Student-to-student sexual harassment is a unique discipline problem for administrators in many ways:

- The potential for incidents of harassment is enormous in every school every day.
- Some people (students, staff, and parents) still don't think it's wrong.
- Many adults, on and off staff, engaged in this type of behavior when they were young and mores were different. This makes them feel awkward and reluctant in vigorously enforcing antiharassment policies.
- Victims are often too ashamed or embarrassed to report infractions (see *Why Students Don't Report Harassment*).

- Some people tend to blame the victim and some victims blame themselves.
- Violators are sometimes viewed as heros.
- Failure to take appropriate action can literally cost responsible authorities their jobs, their reputations, and their life savings.

Why Students Don't Report Harassment

Embarrassment in talking about it

Fear of retaliation or reprisal

Peer pressure

Self-blame

Self-doubt (Am I the only one offended?)

Fear of loss of reputation

Reluctance to cause trouble

Distrust of system

Fear for personal safety

Uncertainty about what constitutes harassment

Concern over harasser's welfare

Fear that no one will understand or take complaints seriously

Lack of information on reporting procedures

In dealing with harassment, school leaders are caught in a cross-fire of mixed messages. On one hand, everyone in the school must learn that overfamiliarity, unwelcome attention and unwanted touching are not acceptable. Conversely, adults and students alike must provide each other with increasing physical and emotional support during times of diminished family unity and heightened social isolation. Large numbers of students need attention, nurturing, and support more than ever before. The challenge to educators is to find ways to make schools safe, secure, and supportive for all students without violating their rights.

The first responsibility of school officials must be to educate students, staff members, and parents about sexual harassment, to inform students of their rights and to establish an atmosphere where it's O.K. to complain. Schools that are winning the battle against harassment send two clear messages:

1. If you're a victim, feel free to report it.

2. If you're a violator, be certain that an investigation will be conducted and appropriate action taken *every* time a substantial complaint is filed.

Many students, at all levels, still aren't sure how to recognize harassment or what to do when it happens. One way to help students identify harassing behavior is to stress that "harmless teasing or flirting feels good, harassment feels bad." Even at a very young age, students can also be taught to say, "no," or to tell someone when any person's actions make them feel uncomfortable or threatened.

Additionally, there are lots of other specific action steps which can be taken in any school to protect students from harassment, while preserving the caring climate essential to successful learning.

HOW TO PROTECT YOUR STUDENTS AND YOURSELF

Sexual harassment in schools is not fun and games. Stopping it is serious business. There's no room for waffling on this issue. The greatest mistake any administrator can make is to ignore the problem or to be unresponsive in dealing with it.

Adopt a Policy

Every school and/or district must adopt an unflinching, no-nonsense antiharassment policy. The policy should be crystal clear in stating that harassing behavior will not be tolerated, that all allegations will be treated seriously and investigated thoroughly, and that swift and certain action will be taken as appropriate. (See sample policies at the end of this chapter.)

Communicate the Policy

Once established, it's important that the policy be communicated widely both verbally and in writing. Post it conspicuously throughout the school and include it in all student, employee, and parent handbooks. Some on-going procedure for informing newcomers, both student and staff, about the policy, should be in place. Likewise, you should establish a system for the annual review and the periodic redistribution of the policy and name someone on the administrative team as the chief compliance officer. Without question the policy must have the complete support of the top management of the school.

Adopt a Fear-Free Complaint Procedure

To be effective, school procedures must include a user-friendly system for filing complaints. The mechanics of reporting should be as simple and nonthreatening as possible.

Sample Sexual Harassment Report Form

Name of person filing this complaint: _____

Address: _____

Phone #: _____

Name of accused harasser: _____

Description of the incident(s) (include time and place): _____

_____

_____

_____

Date incident occurred: _____

List of persons witnessing the incident of harassment: _____

_____

_____

_____

_____   _____

(Signature of complainant)   (Date)

Students should be encouraged to report incidents of sexual harassment to any responsible adult in the school with whom they have confidence and trust and feel comfortable. Complaints should be accepted either verbally or in writing (see *Sample Report Form*). *Every* complaint must be investigated thoroughly and promptly following due process procedures as outlined in the next section. Constant and consistent enforcement is a "must."

Create a Sexual Harassment Education Program

Since many students as well as staff members don't fully understand what the law requires or what sexual harassment really is, a comprehensive program of education must go hand-in-hand with enforcement efforts. The kind and extent of training will vary according to the level of the students. Some schools have found it useful to survey students about their understanding of sexual harassment and then build a training program based on what they need to learn.

In most situations, the goals of the educational program are to develop and heighten awareness of:

1. School policy on harassment;
2. What constitutes sexual harassment;
3. Misconceptions about harassment;
4. Liability and legal requirements;
5. Procedures to follow in reporting;
6. What will happen when a complaint is filed.

The earmarks of a solid training program include the following:

- The audience is *everyone*, including special groups such as part-time students, in-coming students, bus drivers, coaches, volunteers, and so on.
- A variety of delivery options are employed such as class discussions, school assemblies, guest speakers, theatrical presentations, videotapes and roleplaying.
- The program is repeated annually.
- All training sessions are documented.
- All parties sign-off after participation.

Eradicating illegal harassment takes time. Schools staffed predominantly by mature males may be particularly entrenched in "doing business as usual." Nevertheless, by following the steps outlined above, you will have gone a long way toward preserving students' rights and protecting them from harmful, unwelcome harassment on the part of adults or other students in the school.

Protect Personnel

Another dimension of dealing with the issue involves protecting administrators and other personnel from the litigation and liability that often accompanies incidents of sexual harassment in a school setting.

Today's society seems to suffer from a "lawsuit mentality." Frequent headlines chronicle enormous settlements for not handling sexual harassment claims appropriately. In many cases, the generosity of judges and juries seems to know no bounds.

To feel safe and free to act quickly and responsibly when harassment occurs, school leaders should adopt certain risk management strategies as precautionary steps to avoid litigation and/or limit liability. Without proper protection, administrators and supervisors face the danger of jeopardizing their jobs and their reputation and of being strapped with paying substantial punitive and/or compensatory damages should legal claims be made against them.

Risk Management

Lawsuits are scary and the fear of legal action can cause officials to become paralyzed by paranoia. You can't afford to be fettered by fear of liability. The answers are to refuse to panic, to do your job right, and to minimize your risks. The basics of risk management for school administrators include the following:

- Know the law and be sure that those who work for you understand it.
- Be aware of your liability. Today's courts judge actions by the standard of what a "reasonable woman" would do or think about alleged harassment. Ignorance is no defense. Officials can be held liable if they "should have known" about what's going on.
- Insist on a forthright policy against sexual harassment and follow the enforcement and education guidelines spelled out earlier in this section.
- Be scrupulous about detailed documentation and record keeping.
- Be sure you are covered adequately by your school's or district's liability insurance. Some districts add an inexpensive "umbrella clause" which supplements regular coverage in case of unusually high settlements. Review your insurance coverage and update it on a regular basis.

By taking these protective steps, you are freed up to enforce antiharassment policies without undue fear of legal action. Should such action occur, however, the first thing to do is immediately notify the school's legal counsel and insurance carrier. (You may also want to alert your personal attorney depending on the circumstances). It's always advisable to determine from legal counsel whether or not you are free to discuss the case. Sometimes, commenting on the situation can compound the problem and subject you to additional charges.

While litigation is pending or underway, administrators involved are well-advised to cooperate with any outside investigators—state and federal human rights officials—and to monitor the progress of the case to avoid being blind-sided by any surprise developments or outcomes.

Lawsuits involving sexual harassment in schools are often highly charged, emotional situations. When this happens, your role should be to do everything possible to keep things from becoming a circus. Teaching and learning should go on as usual. If extreme distortions of fact become prevalent, it may be helpful to find ways to get out the school's side of the story without violating confidentiality. Word-of-mouth campaigns and supportive parent letters to the editor are often effective in setting the record straight. Lastly, if the school and/or individual staff members are found legally liable, an appeal should be pursued where warranted.

Once the school has taken a stance against harassment by implementing the measures above, the acid test of success will rest on the quality of the school's investigative process.

HOW TO INVESTIGATE COMPLAINTS

When someone claims sexual harassment, it's the school's job to determine the credibility of the allegation, to reach a judicious conclusion and to take appropriate action. All of these outcomes hinge on conducting a comprehensive, objective, and timely investigation. Failure to investigate conveys tacit approval of illegal behavior and implied support of the harasser.

Even if a criminal investigation is undertaken by law enforcement officials, the school is obligated to conduct its own inquiry. An act of student-to-student harassment may not qualify as a crime, but still may be inappropriate behavior by school standards. The depth and breadth of the school's investigation will depend on the particular circumstances involved.

Where possible, there is some advantage in having an outside investigator, such as the school's legal counsel, handle sexual harassment complaints. These agents of the school are often experienced in investigative techniques and can invoke attorney-client privilege in preserving confidentiality. As the number of incidents increase, however, this approach often becomes too costly and impractical.

In most situations, regular school personnel—principals, assistant principals, counselors, and social workers—will have to conduct the inquiry. Whoever is involved, the role of the investigator is to be a fact-finder, not a judge or jury. Since educators aren't detectives, be sure that anyone responsible for investigating sexual harassment allegations receives specific training.

The timing of the investigation is crucial. Any delay may be construed as disinterest or unresponsiveness. All investigations should be initiated as soon as possible. A common rule of thumb is that serious complaints (touching, pornography, date rape) should be investigated immediately; less serious complaints (name-calling) should be investigated, at least, within a three-day period.

Whether a staff member or an outsider is involved, the most common tools of the investigator are interviews, observations, and reviews of student records. In extreme situations you may have to use such techniques as surveillance, sting oper-

Process for Investigation

For most school situations, the architecture of the investigation includes the following components:

1. *Notification.*
   Inform the parents of all involved students about the nature of the allegation and let them know that an investigation is being initiated.

2. *Interviewing.*
   Interview all involved parties separately. The order of interrogation usually follows this pattern: accuser, witnesses identified by the accuser, accused, additional witnesses identified by the accused.

3. *Conclusion.*
   In reaching judgments about the credibility of complaints, you need to consider corroborating evidence, motivation, attitudes, demeanor, student history and/or extenuating circumstances. The combination of these factors should enable you to conclude that the charges are substantiated or unsubstantiated or that you cannot complete the investigation and are unable to confirm or deny the allegations.

4. *Action.*
   Any action must fit the infraction. If there is no substance to the charge, no action is necessary and all parties should be informed. If the violation is a first-time and/or minor offense you may want to consider appropriate progressive discipline in the form of reprimand, detention, transfer to another class, denial of bus privileges or other appropriate action. If the violation is serious, consider suspension or expulsion. This level of action requires consultation with district personnel.

5. *Documentation.*
   Accurate recordkeeping is essential (see next section of this chapter).

6. *Reporting.*
   All parties involved directly (students, staff, and parents) need to be informed of the outcome. Send a wrap-up report to the district office and place a basic disposition report in the student's file.

ations, and/or voice or handwriting experts. Of these, the interview is, by far, the most common and important.

In implementing these investigative steps, the list of "do's and don'ts" below have proved helpful to many school leaders:

Do	**Don't**
• Find a private spot for interviewing	• Do nothing and hope that "this, too, shall pass."
• Be sensitive to gender considerations.	• Insist on a formal, written complaint before taking any action.
• Use females to question females when possible.	• Promise that you won't tell anyone about the complaint.
• Have a third party sit in on all interviews.	• Try to suppress or finesse the problem without investigating.
• Interview all parties separately.	• Say or do anything to blame the victim.
• Use open-ended questions.	• Assume that males can't be victims.
• Dig for details.	• Make snap judgments.
• Watch for body language clues.	• Be swayed by personal biases or previous impressions.
• Inquire about feelings as well as facts.	• Protect the accuser.
• Get names of witnesses.	• Make promises of confidentiality that you can't deliver.
• Remain neutral.	• Tape-record interviews. Recorders may intimidate some interviewees.
• Keep accurate, detailed notes.	• Be confrontational.
• Continue investigation as best you can even if key parties won't cooperate or refuse to be interviewed.	• Ask leading questions.
• Call for help if needed.	• Threaten the accused.
• Tell accuser to report any reprisals or reoccurances.	• Leave the false impression that the accused is entitled to confront the accuser.
• Continue to monitor the situation after the case is closed.	• Tell witnesses more than they need to know.
	• End the inquiry too soon.

Throughout the entire process, experts caution that investigators should consistently stress to the accused that any form of retaliation or reprisal will not be tolerated and will result in additional penalties.

TIPS ON PROPER DOCUMENTATION

Once a systematic investigation has been completed, the final step is to "document everything in sight." Proper documentation is the best liability protection you can obtain. Comprehensive records should be kept at every step throughout the investigative process. To the extent possible, interview notes should include exact quotes and descriptive notations of demeanor, body language, and attitude (see *Note-taking Hints*). One advantage of involving a third party is that one person can concentrate on conducting the interview and the other can record the questions and the responses.

Once an investigation is finished, the complete file should include records of the following:

- Allegations
- Witnesses interviewed
- Interview notes
- Conclusions
- Actions/recommendations. (See *Sample Letter of Reprimand*.)

Note-taking Hints

- Don't try to write down everything word for word, except direct quotes of what was said by the victim and the accused during the incident.
- Use abbreviations whenever possible.
- Identify the victim and the accused by initials.
- Use margin to note attitudes and behaviors such as defensiveness, nervousness, fidgeting, and perspiring.
- Be sure notes reflect specific details such as the following:
  —What happened.
  —How often it occurred.
  —Where the incident took place.
  —How close the parties were to each other.
  —How the victim was touched.
  —What the accused said (exact quotes).
  —What the victim told the accused (exact quote).
  —List of witnesses. Ensure accurate spelling of all names.
- Date your notes and list all parties present during the interview.

All notes should be accurate, detailed, and dated. Don't editorialize. Avoid such comments as "I think he's lying;" "This sounds made up;" "She shouldn't be so touchy;" "She must have done something first:" and so on. Keep in mind that administrative records may be subject to subpoena and disclosure in the event of any formal legal hearing. When legal counsel conducts the investigation, however, notes may be protected by attorney-client privilege and remain confidential.

How long should records be retained? Since most states now have virtually no statute of limitation on cases of sexual harassment, violence, or abuse, the best advice may be to keep records forever. At least, records on each incident and investigation should be retained for three to five years after the students involved have left the school system.

In addition to files on all investigations, schools are also well-advised to document all proactive measures taken to alleviate harassment, including all training sessions and lists of participants.

Sophisticated documentation is an essential tool in handling student harassment problems and an effective risk management strategy for protecting administrators.

SEXUAL HARASSMENT CHECKLIST

Sexual harassment issues are always sensitive, delicate, and emotional, and often must be resolved under pressure. School officials frequently find themselves dealing with three or more student-to-student cases simultaneously. To successfully handle several cases at once, you should follow a structured, systematic process in handling each incident. Use of a simplified step-by-step checklist, like the one shown here, can help to assure that you have touched all bases and will expedite the disposition process (see sample checklist below).

Sample Letter of Reprimand
(school letterhead)

Dear:

This letter constitutes a formal written reprimand in regard to your conduct in violation of School District policy #_____, Prohibition of Sexual Harassment. This notice sets forth inappropriate and illegal acts requiring your immediate attention and correction. Failure to correct these actions will result in further disciplinary action which may include suspension and/or expulsion from school. The specific complaints are as follows:

1. Engagement in inappropriate teasing and "horseplay" with female students in physical education class.

   The teacher received complaints from students that on four different occasions from November 1–November 15, 1993, you made obscene gestures toward three female students and made inappropriate remarks about the size of their breasts.

In the future, you are directed to:

1. Refrain from making obscene gestures in the company of female students.
2. Do not make sexually oriented remarks to any other students.

If you do not correct these actions and follow the directives listed above, you will be subject to progressive disciplinary action.

You are also advised that any acts of reprisal or retaliation will also result in additional penalties.

If you have questions regarding these directions please contact me.

Sincerely,

Sexual Harassment Checklist
(Sample)

General

Develop a specific policy against sexual harassment, including a grievance procedure for handling complaints.

Post the school's policy conspicuously throughout the building.

Implement a plan to inform all students verbally of the policy.

Include policy in student, staff and parent handbooks and other printed communications as appropriate.

Implement a training program to educate students and staff about sexual harassment.

Identify a Compliance Officer for the school.

Reporting

Students should be encouraged to report to the Principal or any employee/adult with whom they have a comfortable relationship.

Employees should report to Principal or designated Compliance Officer.

Reporting Forms should be available, but not made mandatory.

When a Complaint Is Received

If abuse or violence is suspected, report immediately to Police or Child Protection Agency. Proceed with school investigation regardless.

Determine if allegation is serious enough to involve the District Office. If so, inform the appropriate District Office representative immediately who will advise, investigate or arrange for a third party investigation.

In any event, inform the District Office in writing within 24 hours. (Verbal complaints should be reduced to writing.)

Initiate investigation as soon as possible.

Inform involved parents of nature of allegations and that an investigation is in progress.

Interview all parties *separately*. (Involve a third party and use females to interview females when possible.)

Inform accused that any reprisal will result in further disciplinary action.

Take steps to minimize rumors when necessary.

If allegations have no substance, inform all parties (including parents).

If infraction is a first-time or minor offense, take appropriate progressive disciplinary action.

If infraction is major, consult with District Office regarding appropriate action.

Document entire investigation. Save *indefinitely*.

Report general outcomes to all parties in writing. (Respect confidentiality and data privacy guidelines.)

Submit a final report to the District Office.

Place a basic disposition report in appropriate student or personnel file.

Final Advice

- Take it seriously.
- Respond quickly.
- Use good judgment.
- Ask for help if you need it.

SAMPLE POLICIES DEALING WITH SEXUAL HARASSMENT

Addressing concerns about sexual harassment begins and ends with a well-formulated policy statement. The school's policy serves as a platform for redressing wrongs and protecting everyone's rights. It sends a powerful message about what's expected and accepted, and provides a framework for dealing with unacceptable behavior.

The following are two generic antiharassment policies adapted from the philosophy and procedures used in a variety of effective schools across the country.

A Sample School Policy on Sexual Harassment

I. The Policy

A. It is the policy of the Public Schools to maintain a learning and working environment that is free from sexual harassment.

B. It shall be a violation of this policy for any member of the Public Schools staff to harass another staff member or student through conduct or communications of a sexual nature as defined in Section II. It shall also be a violation of this policy for students to harass other students through conduct or communications of a sexual nature as defined in Section II.

II. Definition

A. Sexual harassment shall consist of unwelcomed sexual advances, requests for sexual favors, and other inappropriate verbal or physical conduct of a sexual nature when made by any member of the school staff to a student, when made by any member of the school staff to another staff member, or when made by any student to another student.

III. Procedures

A. Any person who alleges sexual harassment by any staff member or student in the school may use the available Report Form or may complain directly to his or her immediate supervisor, building principal, or district Ombudsman. Filing a grievance or otherwise reporting sexual harassment will not reflect upon the individual's status nor will it affect future employment, grades, or work assignments.

B. The right to confidentiality, both of the complainant and of the accused, will be respected consistent with the school's legal obligations, and with the necessity to investigate allegations of misconduct and to take corrective action when necessary.

IV. Sanctions

A. A substantial charge against a staff member in the school district shall subject such staff member to disciplinary action, including discharge.

B. A substantial charge against a student in the school district shall subject that student to student disciplinary action including suspension or expulsion.

Prohibition of Sexual Harassement and Sexual Violence
(Sample Policy)

I. General Statement of Policy

Sexual harassment and sexual violence is a form of sex discrimination. It is the policy of the School District to maintain a learning and working environment that is free from sexual harassment and sexual violence. The District prohibits any form of sexual harassment and sexual violence.

It shall be a violation of this policy for any student or employee of the District to harass a student or an employee through conduct or communication of a sexual nature as defined by this policy.

The District will act to investigate all complaints of sexual harassment and sexual violence, either formal or informal, oral or written, and to discipline any student or employee who sexually harasses a student or employee of the District.

II. Sexual Harassment Defined

A. Sexual harassment and sexual violence consists of unwelcome sexual advances, requests for sexual favors, sexually motivated physical conduct or other verbal or physical conduct or communication of a sexual nature when:

1. Submission to that conduct or communication is made a term or condition, either explicitly or implicitly, of obtaining or retaining employment, or of obtaining an education;

2. Submission to or rejection of that conduct or communication by an individual is used as a factor in decisions affecting that individual's employment or education;

3. That conduct or communication has the purpose or effect of substantially or unreasonably interfering with an individual's employment or education, or creating an intimidating, hostile or offensive employment or education environment.

B. Sexual harassment and sexual violence may include but is not limited to:

1. verbal harassment or abuse;

2. subtle pressure for sexual activity;

3. inappropriate patting or pinching;

4. intentional brushing against a student's or employee's body;

5. demanding sexual favors accompanied by implied or overt threats concerning an individual's employment or educational status;

6. demanding sexual favors accompanied by implied or overt promises of preferential treatment with regard to an individual's employment or educational status;

7. any sexually motivated unwelcome touching.

III. Sexual Harassment and Sexual Violence As Abuse

Under certain circumstances, sexual harassment and sexual violence may constitute sexual abuse as defined by state and federal statutes. Nothing in this policy will prohibit the school from taking immediate action to protect victims of alleged sexual abuse.

Initially, it may seem overwhelming to try to stem the tide of harassment that prevails in many schools and to reverse long-standing habits and entrenched behaviors. It helps, however, to remember that not too long ago, officials threw up their hands in the belief that they could never reduce or eliminate smoking problems in schools. Today smoke-free schools are becoming the norm.

Change happens when sincere people take it seriously. The action steps spelled out in this chapter provide a guide to changing student and staff attitudes about sexual harassment. The "harassment-free school" can become a reality.

New Approaches

to Traditional

Discipline Problems

Trouble can come in many forms. Not only must schools today deal with the unprecedented threats of gangs, violence, weapons, and drugs, but they must also continue to contend with age-old discipline concerns such as truancy, student theft, and vandalism. Even these traditional bugaboos have taken on some different twists as practiced by a new generation of street-wise students. Fortunately, smart schools have come up with some new ways of their own to handle these old problems.

Workable Ways to Reduce Truancy

Truancy is a cancer which can kill a school. Students can't learn in absentia. Likewise, schools can't fulfill their mission when large numbers of students are absent on a regular basis. When absenteeism reaches a certain level, "nonschool" is in session. Truancy can become part of the school's culture. If it becomes the norm then, learning is only incidental.

Chronic absenteeism has increasingly become a major problem in many schools. In Minneapolis, approximately 4,300 students are absent on any given day. This represents 10% of the student population. More than half of these are unexcused absences. In some hard-core areas of the country, the rate of student absences is much higher.

Students who skip school regularly often end up in other kinds of trouble. There was a time when students "played hooky" just to go fishing or sneak off to a ball game. There was a certain innocence associated with skipping school. That's not what truancy is all about anymore.

Today when students are truant, they're often hanging out in the streets or in malls or arcades or wherever gang members congregate. Truants are trouble waiting to happen and truancy is the beginning of a trip to nowhere for countless numbers of at-risk students.

For lots of students, truancy is the first step toward dropping out of school, and in the eyes of many veteran observers, there is a higher correlation between dropping out of school and ending up in prison than there is between smoking and lung cancer. Evidence of this correlation exists in the experience of cities which have dramatically reduced daytime burglaries by improving school attendance. After implementing comprehensive student attendance incentive programs, San Jose (CA) reduced daylight break-ins by 68% and Oklahoma City cut them by one-third. Staying in school is one way of staying out of trouble.

There are numerous reasons for unexcused student absences (see *Why Kids Skip School*), but truancy almost always indicates a young person with serious problems at school and/or at home. Truancy is a symptom.

© 1994 by Prentice Hall

Why Kids Skip School

- Boredom
- Fear of School (School Phobia)
- Conflicts with Teachers/Administrators
- Fear of Bullies or Gangs
- Falling Behind in School Work
- Depression
- Low Self-esteem
- No One at Home to Get Them Off to School

Unfortunately, neither the symptom nor the cause gets prompt attention in many school districts. Truancy by underage students is a violation of the law in all states, but the law is of little help in keeping kids in school.

Court dockets have become so jammed in most places that truancy cases seldom receive prompt action. Juvenile judges have many more pressing problems to deal with than school absences. In many situations, by the time a truancy case works its way through the gridlock of the court system, a year or more may have elapsed and the student is lost to the school forever. Schools can't count on the courts to solve truancy problems.

In some schools, truancy gets progressively worse simply because nobody does anything about it. The courts are too busy with other things. In addition, some teachers and administrators are inclined to be soft on truancy, because absent kids don't cause any trouble in school. Likewise, more and more parents take school attendance lightly or have their hands too full to be of help in getting their children to school.

Sometimes, the parents themselves are truant. There are districts around the country where an alarming number of parents give the school bogus addresses and phone numbers because they don't want to be reached if there is a problem. Some schools now even have to hire a full-time locator to help find phantom parents.

When nobody does anything about truancy, it only gets worse and education fails by default. This doesn't have to happen. We can get kids to come to school in any community setting.

Schools that eliminate excessive student absenteeism are schools with an attitude—an attitude that school is crucial and that showing up is the first step in productive learning. These schools send a clear-cut message that attendance is important for success now and in the future. As with most problem areas, the solution starts with a no-nonsense policy statement that defines the school's position.

Until recently, many schools had fairly lenient attendance policies based on a belief that school is merely "preparation" for life and mistakes are allowable. As attendance has become a more critical issue, more and more schools are adopting tougher policies with stricter penalties. The current philosophy in many districts is that "school isn't preparation for life—it *is* life" and accountability is important.

A workable attendance policy for today's schools must meet the following tests:

1. The policy is understandable;
2. It is enforceable;
3. Some flexibility is permitted for accommodating the needs of special education students with disabilities;
4. An appeals process is included for instances where students or parents feel treated unjustly.

The sample policies that follow show how some schools are treating truancy in this manner.

(Sample Policy #1)

Truancy
Wayland (MA) Public Schools

Unauthorized absence from school is considered truancy and will be treated as such.

This includes absence from any class, study hall, or activity during the school day for which the student is scheduled. It also includes any after-school, special-help session or disciplinary session which the student has been directed to attend.

Disciplinary action shall be taken in such cases, beginning with notification of parents. Continued violation will lead to suspension from school, with readmittance allowed only through the superintendent's office.

(Sample Policy #2)

Student Attendance Policy
Eden Prairie (MN) Public Schools

The purpose of the Attendance Policy is to do the following:

1. To encourage better student attendance, both in reference to full-day attendance and individual class attendance.
2. To stress parent participation both in reference to communication with parents and their involvement in the encouragement of a good attendance pattern by the student.

If a student is absent from any class 12 times during a semester, s/he will be removed from the course, receive no credit, and will be assigned to a restricted study hall.

Upon the 12th absence from any class, the parents will be informed of the action to remove their student from the class; included will be the process for an appeal of the decision.

Students who are truant three times will be removed from the class with an "F" for the semester and will be assigned to a restricted study hall.

(Sample Policy #3)

Appeals Process—Attendance
St. Louis Park (MN) Senior High School

The student and parent have the right to appeal the loss of class credit to an Appeals Board. The board will consist of 1) the principal, 2) one counselor, 3) two teachers (one representing students in grades 9/10, the other representing the students in grades 11/12), and 4) one student.

Appeals procedure

1. Student must present his/her case in writing to the principal.
2. Student will be allowed to present his/her case to the Appeals Board after the written appeal has been presented.
   a. The Appeals Board will meet one hour weekly.
   b. Each student will have seven (7) minutes to present his/her case orally.
   c. The decision of the appeal will be rendered in writing to the student in question within two (2) school days.
3. Prearranged Absences can be presented to the Appeals Board, the Principal or Dean. These absences are cumulative and will count toward the maximum absences allowed. Vacations should be planned to coincide with scheduled school breaks.

Making the school's attendance/truancy policy work is a joint responsibility shared by students, parents, and school personnel as outlined:

1. *Student Responsibility.* It is the student's responsibility to be in school. It is also the student's responsibility to attend all classes regularly and on time and to follow the correct procedures when absent from a class.
2. *Parent/Guardian Responsibility.* It is the responsibility of parents or guardians to see to it that the student attends school and to inform the school in the event of a student's absence. It is also their responsibility to work cooperatively with the school and student to attain regular attendance. This may include special conferences scheduled by the school when problems arise.
3. *Teacher Responsibility.* It is the teacher's responsibility to maintain an accurate attendance record and communicate attendance concerns to the student, parents/guardians, and administrators.

4. *Administrator Responsibility.* It is an administrative responsibility to encourage students to attend all classes. It is also the responsibility of the administration to inform the parent or guardian of the student's attendance and to work cooperatively with the parent or guardian and the student in developing acceptable attendance patterns. The administrator will ensure all students their rights according to due process.

The key to successful enforcement of any antitruancy policy is communication among all the parties involved. With the increase in single-parent and two-job families, parents are often difficult to contact. Some schools are attempting to overcome this problem by using an automated attendance calling system to inform parents of their student's absence.

Typically, such systems call homes of absent students every evening from 5–10 P.M. If the line is busy or there is no answer, the system will continue calling until 10 P.M. Each morning, the school receives a print-out identifying which homes have been contacted and at what time each call was completed. Although computerized systems have some limitations and sacrifice some of the personalized touch, they are the fastest, most economical way to reach a large number of parents to report school absences.

In addition to phone contact, schools should rely on regular, registered, and certified mail to handle essential communications about attendance (see *Sample Truancy Notice*).

Some of the best results in reducing absenteeism have occurred in schools with a specific *Truancy Intervention Program* (TIP) carried out by a selected team of teachers and counselors. These teams can initiate a variety of intervention strategies such as:

1. Contacting parents and students at the first sign of trouble.
2. Conducting evening programs for parents to develop cooperative attendance improvement plans.
3. Developing a community service option in lieu of detention for truancy. Often, the community education department or a cooperative YMCA can supervise community service work after regular school hours.
4. Implementing a program of incentives (or rewards) for improved attendance.
5. Providing tutors for students who have fallen behind because of excessive absences.

Other effective measures for limiting truancy which have succeeded in some schools include:

Sample Truancy Notice

Student: _____ Grade: _____ Date of Truancy: _____

Teacher: _____ Class: _____ Period: _____

_____ Truancy #1   _____ Truancy #2   _____Truancy #3

Dear Parent:

Your son/daughter was truant from the class indicated above. Truancy results when the student:

1. Is *not* in class.

2. Is *not* on the absence list.

3. Has *not* made prior arrangements to miss the class.

Continuing truancy from this class could result in loss of credit. If this is a *second* truancy, your student will be allowed to remain in the class, but on an audit basis (without a guaranteed credit).

A *third* truancy from this class means the credit will be lost, the student receives an "NC" grade and is placed in a structured study hall for the remainder of the semester.

If you have questions, please contact the school office.

Sincerely,

Principal

---

1. Conducting a media blitz to heighten awareness of the consequences of truancy and dropping out of school.

2. Using technology to monitor and record attendance. Some schools are experimenting with the use of personalized bar-coded ID cards. Students use the cards as they pass through entry and exit terminals at school entrances. Student attendance then, is monitored and recorded electronically. Such systems are designed to reduce or eliminate tedious manual attendance record keeping.

3. Establishing a voice mail system for teachers so that parents can leave messages regarding necessary absences and teachers can respond to questions about attendance.

4. Providing incentives for good attendance as discussed previously (special field trips, concert tickets, and so on). Some schools give raffle tickets for a new car to students with near-perfect attendance.

5. Stressing the importance of a good attendance record as viewed by prospective future employers; tie attendance to employability.

6. Requiring truants to make up the specific classroom work and assignments missed, rather than just "serving time" in detention or suspension.

7. Working with parents to develop guidelines for how many hours students may work at after-school jobs each week. (Many communities use 20 hours per week as a guideline).

8. Eliciting the cooperation of local employers in monitoring student progress and reducing hours worked if grades slip. (The local Chamber of Commerce can often assist in introducing this concept into the business community.)

9. Meeting with small groups of at-risk students and their parents to discuss attendance problems and solutions. (Often, parents of at-risk students are genuinely concerned, but lack skills or knowledge of strategies for helping their child get to and stay in school.)

10. Initiating joint home visits by school and police representatives when truancy problems occur.

11. Working with city and court officials to create Student Service Centers to process cases of students found hanging out in malls or on the streets during school hours without going through traditional, time-consuming court procedures.

Truancy doesn't have to be a way of life in any school. Students at any age will attend school if it's a place where they are recognized, valued, helped, and honored for their accomplishments. If something exciting and worthwhile is going on, they will come.

MODERN STEPS TO STOP STEALING

Whenever large numbers of people (of any age) congregate in limited space for long periods of time, some stealing may occur. Schools are no exception.

Stealing in schools can follow different patterns—

- Students stealing from adults;

- Students stealing from other students;
- Students stealing from the school itself.

Whatever form it takes, student stealing is a major discipline concern, not only because of the act itself, but because of the impact it has on the learning culture of the school.

Stealing undermines morale, destroys confidence, and threatens school climate. Anything that erodes trust impedes learning. That's why effective schools take student theft seriously, even when occurrences are rare and losses are minimal. (Most student thefts involve amounts of less than $10.)

Limiting and/or eliminating student stealing involves reducing temptation, tightening security, following up on evidence, and punishing offenders. Here are the steps most commonly used to halt students stealing in today's schools:

- Heighten school security as detailed in Chapter 6, particularly in high risk areas such as band rooms, TV studios, computer labs, and so forth. Video monitoring systems which provide random recording so that students are not aware when the system is active have proved to be a cost-effective deterrent to theft and other forms of student misbehavior.
- Stress the importance of personal security for staff members. If teachers and other employees would consistently lock up purses and other valuables, school theft would be reduced dramatically.
- Organize a schoolwide Crime Stoppers Program whereby a student panel determines rewards for tips from anonymous informants.
- Hold staff members liable for any money under their control.
- Don't permit locker sharing (by either students or staff members).
- Adopt a "no cash after hours" policy.
- Rotate student locks and combinations regularly.
- Provide vault space for student and staff valuables.
- Identify/mark school equipment, including videotaping valuable items for possible use by the police or insurance investigators should theft occur.
- Schedule evening cleaner hours.
- Insist that all rooms be locked when vacant.
- Discourage staff and students from bringing valuable items to school.
- Spot check student lockers for stolen merchandise when probable cause exists.
- Make a rule never to give keys to students.
- Provide extra supervision and surveillance to locker rooms and parking lots. These are especially vulnerable areas.
- Offer personal security minicourses for students on how to avoid becoming a victim.

- Don't store valuable items in unlit areas.
- Inform parents of any outbreak of theft (minicrime wave) at schools.
- Use stake-outs and sting operations if stealing is a frequent or on-going problem. This is where having a police liaison officer on board is particularly helpful.
- Offer rewards for stolen merchandise when appropriate.
- Provide opportunities to return stolen goods undetected with no questions asked.
- Keep in touch with local police to be informed of changing patterns in stealing by school-age offenders.
- Don't replace popular items stolen from the school right away. If the student body misses things they like or have come to expect, peer pressure builds against student offenders.
- Provide sure-fire consequences for all acts of stealing including suspension, Saturday School classes, "working off" fines by helping the custodial staff or cafeteria personnel, prosecution, and restitution.

If stealing becomes commonplace, the whole school is the loser and everyone is a victim. Student theft may be more than an infraction and an inconvenience. It can be a symptom that the system isn't working for some students.

Don't take any incidence of theft in school lightly. Student stealing doesn't have to be tolerated. It can be controlled through cooperative vigilance and action. It's worth the effort. Honesty should be part of every school's curriculum.

Tested Tips to Reduce Vandalism

Vandalism is violence against the school or its property. It may result from student anger directed at school personnel, be part of a conscious campaign to announce gang presence, or simply be the outcome of senseless, random destruction. Levels of vandalism may range from a few broken windows to the total devastation of a building by fire or explosion. Whatever form it takes, vandalism causes both students and staff members to feel violated.

It's hard for students to feel pride for a vandalized school. Staff members don't want to work in defaced surroundings. Taxpayers don't want to pay for repairing needless damage. Repeated acts of vandalism demean learning and learners.

The school should be more than an extension of the street or the ghetto. It should be a special place where special things happen to all children.

It's important for every school to maintain the appearance of a place where students can feel safe, learn successfully, and have fun. This means you should take every step possible to prevent, eliminate, or minimize vandalism in your building.

The greatest protection against vandalism is to create a positive school culture based on mutual respect (see Chapter 2). Any effort which boosts student pride in the school decreases the likelihood of vandalism. Nevertheless, no school is 100% vandalism-proof.

Based on experience of elementary and secondary schools around the country, we know these things about vandalism:

1. Most vandalism occurs after school hours and on weekends.
2. Vandalism occurs in cycles.
3. Arson is the most costly form of vandalism.
4. Vandalism breeds more vandalism.
5. Vandalism can destroy more than just property or the school building itself. If left unaddressed and unpunished, it can destroy the spirit of the school.

With this information, it's possible for any school to develop a comprehensive antivandalism campaign. Some of the most effective measures to reduce vandalism include the following:

- Adopt the security measures outlined in Chapter 6.
- Install vandalism-resistant windows (plastic or other glazing). All glazing should be from the inside.
- Require students to repair or clean up even minor acts of vandalism (for instance, defacing school desks).
- Always notify parents when their child is involved in any act of vandalism.
- Lobby for a reasonable curfew for all underage students.
- Repaint, replace, or repair any defacing or destruction of property immediately.
- Eliminate anything climbable on the building's exterior.
- Establish an antivandalism incentive program by making some of the building's repair budget available for student use if it isn't needed for vandalism repairs.
- Beef up lighting for highly vulnerable or frequently vandalized areas. (Be sure that the lights themselves are as vandal-proof as possible.)
- Encourage student art work or murals on all appropriate walls or surfaces.
- Create a Neighborhood Alert by informing residents living close to the school of any vandalism problem and urging cooperation in apprehending offenders.
- Take tempting targets out of washrooms (for example, place towel dispensers in the hallway next to restrooms where they are noticeable and easy to monitor).

- Replace metal partitions with masonry where feasible.
- Recess fixtures where possible throughout the building, especially in washrooms.
- Don't use gravel or rock in any landscaping around the building.
- Designate a graffiti wall for student use (no obscenity allowed).
- Replace frequently broken windows with acrylic plastic or other hard-to-break material.
- Teach students the economics of vandalism (for instance, the cost of window replacement or exterior wall cleaning).
- Always require restitution or the "working off" of any damage done to school property by students.
- Sponsor clean-up or school improvement projects by student groups (Student Council, Environmental Club, and so on).

Controlling vandalism does more than preserve the appearance of the building. It maintains the dignity of the school and helps create an environment conducive to efficient and effective learning.

HOW TO HANDLE BUS DISCIPLINE

It's hard enough being fully responsible for the discipline and safety of large numbers of children or teenagers every day. Imagine what it would be like if you had to do it with your back turned toward them and had to drive at the same time. That's what school bus drivers contend with all the time, which makes them unique members of the school's overall discipline team.

School buses are extensions of the classroom and misbehavior doesn't stop at the edge of the school grounds. Arguments and other trouble that begin in class or in the locker room often continue on the bus ride home. As behavior problems have increased and intensified in schools, discipline has often gotten worse on school buses as well (some of the nation's most costly civil suits alleging sexual harassment among students originated on school buses.).

Safety issues have made bus discipline especially important to parents and school personnel. When kids cause trouble on the bus, lives are in jeopardy.

Some of the most frequently reported school bus infractions include:

- Use of profanity and obscene/abusive language;
- Shouting and other distracting noises;
- Throwing of objects;
- Ripping up seats and/or breaking seat frames;

- Window breakage;
- Stealing first aid supplies;
- Fighting;
- Hazing;
- Harassment;
- Smoking;
- Mooning;
- Drug use;
- Weapons possession.

Most districts report that middle school/junior high-age students are the worst offenders.

As with any form of discipline, the positive control of bus behavior must be based on uniform, unambiguous policies and rules which carry predictable and consistent consequences (see *Sample Policies and Rules*).

Typical consequences for bus misbehavior must follow a pattern of progressive discipline such as:

1. Verbal warning/reprimand.
2. Report to parents (see *Sample Bus Misconduct Form*) and/or parent conference.
3. Temporary suspension of bus privileges.
4. Complete withdrawal of transportation privileges. Naturally, certain violations (assault, drug use, weapons possession, and so forth) often bypass the routine sequence of consequences, resulting in immediate removal from bus service.

Of course, the front-line enforcers of bus policies and rules are the drivers themselves. In many places, lack of driver training and large turnover of bus personnel compound on-board discipline problems.

Anything you can do to "professionalize" the district's cadre of drivers will go a long way toward improving bus behavior and control. Unfortunately, this usually means providing competitive wages and attractive benefits which are costly. With both discipline and safety at stake, however, the investment is worth some sacrifice.

Whether employed by the school district or by an outside independent contractor, bus drivers should be screened carefully, including criminal records background checking (see Chapter 4). Once hired, drivers should receive continuous inservice training on safety, discipline techniques and human relations skills (see *Directions for School Bus Drivers*).

(Sample Policy #1)

Student Conduct on School Buses
Billerica (MA) Public Schools

Buses are provided for those pupils whose distance from school or health make this service essential. Children should be instructed in the following rules of behavior.

1. Pupils shall remain well back from the roadway while awaiting the arrival of the bus. They should refrain from throwing things or playing at a bus stop.
2. Pupils shall enter the bus in an orderly fashion and go directly to a seat and remain seated until the destination is reached.
3. Younger pupils should be permitted to enter first.
4. Seats in the rear of the bus should be filled first.
5. Pupils shall keep their hands, arms, and heads inside the bus.
6. There shall be no shouting, roughhousing, or throwing things on the bus.
7. All articles such as athletic equipment, books, musical instruments, and so forth, must be kept out of the aisles.
8. The emergency door must be used for an emergency only. Children shall not touch safety equipment on the bus.
9. People who must cross the street at a bus stop shall not do so until they receive a signal from the bus driver.
10. There shall be no smoking at any time on school buses.
11. All directions given by the bus driver are to be followed.

(Sample Policy #2)

Student Conduct on School Buses
St. Louis Park (MN) Public Schools

While the law requires the School District to furnish transportation, it does not relieve parents of students from the responsibility of supervision until such time as the child boards the bus in the morning and after the child leaves the bus at the end of the school day.

Once a child boards the bus—and only at that time—does he or she become the responsibility of the school district. Such responsibility ends when the child is delivered to the regular bus stop at the close of the school day.

In view of the fact that a bus is an extension of the classroom, the School District shall require children to conduct themselves on the bus in a manner consistent with established standards of classroom behavior.

In cases where a child does not conduct himself/herself properly on a bus, such instances are to be brought to the attention of the building principal by the transportation contractor.

Children who become a serious disciplinary problem on the school bus may have their riding privileges suspended by the principal. In such cases, the parents of the children involved become responsible for seeing that their children get to and from school safely.

(Sample Policy #3)

Bus Rider Rules and Disciplinary Measures
New Richmond (WI) Public Schools

A. General

Bus riders will:

1. Ride on assigned buses.

2. Board and disembark from assigned bus at the selected destination unless written permission is granted to be left off at other than the regular stop.

B. Prior to Loading the Bus

Bus riders will:

1. Be at the designated bus stop on time.

2. Stay off the road while waiting for the bus.

3. Conduct themselves in a safe manner while waiting for the bus.

4. Wait until the bus comes to a complete stop before attempting to board.

5. Line up in an orderly, single file manner.

6. Not rush to get on the bus.

7. Be courteous.

8. Not take advantage of younger students in order to get a seat.

9. Walk to the side of the road facing traffic to get to the bus stop if there is no sidewalk or path.

10. Use the handrail and watch their step when boarding the bus.

C. While on the bus

Bus riders will:

1. Keep hands and head inside the bus at all times.

2. Assist in keeping the bus safe and sanitary at all times.

3. Remember that loud talking, laughing, or unnecessary confusion diverts the driver's attention and may result in a serious accident.

4. Treat the bus equipment as valuable furniture in their home. Damage to seats must be paid for by the offender.

5. Never tamper with the bus or any of its equipment.

6. Do not leave books, lunches, or other articles on the bus.

7. Keep books, packages, coats, and all other objects out of the aisles.

8. Remain in the bus in case of a road emergency unless directed to do otherwise by the bus driver.

9. Do not throw anything out of the window.

10. Always remain in seats while the bus is in motion.

11. Always be courteous to fellow students, the bus driver, the driver's assistant, and passers-by.

12. Keep absolutely quiet when approaching a railroad crossing stop.

13. Obey the driver promptly and cooperatively.

D. After Leaving the Bus

Bus riders will:

1. Cross the road at least 10 feet in front of the bus, but only after checking to be sure no traffic is approaching and/or receiving a signal from the driver.

2. Help look after the safety and comfort of small children.

3. Be alert for the prearranged danger signal from the driver.

(Sample Policy #4)

School Bus Misconduct Form

Student Name:_____ Date: _____

School: _____Driver's Name:_____

Grade:_____ Bus #: _____ Time: _____

Bus driver's description and comments regarding the incident:

_____

_____

_____

This is the student's:
    1st violation: Misconduct Form to Parents
    2nd violation: Second Warning
    3rd violation: Parent Conference
    4th violation: Loss of Bus Privilege

_____

(Official Signature)

Directions for School Bus Drivers

Be sure to	Avoid
Inform students of bus rules.	Being overly familiar.
Remember your riders are just kids.	Using physical force. Embarrassing kids
Be courteous and respectful.	publicly.
Control your temper.	Making threats you can't
Make it clear you're in charge.	deliver. Generalizing blame.
Keep your sense of humor.	Trying to discipline while
Seat troublemakers in an "isolation seat."	bus is in motion. Putting offenders off bus
Report all problems.	without informing parents.
	Talking over your shoulder.

Maintaining bus discipline is sometimes complicated by confusion over who's in charge and who does what. Drivers must handle many situations on the spot, but they are not always the best parties to deal with parents or enforce long-term consequences. Questions of who is responsible for discipline on buses and particularly at bus stops must be clarified.

In most situations, building principals handle bus incidents involving disciplinary action. When and if others (such as district transportation personnel and representatives from the bus contractor) get involved needs to be agreed upon in advance.

Some systems, such as the Adams County School District in Northglenn, CO, have had success by assigning responsibility for bus behavior to the district transportation department exclusively. Advantages include providing relief for overburdened principals and promoting consistency of enforcement.

Whoever is in charge, it's important that bus discipline efforts include positive proactive, as well as punitive measures.

Many schools have initiated "safe ridership" training programs which teach students and parents bus etiquette and expectations for proper bus conduct. It sometimes helps to have parents sign off on bus rules. Forming a *Bus Safety Advisory Council* comprised of school staff, parent, driver, and student representatives also demonstrates concern and enhances proactive planning.

The most sweeping innovation in bus discipline across the country in recent years has been the introduction of *video monitoring*. More and more districts are installing video cameras on school buses. To curb costs, most school boards favor the use of concealment boxes on all buses with the rotation of "live" cameras on a daily basis. A continuous red light gives the appearance that every camera is taping actively. Neither drivers nor students know with certainty which cameras are actually recording behavior.

Opponents of video monitoring on buses argue that it is an Orwellian approach that sends a message of distrust. Supporters maintain that improved safety justifies the use of video cameras. They cite better supervision, reduced discipline problems, and improved driver performance as sufficient reason for video monitoring. Despite the philosophical arguments pro and con, experience across the country clearly established that discipline problems go down when video cameras go up.

In addition to video monitoring, other tested techniques that successfully reduce bus behavior problems include the following:

- Ensure that complete rules are posted in all buses all of the time.
- Discourage taking valuables on school buses.
- Allow only assigned students to ride the bus.
- Equip drivers with walkie-talkies or cellular phones for emergency communication.
- Hold regular meetings of principals and drivers to analyze behavior patterns, identify problem areas, and brainstorm solutions.
- Encourage parents and older students to monitor bus stop behavior.
- Change bus seating or bus assignments when necessary.
- Separate boys and girls on buses. (This is controversial, but some veteran operators claim it improves discipline.)
- Require students to sit in numbered seats to increase accountability.
- Conduct spot checks of bus routes and bus stops.
- Use AM/FM radio music to provide a calming background effect.
- Provide incentives (for instance, treats) for respectful ridership.
- Use volunteer bus liaisons to greet buses when they arrive and take student reports about discipline incidents.
- Place aides on problem buses to assist with discipline (similar to the practice of having a second guard ride "shot gun" on stage coaches in the old west). Districts are advised to check if liability insurance covers nonstudent riders before adding aides.
- Instruct drivers to stop the bus if things get out of control and safety is endangered.

- Conduct an annual review of discipline problems on buses and adjust procedures as needed.

School administrators often don't like to deal with bus discipline problems because they feel one step removed from the scene and source of the difficulty. Nevertheless, these are three compelling reasons why bus discipline is as much or more important than any other area of behavior concern:

1. Discipline problems on school buses can be life-threatening situations.
2. What happens on the bus on the way to school sets the tone for the rest of the day.
3. What happens on the bus on the way home from school is the first (and sometimes the only) thing reported to parents.

Bad behavior on the school bus causes distractions which can cause an accident, injury, or death.

There are lots of nightmarish stories about uncontrolled school bus behavior, but there are many more examples of relatively trouble-free transportation programs. There's nothing more important that you do in the area of discipline than making the school bus as safe and well-behaved as your best classroom. Lives depend on it!

WHAT TO DO ABOUT TEEN PREGNANCIES, AIDS, AND OTHER STDs

Student sexual activity is a given. Like it or not, the average age of student sexual exposure and experimentation has consistently gone down in recent years for a variety of reasons including:

- Earlier maturation;
- An increased sexual orientation throughout the culture;
- Mixed messages from society regarding what's O.K. and what's taboo;
- Emergence of alternative lifestyles;
- Lower age of legal majority;
- Saturation of sex-oriented stimuli through music, fashion, and the media;
- Expanded freedom, mobility, and privacy for young people;
- Protracted period of adolescent nonproductivity in our society;

- Promiscuous behavior fostered by gangs and the drug culture;
- Teenage isolation and loneliness.

With the average age of initial sexual activity now occurring between 12 and 14, concerns about teenage pregnancy and the spread of sexually transmitted diseases (STDs), including AIDS, have intensified debate about what role schools should play.

Many parents and public policy makers clamor for schools to take the lead in providing education and information on contraceptives, safe sex, and planned parenthood. Conversely, opponents assert that sex is none of the school's business. Whatever approach schools take, they confront countless legal hurdles, ideological battlegrounds, political concerns, and financial problems.

No matter how politicized the issues of teen pregnancy and STDs become, these are real problems which directly affect learning, student health and safety, school climate and morale, community confidence and public support. Schools can't solve these problems alone, but neither can they back off or walk away.

In dealing with all of the politics surrounding student sexuality, the guiding principle for every school leader should be to *do everything community conditions allow to provide students with information and counseling they need regarding sex, pregnancy, AIDS, and other STDs*. It's counterproductive to lose your job over these issues, but the welfare of students demands that administrators push the limits in getting help for all kids—even those who have made big mistakes and need a second chance—either within the school or elsewhere in the community.

For starters, every school should have an appropriate, meaningful sex education component integrated into the overall health curriculum. All such programs should include self-esteem building exercises and the teaching of refusal skills.

Likewise, every school needs to take steps to ensure that pregnant students and students who are already parents are treated fairly by:

1. Providing continuous education within the regular school program or through an appropriate alternative program. Training in prenatal and infant care and in parenting skills should also be available.

2. Ensuring that pregnant students and student parents are not excluded or discriminated against.

3. Providing for easy exit and reentry with no adverse status, penalty, or stigma.

4. Establishing peer support groups.

5. Providing free or affordable infant care for students with babies.

Beyond these basics, anything else the school can do is often defined by the local political climate. Probably the most controversial question on the subject nationwide is whether or not schools should distribute condoms to students.

As explained by Kristine Gebbie, the Clinton administration AIDS spokesperson, "Condoms are not a mystery to kids. They've been making water balloons out of them for years." The critical issues, however, are whether students know how and when to use them, how important such use is, and whether or not they should be able to obtain them at school.

The Center for Population Options reports that more than 60 school districts across the country now have school-based clinics which distribute condoms to students. At least 10 other districts have some other kind of condom distribution program. Many other districts throughout the country, however, have rejected the idea.

The controversial nature of the condoms-in-schools issue is reflected in the noncommittal position/resolution adopted by the National Education Association (NEA) in 1993 which reads:

> The Association urges that, *if appropriate by local choice,* health care services (at school-based clinics) include family-planning counseling and access to birth control methods and instruction on their use. (Underlining added.)

Whether or not condoms are distributed, it's important for the school to send a clear message that the *use of condoms promotes health*!

Separate from the condom controversy is the issue of what else the school can and should do about AIDS and other STDs. The question is twofold:

1. What should the school do about students who are HIV infected or have AIDS?
2. What should the school do to protect students from AIDS?

AIDS constitutes one of the most critical public health threats in the nation's history. Deaths attributed to AIDS in this country increased each year from 135 in 1981 to over 30,000 in 1991. The Center for Disease Control now estimates that approximately 1 million Americans are currently infected with HIV. Students who are sexually active and/or use drugs are vulnerable to this epidemic. Approximately 3 million teenagers get some sexually transmitted disease every year. Schools can't remain silent on AIDS.

Despite the panic and paranoia often associated with AIDS, there can be no doubt that HIV-infected students are entitled to equal treatment and the best possible education. School attendance should not be denied to any HIV-infected student as long as his/her health permits it (see *Model Guidelines for School Attendance*).

Model Guidelines for School Attendance
of Children with
Human Immune Deficiency Virus
(Virginia Board of Education)

Mandatory screening for HIV infection is not warranted as a condition for school entry. Upon learning a student is HIV infected or has AIDS, the Superintendent shall consult with the individual's family and a physician or health officer from the local health department to determine whether the student is well enough to stay in school. Since it is known that HIV is not transmitted through casual contact, any student who is HIV infected will continue in a regular classroom assignment unless the health status interferes significantly with performance. If a change in the student's program is necessary, the Superintendent or designee, family, and physician or health officer will develop an individual plan which is medically, legally, and educationally sound. If the HIV student is receiving special education services, the services will be in agreement with established policies.

Parents/guardians may appeal decisions for restriction or exclusion as determined by the school division's established procedures.

All persons privileged with any medical information about HIV-infected students shall be required to treat all procedures, discussions, and documents as confidential information. Individuals will be informed of the situation on a "Need to Know" basis with written consent of the parent/guardian.

Having an HIV-infected student in attendance may, in fact, be healthy for the school culture by serving as a powerful educational experience for both the young people and the adults in the school.

For all students, access to full, complete, and accurate information about AIDS and other sexually-transmitted diseases is essential. School counseling and health personnel should be sure that all students and parents are aware of the National AIDS Hotline (1–800–342–AIDS), a toll-free service provided by the Center for Disease Control which offers confidential information, referrals, and educational materials in both English and Spanish. With a database of over 10,000 service organizations, the Hotline can often make referrals to agencies in the student's local community.

Additional sources of information available in most areas include a variety of private Community-Based Organizations (CBOs) which provide family-based condom distribution and safe sex education, and local health departments which offer HIV counseling, testing, referrals, and partner notification.

Obviously, student sexual activity isn't a typical student behavior problem for schools. You can't pass a policy against it. The best you can do is to be sure that students get the guidance and information they need to make healthy choices using resources inside and outside of the school.

Since schools can't solve student sexual behavior problems by themselves, smart administrators look for help wherever they can get it. Two current developments that emphasize a new approach to student sexuality are the "Sexual Touch-Tell Policy" originated at Antioch College and the "True Love Waits" campaign initiated by the Southern Baptist Church.

The Sexual Offense (Touch-Tell) Policy begun by students at Antioch College has sparked interest at other campuses and high schools and may spread elsewhere. The policy, rising out of concerns about date rape, serves as a sex code for students. The policy requires that both males and females get and give verbal approval every time before any touching, hand-holding, kissing, and so forth, occurs. Offenders must appear before a Hearing Board and may receive penalties ranging from simple reprimands to dismissal.

"True Love Waits," started by the First Baptist Church in Houston, is a nation-wide campaign to get teenagers to pledge abstinence/chastity until marriage. Thousands of school age youth have signed a formal pledge statement which reads:

> Believing that true love waits, I make a commitment to God, myself, and my family, those I date, my future mate and future children to be sexually pure until the day I enter a covenant marriage relationship.

It's going to take more than school programs to solve the problems of premature sexual activity, unwanted teenage pregnancies, and sexually transmitted diseases among students, but schools have to show the way. Schools are in the information business. This is one area in which we must deliver.

BETTER METHODS OF CROWD CONTROL

In a volatile world, any crowd may be mayhem in the making. Schools are in a Catch 22 situation regarding crowds. Every school wants widespread participation and support at school activities. Attendance is rigorously sought and encouraged and large crowds are often a measure of success for many school functions.

On the other hand, every crowd situation poses some danger. The increased incidence of violence and weapons throughout society raises the risks whenever large crowds congregate. Anonymity, "mob psychology," and the presence of outsiders can also heighten the explosive potential of crowd behavior. At events where school rivalries, pride, and competition are the focal point, the atmosphere may be particularly incendiary and charged with emotion.

Crowd control has to be an important part of maintaining discipline, order, and safety, and for making school-sponsored activities successful, positive experiences for all those involved. The following suggestions for crowd management have been found effective in a variety of schools and school systems:

- Involve students and parents in developing reasonable rules for spectators and audiences.
- Sponsor Fan Education programs for students and adults prior to all sports seasons. These miniclinics can review rule changes and stress the proper role of participants, spectators, and officials.
- Adopt and publicize *Guidelines for Spectator Sports Conduct (see Sample Guidelines)*.
- Don't tolerate any coach or advisor who condones disruptive conduct.
- Follow up on rumors of pending problems at any activity. You may be able to head off trouble before it starts.
- Ban inflammatory or offensive cheers, chants, or songs at any school event.
- Limit attendance to students of the schools involved when necessary.
- Print expectations for behavior on programs handed out to all in attendance.
- Park squad cars near the entrance to the contest area to dissuade potential troublemakers.
- Use assigned seating to separate opposing or rival factions when appropriate.
- Use music to establish an appropriate mood where feasible.
- Be conscious of lighting at all evening indoor and outdoor events. Eliminate all pockets of darkness which may encourage misconduct.
- Require the checking of all backpacks and sports bags.
- "Stack the stands" or audience with security personnel, aides, or off-duty police when any trouble is anticipated.
- Use *Parent Patrols* or *Dads-in-the-Stands* programs to place responsible adults in strategic locations throughout the crowd.
- Always alert the local police whenever a major event is going on.
- Have first aid supplies and personnel available at all activities involving sizable crowds.
- Provide Good Sports Awards for teams and schools at the end of each athletic season.
- Sponsor a Fan-of-the-Month Award to spotlight positive crowd behavior.
- Work with city officials to design a traffic flow to cut down on wait time and driver frustration at major school events.

Guidelines for Good Spectator Sportsmanship

(These guidelines are based on the Minnesota State High School League's Sports Project)

1. Maintain self-control at all times. Good sports conduct is concerned with the behavior of all involved in the game.
2. Show respect for the opponent at all times. Good sports conduct is the Golden Rule in action.
3. Show respect for the officials. Good conduct implies the willingness to accept and abide by the decisions of the officials.
4. Know, understand, and appreciate the rules of the contest. A familiarity with the current rules of the game is essential. Good sports conduct is conforming to the spirit as well as to the letter of the rules.
5. Recognize and appreciate skill in performance regardless of affiliation. The ability to recognize quality in performance and the willingness to acknowledge it without regard to team membership is one of the most commendable gestures of good sports conduct.
6. Show a positive attitude in cheering, refraining from intimidating or any negative type of cheering. Good sports conduct is cheering your own team on to victory.

Certain undesirable acts or actions by you, the viewing public, cannot be condoned. Anyone found in violation of the following may be asked to leave the contest:

1. Use of obscene or abusive language that seeks to offend or intimidate a player, official, or spectator.
2. Use of noise makers—whistles, compressed air horns, cowbells, and so on.
3. Use of banners or placards.
4. Throwing of objects—coins, pop cans, papers, and so forth.
5. Being on the premises of a scheduled contest while under the influence of alcohol or chemicals.
6. Unauthorized entry into any scheduled contest.

Keep in mind that as a spectator you are a guest of the school. Your token payment to an interscholastic contest entitles you to one thing—the privilege of watching students, amateur athletes, exhibit what they have learned in the athletic classroom. Think of the playing field as an extension of the classroom. Interscholastic athletics are justified only in this context. We're happy to have you here. Come again and enjoy amateur athletics at their finest.

- Establish a *Command* Center at all events with large crowds. Locate the center where a responsible authority can monitor both the crowd and the contest/performance and communicate with security personnel stationed throughout the area.

- Videotape audiences/crowds to spot and record persons causing trouble.

- Move the location of the event to a neutral site if necessary.

- Schedule activities for daytime hours or midweek evenings to limit attendance by undesirable elements who have no legitimate business at the activity or event.

- Don't hesitate to cancel or stop an activity if things threaten to get out of hand. This is a drastic step, but is an effective way to establish credibility and convince all parties that you mean business. It usually never has to be done more than once.

- Use the sprinkler system and/or fire extinguishers to stop riot-like behavior if emergency action is imperative before outside help can arrive.

- Don't be too proud to call for help. Some administrators wait too long to get assistance when crowd trouble arises because they fear damaging the school's image or admitting they can't handle the situation alone.

Schools don't want to do away with crowds; but they do want to do away with crowd behavior that turns ugly and jeopardizes the safety and security of students and patrons alike.

Even in the toughest schools, activities can go on, students can continue to compete and perform, and the public can still attend school events in a safe atmosphere. It's worth whatever extra efforts it takes to go public with the school's culture, to showcase student accomplishment, and to model that we can all get along.

IMPROVING SUBSTITUTE TEACHER DISCIPLINE

The fabric of discipline within any school can unravel quickly in the hands of ineffective substitute teachers. Substitute (Reserve) Teachers are the unsung heroes in all schools. Their service is essential to maintain continuity, order and quality of instruction in the day-to-day program. If the substitute system is operating effectively, the school program flows smoothly throughout the year. If it is in disarray, daily operations can be reduced to a shambles in a hurry.

Overuse of substitute teachers or use of weak substitutes can seriously threaten school discipline. Most reserve teachers come to the classroom at a disadvantage because they don't know the students, the specific rules of the classroom, or the regular routine students are accustomed to following. To make matters worse, students at all levels often seize on this disadvantage as an opportunity to stretch the limits and create havoc in the classroom.

It's wasteful to painstakingly develop a schoolwide learning culture based on positive discipline and then let it slip away because too many substitute teachers lose control too often. It doesn't have to happen if you follow the ten step program used in many schools to assure substitute teacher success:

1. Select reserve teachers as carefully as you do regular staff members. In most parts of the country, there is a sizable pool of substitute teaching talent. You don't have to accept mediocre subs or settle for the friend of a friend of someone on your staff.

    Take the time to screen prospective reserve teachers and check references thoroughly. It will pay off later when your well-chosen subs step in and take over classroom programs without missing a beat.

2. Hold building-orientation programs for reserve teachers you intend to use regularly. If substitutes understand the school's culture, routine, and specific discipline plan in advance, there will be a more seamless transition every time they take over a classroom in your building.

3. Cut down on the number of reserve teachers used. Some schools fall into a pattern of relying heavily on reserve teachers to free up regular staff members to participate in staff development programs. This results in better-trained teachers, but poorly run classrooms due to overuse of subs and disruption of program continuity. Usually, students don't like to have a lot of substitutes; parents don't like it, and teachers themselves often dislike the extra effort required to prepare for a substitute and to regroup after frequent absences.

    Some schools have established guidelines for how many substitutes may be used for staff development programs during any given day, month, or year. Review your use of reserves carefully. Substitute teachers can be lifesavers, but they shouldn't be a way of life.

4. Develop a Substitute Teacher Handbook for use in your school. The handbook should contain pertinent information on responsibilities, schedules, discipline policies, daily procedures, event calendars, emergency plans, parking rules, and so on. The handbook can serve as a user-friendly manual for every substitute who comes into your building.

5. Insist that teachers leave daily lesson plans for use by substitutes. Good subs can "wing it;" but things always work better when the teacher leaves specific instructions which provide continuity in learning. Teachers don't always like to have to leave detailed lesson plans; but they like it less when discipline gets out of hand during their absence.

6. Treat reserve teachers as guests. Some schools have had success by referring to subs as "Guest Teachers" and training students to treat them accordingly. Usually, a designated student will meet and escort the guest to the classroom and introduce him/her to the class. Changing the title changes the perceptions held by students and can improve behavior as well.

7. Assign a faculty host to each substitute. Many schools make life easier for substitutes by having a particular staff member assigned to them as host and contact person for the day. The staff member can assist in familiarizing the substitute with the daily schedule, showing him/her around the building and answering questions. It helps if the host/contact checks with the sub throughout the day to see if things are going O.K. Often the host responsibilities replace other supervisory duties which might be assigned to the regular teacher.

8. Include reserve teachers in staff development programs. It doesn't cost anything to invite your regular substitutes to participate in building-level in-service training programs. The result is better prepared reserves who feel more a part of the staff and who are more attuned to your school's unique culture and goals.

9. Evaluate every reserve teacher every time he/she works in your building. Most schools fail to conduct any kind of formal evaluation of reserve teachers. This is unfair to the reserve and to other teachers who may end up using a weak sub because they were unaware of any past problems.

   It doesn't require much time or effort for the regular teacher to complete a short evaluation form whenever a reserve teacher is used (see *Sample Evaluation Form*). The information gained can help guide the principal or district substitute caller in determining future assignments for each reserve.

10. Recognize successful substitutes. Reserve teaching is some of the toughest teaching in the business. Professionals who are good at it deserve recognition. Their performance can serve as a model for others. Some schools and school districts present "Reserve Teacher of the Year" awards to outstanding subs who are nominated and voted on by the regular teaching staff.

Substitute teachers are your back-up system for positive discipline. During peak periods of absences, your school may have to operate with more subs than regular teachers for days at a time. You want professionals who can come off the bench and save the day in the classroom.

(Sample Evaluation Form)

Substitute Teacher Performance Appraisal

Substitute Teacher: _____ _____

Date(s) of Substitute Teaching

Subject/Grade Taught:_____ School:_____

Rating: _____ Excellent (Comments optional)

_____ Satisfactory (Comments optional)

_____ Unsatisfactory(Explanation required)

Comments:_____

_____

_____

_____

Would you request this substitute again?

_____ Yes _____ No

_____ _____

Regular Teacher(s) Signature Date

_____ _____

Principal's Signature Date

Please forward to the Personnel office. A copy will be provided to the substitute teacher.

Don't take the reserve teacher program lightly. Seek out winners, make them feel at home, and be sure your school is a place where the best substitutes always want to work.

Do's and Don'ts of Due Process

Concerns about due process must permeate all actions regarding student discipline. No matter what type of new or historic behavior problem you're dealing with, the rights of every student must be protected and ensured at each step of the way. Although some school leaders are frustrated by the limitations and delays imposed by due process requirements, there are no options or short cuts.

All students must have some way to stand up for their rights, to challenge the system, and to keep it honest. This is what due process is all about. If the school doesn't model the principle of protecting student rights to due process, who will? School leaders must be champions of due process for all students—even the most "challenging" kid in school!

The right of every student to: (1) equal protection; (2) procedural guidelines; and (3) unequivocal application of equitable standards and consistent consequences should be spelled out in school policy or rule (see *Sample Policies and Rule*).

The essential elements of due process which must be followed in all discipline situations include the following:

- Reasonable rules (necessary to the orderly operation of the school).
- Proper notification and explanation of all rules/regulations.
- Objective investigation of all allegations and infractions.
- Documentation of all investigations, findings, and actions.
- Disciplinary action which is comparable and consistent with that imposed on others disciplined in similar circumstances.
- Opportunity for grievance filing (see *Sample Student Grievance Form*).
- Right to a hearing.
- Appeals provision.

Democracy guarantees everyone the right to call attention to unfair treatment, to right wrongs, and to overturn injustices. This democracy doesn't stop at the schoolhouse door.

(Sample Policy #1)

Student Due Process Rights
St. Louis Park (MN) Schools

In cases where violations of statute, regulation, or school rule require disciplining of pupils, the following elements of procedural due process shall be present:

1. All Students shall be provided with accurate information as to rules and regulations. The information may come to the student through the school public address system, by means of instructions from teachers or in printed form.

2. The student must be aware of the specific matter(s) giving rise to any proposed penalty or disciplinary action.

3. The student must have a reasonable opportunity to express his/her views to the decision-making authority regarding the incident.

4. All decisions must be based on the incident or matters about which the pupil has been apprised.

As appropriate, the student's parents will be made aware of and/or involved in the implementation of these student rights.

NEW USES OF SUSPENSION AND EXPULSION

With the banning of corporal punishment and the increase of serious student offenses involving weapons and violence, suspension and expulsion are playing a new role in student discipline. Many schools which hadn't expelled a student in 20 years, now regularly expel some students each year for possession or use of a weapon.

Suspension and expulsion have always been acts of last resort in school discipline, but today's crisis mentality and fears about student safety cause administrators to move to the bottom line more frequently. There are situations in today's society where certain students must be removed from the school setting in order to preserve a safe and workable learning environment.

It should be noted however, that even expulsion is never forever. With evidence that he/she poses no further threat, any student may eventually return to regular

---

(Sample Policy #2)

Due Process
New Richmond (WI) Public Schools

In order to ensure a student of his/her constitutional rights and protection of due process of law as guaranteed by the Fourteenth amendment of the Constitution of the United States and state and federal law, he/she shall be entitled to:

1. A notice of the charges brought against him/her;
2. A hearing;
3. Counsel;
4. Confrontation and cross examination of witnesses appearing against him/her;
5. Privilege against self-incrimination;
6. A transcript of the proceedings; and
7. An appellate review.

(Sample Policy #3)

Student Due Process Rights
Supervisory Union School District
North Conway, NH

Before any disciplinary action is taken against a student, the student has a right to the due process guaranteed him by our Constitution. Any student accused of an action and threatened with punishment for this action has the right to request a hearing before the principal or the assistant principal, with the student's parents attending if he or she desires. If the student is still dissatisfied, he or she may request a hearing before the superintendent of schools and, if still dissatisfied, may request a hearing before the . . . School Board.

Before taking any disciplinary action the teacher or principal must advise the student of his or her right to a hearing.

(Sample)
Student Grievance Form

Student's name: _____ Grade: _____

Date of incident: _____

Description of incident: _____

_____

_____

Results of incident (damage, injury, and so forth): _____

_____

_____

Witnesses to incident: _____

_____

Date: _____ Student signature: _____

Parent/guardian signature (optional): _____

school. In addition, most states now require provision of an alternative educational program during periods of expulsion.

Suspension is a discretionary act on the part of the principal to meet immediate or emergency situations. Expulsion is a much more formal and legalistic process, usually involving school board action.

No administrator should undertake expulsion proceedings without seeking legal counsel. Expulsion of any student must follow strict and thorough due process guidelines which may very from state to state (see *Sample Expulsion Letter*).

Suspension and expulsion involving a student who receives special education services is even more complicated by requirements of federal or state legislation such as *The Individuals with Disabilities Education Act, Section 504, Rehabilitation Act of 1973*. Special procedures are often required to suspend or expel a student with disabilities. Note that this terminology is used in place of "handicapped students." (see *Sample Policy*).

(school letterhead)

Sample Expulsion Letter

Dear (Parent's name):

This letter constitutes written notice of the school district's intent to initiate expulsion proceedings pursuant to applicable state statute (enclosed).

These expulsion proceedings are being initiated as a result of *(student's name)* conduct while a student at _____ school during the 1993–1994 school year. Specifically, the school district shall be seeking dismissal on the following statutory grounds:

1. Willful violation of reasonable school board regulations.
2. Willful conduct that endangers the pupil or other pupils, or school property.

FACTS

On *(date)* , the student brought a loaded .22 caliber semiautomatic pistol to the school.

WITNESSES

Witnesses expected to testify at the expulsion are the following:
_____, Police Liaison Officer
_____, Discipline Aide
_____, Assistant Principal

EXPULSION HEARING

The school district is seeking to expel the student for the period beginning *(date)* through the end of the current school year. The hearing on this matter has been set for *(date)* and shall be conducted at the school district offices located at _____ *(address)* _____.

PARENTS' AND STUDENT'S RIGHTS

The student may designate a representative of the student's own choosing, including legal counsel. Furthermore, the school district hereby specifically informs you that the student and the parent have the following additional rights:

1. You may have legal counsel at the hearing;
2. You may examine the student's record before the hearing;
3. You may present evidence;
4. You may confront and cross-examine witnesses.

The hearing shall be closed unless you request an open hearing and the hearing shall take place before an independent hearing officer.

ALTERNATIVE EDUCATIONAL PROGRAM

In the event the final decision of the school board results in expulsion, the student shall be provided an alternative educational program consisting of homebound instruction and shall continue until the final day of the current school year.

WAIVER OF HEARING

If you choose, you may waive your right to said hearing with the understanding that by so waiving these hearing rights the proposed terms of expulsion will be submitted for action to the school board.

If you have questions about these proceedings, please contact the Superintendent of Schools at _(phone number)_.

Sincerely,

Principal's signature

(Sample Policy)

Suspension/Expulsion of Handicapped Students
New Richmond (WI) Public Schools

Suspension

Handicapped students may be suspended from school in accordance with Board policy except that handicapped students may only be suspended for no more than 10 school days if a notice of an expulsion hearing has been sent.

If the conduct for which the student is suspended from school impaired the education of other students in his/her program, the student shall be referred to a multi-disciplinary team (M-Team) for a determination of appropriateness of his/her placement.

Expulsion

Before a handicapped student may be expelled from school, the district shall demonstrate that the behavior for which the student may be expelled is not related to his/her handicapping condition or an inappropriate placement.

Suspension and expulsion are drastic measures, but serious times call for severe responses. You shouldn't hesitate to impose suspension and/or expulsion when required for the greater good and safety of the overall student population.

You need to understand however, that the school's obligation to the student does not end with an expulsion hearing. Good schools never abandon a student; you will need to continue to try to find ways to reach and teach the expelled student.

This chapter has outlined the latest approaches for dealing with traditional discipline problems. Sometimes, these old behavior problems, such as truancy, seem petty compared to new concerns about weapons, violence, and gangs. Nevertheless, school leaders must address all areas of discipline. Overall positive school discipline is won one battle at a time by effectively dealing with all problem areas, large or small, old or new.

Helping Teachers Learn the Secrets of Successful Classroom Management

Principals and other administrators play an important role in establishing effective discipline throughout the school. They lead in creating a vision for the organization, develop a philosophy of positive discipline, and establish an overall orderly environment through reasoned rules and policies. It's up to the leaders of the school to support teachers and model respectful human interaction. They provide positive reinforcement, as well as punishment, and intervene in a supportive and corrective manner when needed.

Nevertheless, positive discipline isn't made in the principal's office. Good teachers make it happen in the classroom, in the hallways, on the playground, and in every other corner of the school every day of the year.

A principal doesn't have to be the best disciplinarian in the school, but does need to know what good discipline looks like and what it takes to achieve it. The most powerful and enduring thing you can do to foster positive discipline in your school is to coach teachers in effective classroom management.

Where teachers are strong, effective principals support them and help them get even better. Where teachers are weak, principals have to teach them the secrets of successful classroom management and overall discipline.

It begins by helping all teachers, beginners and veterans alike, to understand the real-world dynamics of today's classroom. Controlling classroom behavior isn't the same as it was a few years ago.

IT'S A DIFFERENT CLASSROOM TODAY

Everyone who works in or around schools knows that it's a dramatically different classroom today. Kids are different. The problems are different. What teachers can and can't do are different. What works and doesn't work are different. Classroom management is a tougher job than it used to be. (It's not impossible, however, because good teachers are doing it every day with the support of savvy leaders who know how to help.)

Taking charge of an elementary or secondary classroom today means understanding the many differences that have occurred in the last ten years:

- Class sizes are generally larger and classrooms more crowded.

- More handicapped students (some with near life-threatening impairments) are now mainstreamed into the regular classroom.

- Classroom populations are more diverse and racially mixed.

- Noncompliance is common. (Discipline guru Lee Cantor reports that, "Tough kids comply to 40% or less of teacher requests.")

- There is much more verbal abuse and use of profanity and obscenities by students at all ages (even kindergarten).

- Kids have more problems at home.

- Students are more streetwise.

- Younger students are involved in drugs, sex, and gangs.

- More kids are quick to resort to violence to make a point or settle an argument.

- Students and parents are more ready to resist and challenge authority (including all school personnel).

- Weapons are much more likely to be present in the classroom.

- More and more students are unafraid and unmoved by reprimands and other traditional discipline techniques.

- Parental support and involvement have diminished in many areas.

- There are more limits (rules, regulations, case law) on teacher behavior and authority.

- There are a greater number of lawsuits directed at teachers and school administrators.

- There are more mandates and expectations imposed on the classroom. A society under siege wants schools to "fix our kids and make everything O.K. again."

Although many of these changes may influence classroom behavior negatively, the basic elements of a good classroom haven't changed:

1. All students can still learn.
2. Most children need and want some limits and structure.
3. Students respond to honesty and respect.
4. All children thrive on success and recognition.
5. Kids still want a teacher, not another "pal."

Once teachers understand the new nature of the classroom, they can adjust their professional strategies accordingly. Obviously, some of the old techniques, such as writing "I won't" 100 times, standing in the hall, rapping knuckles or corporal punishment, don't usually work very well today. Even out-of-school suspension is now suspect because many students enjoy the time off too much.

Classroom control can't be established solely through punishment anymore—if it ever could be. Today's teachers have to adopt some fresh approaches to classroom management.

DEFINING A NEW ROLE FOR TEACHERS IN DISCIPLINE

Principals must help all teachers realize that: (1) there's no automatic respect any more; (2) classrooms can't be run by teacher edict alone; and (3) adults "can't take scalps" in the classroom without serious repercussions.

Successful teachers *earn* their wings every day by demonstrating confidence, competence, and caring. The tools of effective classroom management in the nineties include:

- Empowering;
- Coaxing;
- Influencing;
- Modeling;
- Facilitating;
- Mentoring;
- Resourcing;
- Negotiating.

More than being an enforcer or punisher, teachers today get better results by serving as coach, cheerleader, and champion of excellence. A major portion of maintaining discipline has become boosting student self-esteem.

The two most significant changes in the role of teacher as disciplinarian in recent years have been the following:

1. Teachers are now sometimes the first and/or only authority figure in a child's life who espouses values of civility, mutual respect, and cooperation. (You can't count on parents teaching manners or social skills at home anymore.)

2. Teachers must be part of a schoolwide discipline team and help out with discipline outside their own classrooms. Effective school staffs operate as a unit, not as a "star system" with each individual striving to have the best classroom and not worrying about anything else. It takes the entire staff working together to create a totally effective learning environment.

To make it in the classroom today, teachers must be risk-takers and mold-breakers. It's not enough to merely enforce the old rules. Good teachers must be willing to bend the rules when necessary, and even throw out the old rules if that's what it takes to save a child from the abyss of the streets. Principals need to teach teachers that rules are tools, not scriptures.

Modernizing Your Classroom Rules

Every group needs some written or unwritten rules in order to function and achieve desirable goals. Classrooms are no different, but some teachers lose themselves and their students in a labyrinth of rules for all occasions.

As principal, you have a responsibility to help teachers develop meaningful and manageable rules to ensure successful learning.

Classroom rules don't have to be identical for all teachers. Students can readily adapt to various sets of rules if each makes sense for the situation involved. Effective rules should be built around the types of activities that will take place in the class and around the teacher's unique style of instruction (for instance, some teachers thrive on ambiguity and some do not).

Obviously, rules have to be in tune with the times. Look at some of the dress codes of the 50s to see how ridiculously outdated rules can become. When kids are killing each other in the streets, rules against gum-chewing seem, somehow, less compelling and important.

The best classrooms and schools often have the fewest rules. Too many rules can be perceived as overkill by students and can become a source of conflict, rather than guidelines for good behavior. If the Christian religion can survive on ten commandments and one golden rule, it shouldn't take much more to run a classroom.

As a case in point, staff members of the Cedar Manor Intermediate Center in St. Louis Park, MN, recently reduced a list of over 40 rules and specific behaviors to three basic expectations for all students. The staff now uses the acronym *T.U.F.* ("Be TUF") to remind students and parents of the three essential school rules:

1. <u>T</u>reat each other with respect;
2. <u>U</u>se school supplies and equipment appropriately;
3. <u>F</u>ollow adult directions.

The purpose of all school rules is simply to define the borderline between what's O.K. and what's not in the classroom. To be effective, rules for students should be simple, specific, worded clearly and stated in positive terms whenever possible. Avoid too many "don'ts." Other characteristics of successful classroom rules include:

- Rules should be brief.
- Rules should be stated in behavioral terms.
- Rules should deal with observable behavior.
- Rules should be measurable.
- Rules must be enforceable.

The difference between workable rules and waste-of-time rules are illustrated below:

Examples

Effective Rules	**Ineffective Rules**
1. Give each assignment your best effort.	1. Be good.
2. Work quietly when directed.	2. Don't bother others.
3. Take care of shared equipment.	3. Practice good citizenship.
4. No hitting.	4. Behave appropriately at all times.

Whatever the rules are, they work best if students have a voice in forming them, if all students are fully informed of the rules, and teachers have good reasons for implementing them. Teachers need to present classroom rules with conviction. If there's any hint of questioning, pleading, or room for negotiating, the rules won't be taken seriously.

Of course, the best rules in the world won't work if class sessions are boring and lessons irrelevant.

Chapter Ten

WHAT TEACHING STRATEGIES WORK BEST WITH TODAY'S STUDENTS

The key to successful classroom management is good teaching, not rules.

Boredom, failure, and frustration teach kids to be troublemakers. In a classroom where learning is fast-paced, relevant, success-oriented, and makes sense to each student, behavior management becomes a secondary concern. When the classroom is a place of learning-excitement, students don't have time to get everything done that they want to do, including getting into trouble.

Obviously, changing times and changing learners call for different teaching techniques and strategies. Teaching can't be a static profession. Teachers who plan to teach tomorrow the way they teach today should have quit teaching yesterday.

It's part of your job as school leader to help teachers stay up-to-date in the classroom, to learn how the best teachers are teaching today, and to understand what works and what doesn't with contemporary students.

Effective teaching today has to be rooted in a curriculum where all students succeed (see Chapter 3). The best curriculum in the world however, won't come alive for learners if teachers don't practice effective instructional strategies.

Certain once-popular techniques (for example, large group lectures, rote memorization exercises and fill-in-the-blank worksheets) are now viewed as turn-offs for kids. Conversely, most classroom experts agree that the following strategies and lesson designs work best with today's students:

- Hands-on learning activities;
- Lessons that accommodate a variety of learning styles (audio learners, visual learners, kinesthetic learners, and so forth);
- Cooperative learning projects;
- Open-ended assignments;
- Seminar situations (where students can give their own answers, instead of just the teacher's answer);
- Lessons tied to student causes (for instance, save the environment);
- Assignments requiring the use of computers and other technologies;
- Activity-oriented lessons;
- Self-paced, continuous progress lessons;
- Self-directed study;
- Interdisciplinary lessons;
- Individualized/personalized lessons;
- Assignments broken down into manageable pieces;
- Lessons involving student choices;

- Learning experiences organized around student learning centers;
- Pupil-centered lessons derived from student questions and built on student interests;
- Alternating active and passive activities;
- Field experiences involving out-of-classroom activities;
- Learning experiences provided by real-world role models;
- Extensions of the curriculum through minicourses;
- Spur-of-the-moment lessons (for instance, nature walks) that capitalize on unanticipated "teachable moments;"
- Opportunities to learn by teaching;
- Lessons that are unpredictable;
- Independent study projects;
- Lessons that help others (for example, projects for nursing homes);
- Real world assignments dealing with everyday student problems (family relationships, neighborhood violence, and so on);

Some teachers become so preoccupied with classroom management that they have little time left for teaching. They have it backwards. Good teaching comes first. Good behavior follows. The better the curriculum and instruction, the better the discipline. If you help your teachers expand and modernize their repertoire of teaching techniques, you help them improve classroom control at the same time.

Of course, it takes more than up-to-date curriculum, lesson designs, and teaching techniques to solve all discipline problems. There are lots of other classroom management methods your teachers need to know about.

75 Discipline Tips for Today's Teachers

Part of leadership is helping colleagues and co-workers learn how to do their jobs better and easier. This is the principal's role in classroom discipline.

The teacher is the school's first line of defense against behavior problems. If discipline is to succeed, it will succeed because of what teachers are and what they do in and out of the classroom. The principal serves as coach, trainer, and backup.

There is no point to public education unless teachers can handle discipline and create an orderly learning environment. The problem is that what works in teaching and classroom management looks easy, but is deceptively difficult.

The elements of good classroom control appear obvious, but the energy and expertise required to make them reality extract the utmost from any professional. Teaching is a tough, draining business. The goal is to achieve and maintain control without realizing exhaustion. The principal has to help.

The following are 75 specific classroom-tested suggestions which can assist your teachers in mastering effective classroom management:

1. Structure classroom space so you can move around and get close to every student. (Some teachers like a U-shape arrangement.) Be everywhere in the classroom.

2. When a problem occurs, have students call their parents in your presence to report the trouble, rather than you doing all the calling.

3. *Always* have a plan!

4. Provide alternative or limited recesses for students with chronic behavior problems.

5. Encourage students to ask directly for extra attention when they *need* it, rather than seeking attention through misbehavior.

6. Minimize "downtime" in the classroom. Have something worthwhile going on all the time.

7. Cultivate (and practice) an appropriate teacher "look" (glare or stare) to communicate nonverbally with unruly students in the classroom.

8. Provide acting-up and acting-out students with a "time out" period in another teacher's classroom (with prior arrangement, of course).

9. Don't employ consequences that are unduly inconvenient or punish the teacher as much or more than the student.

10. Meet students at the door every time the group enters the classroom.

11. Don't overlabel or overpunish kids.

12. Reduce or modify assignments when necessary so that all kids can succeed.

13. Tape or videotape student misbehavior to share with parents and/or administrators.

14. Remember that students frequently choose misbehavior to achieve one or more of four basic goals: a.) attention-getting; b.) power; c.) revenge; or d.) avoidance of failure.

15. Don't nag. After two requests, take action.

16. Recognize/acknowledge your own biases and prejudices. Be honest with kids.

17. Have a one-on-one meeting with difficult students before the school year starts.

18. Give students a choice of punishments/consequences.

19. Make the classroom look like a learning place.

20. Don't take obscenities too personally.

21. Set routines. They work wonders.

(Example)
Behavior Improvement Form

Date: _____ Time: _____

Student's Name: _____

Teacher's Name: _____ Room #: _____

Staff description of problem/situation:

Student description of what happened:

What could you (the student) have done differently?

I understand that if the problem happens again, my parents may have to attend a school meeting.

_____   _____
(Student signature—Date)   (Staff signature—Date)

---

22. Offer rewards as inducements for good behavior. At South Mountain Middle School (Allentown, PA), staff members give students tickets for a monthly "Mountaineer Lottery" prize drawing as rewards for displaying good citizenship, doing a good job, and so forth.

23. Try not to "lose it," no matter how annoying a student becomes. Rage and reason aren't compatible. Whenever students anger you, they beat you at the discipline game.

24. Make secondary classrooms as large and lively as elementary rooms. There's no reason for classrooms to get smaller and more boring as students get older.

25. Use a *Behavior Improvement Form* to get student's attention and to record incidents (see example).

26. Let students know that you won't go away and you won't give up on them or yourself.

27. When an issue is closed, move on. Don't hold grudges.

28. Be on time every time.

29. Remember that short, direct instructions or commands work best.

30. Don't believe everything kids tell you about what other teachers do or allow in the classroom. Don't get conned.

31. Get new students off to a positive start by providing a *New Kid Kit* (see example).

New Kid Kit Items

Welcome banner	School map
Class picture	Points of school interest.
Class roster	School pencil
Class rules	Free lunch coupon
Daily schedule	

---

32. Know when to back off.

33. If students talk excessively, detain them after the period long enough to interfere with their socializing time between classes. Most students will soon get the message.

34. Use school service projects (cleaning up, painting defaced areas, and so forth) as punishments sometimes.

35. Design a group lesson (discussion) around an individual problem (for instance, Why do some people argue all the time?).

36. Set aside an Energy Outlet Space in the classroom where "pumped up" students can scribble, use a punching bag, and so on to release anger and emotion.

37. Establish authority and credibility by *always* keeping your promises and doing what you say you will do.

38. Stop, unexpectedly, by a troublesome student's home.

39. Have your class pick a secret code word (something only the class knows) to signal for cooperation.

40. Make use of eye contact, voice control, body language, and distance management to maintain classroom control.

41. Make criticism of students specific, direct, polite, clear, and immediate.

42. Match consequences to offenses by using progressive discipline as follows:

    a. reprimand;

    b. parent contact;

    c. revoke privileges;

    d. detention;

    e. referral to principal;

    f. suspension/expulsion.

43. Don't tempt students (for example, leave the room during a test).

44. Get everyone's attention before starting any lesson. (It's worth the wait.)

45. Show that you like your job and your students.

46. Don't be too hard on parents. They send you the best they have and most try to do the best they can in raising their children.

47. Remind yourself that the most unpleasant student you have may be the one who needs you most.

48. Allow some constructive noise in the classroom. It can actually help settle down some restless students.

> "Good noise means learning. Bad noise means the children are out of control. No noise means adults don't understand the nature of children."
> —*Dr. Harlen Hansen, University of Minnesota*

49. Give fidgety kids hands-on activities.

50. Understand the cliques in your classroom and how they work for and against different students.

51. Use a chart to help log and analyze patterns of classroom behavior (see example).

52. Don't be afraid to hug or touch a student who needs it (just be careful how and where you touch students).

53. Establish a student grievance procedure in your classroom.

54. Hold periodic "Sound Off" sessions so students can vent frustration and identify problems.

55. Anticipate that students will search out and try to exploit your weaknesses.

56. Use a variety of positive reinforcers such as:

    a. being first in line;

    b. being class captain for the day;

    c. free computer time;

    d. time to sit with a friend.

57. Don't be a historian. Don't prejudge students on the basis of family history or past problems with older siblings.

58. Retain positive expectations for all students. School success is built on a self-fulfilling process.

59. Subgroup in such a way that all pupils can grow in self-esteem. Don't promote or perpetuate stigmas.

60. Use the power of goal setting (individual and class goals) to promote positive discipline.

61. Reduce the number of excuses by limiting occasions when pupils may leave the classroom. This prmotes consistency and eliminates arguments over rule-interpretation.

62. Learn as much as you can about your students' background and lives outside of school. The more you know the more you may be able to help.

63. Teach students to use visualizing/imaging techniques (for example, picture yourself behaving well and succeeding in the classroom).

64. Keep track of your interventions in behalf of difficult students:

    a. Record your intervention strategies;

    b. Document referrals;

    c. Keep a copy of all communications with parents.

65. Don't exhaust your energies fighting "ghosts" ("What ifs").

66. In case of a student tantrum, splash a little cold water in the student's face to get his/her attention.

67. Reserve a "limbo seat" in the classroom for any student who can't function or focus in his/her regular seat for the day.

68. Where necessary, reintroduce a mark or grade for behavior or effort on the student report card (see example). Parents and students must know that accountability counts.

69. If a lesson isn't working, do something else quickly. (Always have a back-up lesson plan in reserve.)

70. Remember that one-on-one encounters are always better than group lectures or punishments.

71. If you make a mistake (for instance, accuse the wrong student), promptly admit it and apologize.

72. Use E-mail or other computerized networks to exchange discipline ideas and techniques with other teachers throughout your district and across the country.

73. Never be afraid to call for help when you need it.

74. Don't give up and refuse to become cynical.

75. Lighten up! Keep your sense of humor.

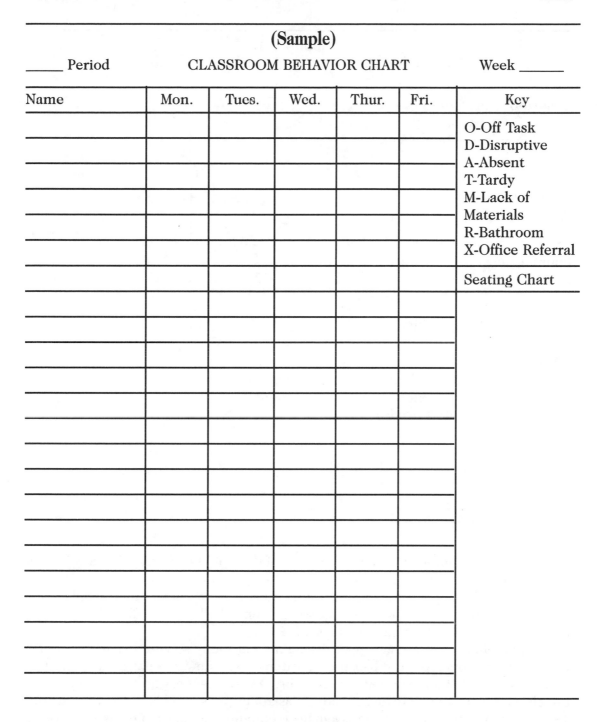

(Sample)

_____ Period   CLASSROOM BEHAVIOR CHART   Week _____

Name	Mon.	Tues.	Wed.	Thur.	Fri.	Key
						O-Off Task
						D-Disruptive
						A-Absent
						T-Tardy
						M-Lack of
						Materials
						R-Bathroom
						X-Office Referral
						Seating Chart

(Examples)
Behavior Marks on Student Report Cards

Behavior/Effort Continuum
   C = Consistently
   N = Needs Improvement

	N	C	Comments:
Works independently			
Follows directions			
Accepts responsibility			
Shows respect			
Cooperates			
Positive attitude			
Resolves conflicts positively			

Effort Key:
   C - Puts forth effort *consistently*
   E - Puts forth effort with *encouragement*
   N - More effort *needed*

Effort Grade:

Jan.	June

If every teacher would follow every one of the tips above every day, any school could become a model of positive discipline in a remarkably short period of time.

Like all leaders, school administrators must work through other people. This is especially true in maintaining classroom control. Without effective teachers, there is no effective discipline in any school.

No teacher wants to have poor discipline; but many sincere teachers struggle with classroom management because they don't know how or what to do to control today's students. Whatever you can do to bring your teachers up-to-date regarding the characteristics of students, effective classroom rules, workable teaching strategies, and modern classroom management techniques advances positive discipline throughout the entire school.

In addition to working with individual teachers, many successful school leaders use a variety of group approaches to upgrading their staff's discipline skills such as:

- Organizing small group discussion and study groups;
- Developing building level staff development programs (see Chapter 12);
- Encouraging peer teacher observation, exchange, and visitation programs;
- Enrolling a number of teachers in a Lee Cantor discipline course;
- Use role playing to simulate common discipline situations;
- Forming a staff committee to develop a new job description for the modern teacher.

One teacher whose class is out of control can infect an entire school. Good principals exercise every means possible to help teachers learn the secrets of successful classroom management. When all such efforts fail, there should be a subtle revolving door to remove misfits or incompetents from the profession. Student learning and discipline are more important than teacher job security.

How to Rejuvenate the Partnership Between Home and School

Maintaining positive school discipline is an interactive process involving the student, the school, the home and the entire community. Since students ages 6–18, spend only an average of 9% of their time in school, the home and community environment are crucial in developing self-disciplined children and youth. The school can't do it alone.

Where schools are succeeding and positive discipline is intact, the partnership between home and school continues to be a healthy, vibrant reinforcer for maintaining prosocial behavior. Where discipline has disintegrated and schools are out of control, the home and school no longer speak with a single voice, nor really listen to one another.

In these situations, the collaboration has collapsed. According to Dr. Ernest Boyer (President, Carnegie Foundation for the Advancement of Teaching), "It's not the school that has failed, it's the partnership that has failed … we cannot have an island of excellence in a sea of community indifference."

In solving school discipline problems, parents must play a key role. Everything in the community, including social agencies and the business community, should make a contribution toward supporting effective parenting.

School discipline is a product of the partnership. Unfortunately, in many parts of the nation, we have reached the point where schools and families must be reconnected and the school-home partnership must be recreated. The alternative is growing chaos, more throwaway kids, and a murky (if not frightening) future for both schools and society.

What Went Wrong with the Partnership?

Both educators and parents are guilty of contributing to the demise of strong home-school partnerships.

Families have changed; but many schools have not. In fact, some schools refuse to admit or accept societal changes which have produced multiple family configurations. These schools steadfastly continue to treat all families alike and to deal with them in the same ways that worked decades ago. Instead, they should be seeking creative new ways to collaborate with today's different family forms.

Likewise, many families have become so dysfunctional that they are no longer strong enough to help the school in disciplining their own children (see *Signs of a Family-in-Trouble*).

For these families, the school is frequently viewed as the enemy, not as an ally. The parents have often lost control to the extent that they are virtually defeated. A few may even be held emotional hostages by their tyrannical teen-age offspring.

Such parents merely want to run and hide and let the school handle all discipline affecting their sons or daughters. Some blame the school for the family's failure. Instead of being interested in forming a partnership, they're more likely to want to file a malpractice suit against the school.

Signs of a Family in Trouble

Lack of mutual respect or appreciation.

Few compliments among family members.

Put-downs become the norm in family communication.

Little physical contact other than abusive behavior or violence.

Blaming and shaming are commonplace.

Absence of family rituals.

Few, if any, special family events.

Part of rebuilding the partnership must be helping families to rebuild themselves.

Other forcing factors which have undermined the home-school alliance include:

- Increase of dual-income families. It's difficult for two working parents to stay connected to their growing children and to the school.
- Proliferation of value choices. Not all of today's families share the traditional values espoused by most schools.

- Growing numbers of single parent families and increased acceptability of having children outside of marriage.
- Expanded masses of children being raised in poverty (1/2 of single parents live below the poverty line).
- Accelerated abuse and violence against children at all levels of society.
- A self-indulgent mentality among growing numbers of adults. Children no longer come first in many households.
- More fatherless families with no male presence, role model or support. ("Deadbeat Dads" deny emotional as well as financial support to thousands of children nationwide.)

These and other influences have relentlessly eroded the bridge between home and school. Where this has happened, students and discipline have been the losers and the partnership has become inoperable.

Bemoaning changing times, however, doesn't solve problems. Families and schools can be reunited as a powerful dual force for positive student behavior. Winning schools are becoming proactive in reinventing the partnership and galvanizing community support. It's happening in lots of schools and communities. It can happen in yours too.

THE SCHOOL'S ROLE IN STRENGTHENING THE FAMILY AND THE PARTNERSHIP

Parents are every child's first teachers, disciplinarians, and role models. All parents and families have strengths (although some are far from obvious) and all parents and families, occasionally, have problems and need help. Every family is "at-risk" sometime.

Schools can't afford to disregard any family anymore than they can ignore any child. Schools can't function without parental support and collaboration. To succeed today, schools need to reach out and help all families to help themselves so that the family becomes strong enough to help the school in return.

There isn't a community in the country where the school/home partnership can't be improved. Even where family involvement is greatest, most parents do little more than talk to their kids about school and attend obligatory PTA meetings and conferences. Less than 1/2 of all parents help their children with homework or read to them daily.

The role of the school in working with today's families is twofold:

1. Strengthening all families;

2. Strengthening the home-school partnership.

Schools must work with parents on several levels to achieve these purposes:

Level I—Supporting the family structure;

Level II—Treating parents as valued customers;

Level III—Keeping parents informed;

Level IV—Bringing parents into the school as visitors and volunteers;

Level V—Encouraging parent participation in learning projects;

Level VI—Collaborating with parents in developing behavior standards and enforcing positive discipline;

Level VII—Involving parents in on-site decision making.

Too often, schools think that crisis intervention and management are the only avenues to building strong families and effective partnerships. Contemporary society is afflicted by a preoccupation with deficits. Too many leaders spend all their time "fixing" specific problems (drugs, gangs, violence, vandalism), rather than nurturing resources (assets) which enable young people to avoid, cope, and overcome *all* problems. As Don Fraser (former mayor of Minneapolis) laments "…we keep ordering more parachutes as the wings of our airplanes continue to fall off." The best programs for strengthening families and bolstering home-school cooperation, however, focus on enhancing student *assets*.

Schools and families need to work together to develop individual student strengths and provide a positive safety net of support and nurturing for all children. Providing children and youth with tools for effective living has more long-range impact than constantly picking away at specific problem areas.

One nationwide asset-oriented effort which has proved successful is the Family Education Program sponsored by the Sears Roebuck Foundation (SRF). This program is designed to help parents help kids stay, behave, and achieve in school. Through a series of workshops conducted by the Home and School Institute, parents are shown how to use normal family routines and activities as learning opportunities. The workshops focus on 10 life-essential skills:

1. Confidence;

2. Motivation;

3. Effort;

4. Responsibility;

5. Initiative;

6. Perseverance;

7. Caring;

8. Teamwork;

9. Common sense;

10. Problem solving.

Results of the Sears program, which has now been successfully introduced in 42 states reaching over 500,000 families, have shown that building on these megaskills helps children stay out of trouble and do better in school, while parents become more involved in all aspects of school life. The Sears model can be adapted in any community and funded by local contributions.

Other tested ways to link up the home and the school to promote achievement and good discipline include the following:

- Vary school schedules so that more parents can come to school to work as volunteers and/or to serve as audiences during different times of the day and early evening.

- Initiate family literacy programs where needed. There's nothing wrong with three generations of learners in a family all mastering reading together.

- Step-up home visits by teachers and other professional staff members.

- Establish a Parent Center in your school where parents can meet, plan car pools, get information on school events, and share ideas and solutions to problems.

- Stress interactive homework assignments which require family members to work and learn together.

- Let parents know specific ways they can help with their child's learning (see example).

- Provide parents with on-going information on health, nutrition, safety, discipline and parenting skills as long as they have children or teenagers in school.

- Lobby for quality and affordable day care and after-school care in your community.

- Recruit a corps of fathers as volunteers to help chaperone/monitor school events. Students will often respond to and respect their classmate's father more than a security officer who is a stranger to them. Arlington High School (Indianapolis) has had success in reducing rowdyism at school activities and in increasing overall parent involvement through this type of a "Security Dads" program.

- Incorporate a community service component into every child's educational experience.

Education on the Home Front

(16 Ways to Help Your Child Stay Out of Trouble and Succeed in School)

1. Establish regular bedtimes.
2. Subscribe to magazines and newspapers.
3. Limit TV time.
4. Talk about school and life-long learning.
5. Have maps around the house.
6. Celebrate big and little successes at school.
7. Make a big deal out of reading.
8. Model patience and sticking to a task.
9. Talk about the values you believe in and live by.
10. Spend time in the classroom.
11. Don't stop learning yourself.
12. Show your children how mature people solve problems without violence.
13. Model goal setting.
14. Communicate with teachers.
15. Show interest in your child's school work (even at the high school level).
16. Support positive peer groups such as SADD.

- Use native speakers and interpreters to involve non-English speaking parents.
- Create a Family Resource Center in the school where parents can get art/craft ideas, check out videos, compact disks, and toys, and pick up the latest information on parenting.
- Promote tutoring and mentoring programs available to all families.
- Set up and facilitate Parent Support Groups where needed.
- Make use of parents on Site Councils or Principal Advisory Committees to solicit input for important school decision making.
- Remove barriers which inhibit parents' access to trained professionals for crisis management, health care issues, and legal problems.
- Establish Neighborhood Block Clubs.
- Expand the role of teachers outside the classroom to work with families over extended time. The Hopkins (MN) schools have extended the contracts of

selected "Career Teachers" (CTs) to work with families during evenings, summers, and off-school days. Each CT is assigned seven families. The role of the CT is to: (1) coordinate year-to-year progress; (2) provide parenting information; (3) serve as a resource and make referrals; and (4) help with transitions from one level of schooling to the next.

- Educate parents about the need for their involvement in their child's learning. (Research is unequivocal in validating that kids do better in school when their parents are interested and involved.)

- Promote family-friendly employer practices in your community (making it "O.K." for the school to call parents at work, releasing parents from work to attend school functions, job-sharing for workers with children, and so on.).

- Hold frequent family-type celebrations for learning successes at school.

Many families have lost the traditional support of two parents, nearby grandparents and/or true neighbors. Good schools are looking for ways to fill the void. The school has to help families, so families can help the school.

If the partnership between the home and your school is weakened or broken, fix it. There is no effective discipline without parental involvement and support.

HOW TO HELP FAMILIES BOOST SELF-ESTEEM IN THEIR STUDENTS

The closest thing to a single root cause for student misbehavior is low self-esteem. Students join gangs to seek some recognition and status. Students take drugs to feel better about themselves. Students do lots of bad things to get attention. Some even commit suicide because they think so little of themselves. Conversely, children with high self-esteem are willing to take risks and stick to tough tasks and don't need to act up or act out to get attention.

How children and teen-agers view themselves shapes how they engage the world and react to problems and peer pressure. The biggest difference between "good kids" and "bad kids" is that the good kids believe in themselves and see themselves as being able to succeed in school and in life.

Helping children to like themselves and to have a positive self-image is the greatest gift parents and schools can bestow. High self-esteem is the key to good discipline and school achievement. If the power of the home-school partnership could be focused on boosting every child's self-worth, the battle for better discipline would be won.

Schools must lead the way in showing parents how caring, listening, praising, reinforcing, and taking children seriously can give the gift of self-esteem to any child. As champions of all children, you and your school staff should help parents

---

Parent Tips on Building a Child's Self-Esteem

- Communicate one-on-one with your child every day.
- Act like your children are important in your life.
- Treat kids as people, not objects.
- Don't put work or self before your children.
- Show your human side and admit vulnerability.
- Be honest; keep promises; don't lie.
- Celebrate differences among your children.
- Hold high expectations; but remain flexible.
- Don't try to be perfect and don't expect your kids to be.
- Help children overcome weaknesses without feeling inferior.
- Never belittle a child's dreams.
- Downplay competition with others and emphasize self-growth.
- Insist that no one is worthless.
- Show pride in yourself, your family, and your children.
- Reinforce successes and desired behavior.
- Do lots of little things that show you care.

---

learn the importance of student self-esteem and how to nurture it (see suggestions that follow).

All children need to know that their parents want to spend time with them and give them attention. The school can help by showing busy single and working parents how to stay connected with their children through using notes when face-to-face contact is impossible, inventing short/quick family rituals and capitalizing on spontaneous opportunities to be with their children.

Schools should offer parents guilt-free guides to boosting student self-esteem. There's no more important goal of the home-school partnership than promoting and protecting every child's self-concept. This is the best kept secret for improving discipline at home and in school.

HOW TO REACH AT-RISK FAMILIES AND GAIN THEIR SUPPORT

Any veteran teacher or administrator will tell you that the parents who most need to dialogue and/or work closely with the school to improve their child's behavior are the same parents who never visit school or attend conferences. And the number of such families is increasing.

For naysayers this is ample cause to give up in futility. For problem solvers, however, it merely suggests that it may be time for the school to go to the parents.

The day when most families had one parent at home full time who was always available to volunteer, be a room mother, or visit school on short notice is gone forever. Today's schools have to invent new ways to reach and connect with nontraditional families of all kinds. It's called survival.

According to "Kids Count," an annual survey conducted by the Center for the Study of Social Policy, one-half of all new families in America start out with one or more of the following deficits:

1. The mother is under 20 years of age when the first child is born;
2. The mother has not finished high school;
3. The parents are not married.

Ten percent of new families have all three of these strikes against them from the outset. With this kind of negative beginning, the chances are great that these families will live in poverty, that the parents will split up and that the children will be unsuccessful students and will get into trouble at school and in the community.

The barriers to positive interaction and teamwork between such at-risk families and the school are formidable; but they are also self-made and can be overcome. The main blockers to a productive partnership with at-risk families include:

- Parental feelings of inadequacy and/or guilt.
- A legacy of bad experiences with school personnel and other authority figures.
- Language and other communication barriers.
- Lack of parental time or energy for school involvement.
- Transportation problems.
- Child care problems.
- Schools project an unwelcoming image.
- Middle class teachers are uncomfortable and unskilled in dealing with nontraditional families.
- Schools discriminate (intentionally or unintentionally) against single-parent families.
- Parents want to leave it to the school to solve learning and discipline problems.
- School staffs are not committed to parental involvement (fear loss of status and/or turf).
- Schools focus on negative issues only.

- Mutual suspicion and disrespect between the home and the school.
- Teachers don't expect much from at-risk kids or parents.

Schools can't succeed by ignoring or giving up on half of the families they serve. Pointing fingers is not a process for improvement.

Blame is a worthless commodity. Blaming the schools or shaming the parents for the unacceptable behavior of youth won't make things better. Working together will. School authorities need to take a "no-fault" attitude in engaging the trust and cooperation of at-risk families.

Maybe the place to start is to eliminate the label. Using the term "at-risk" perpetuates an undesirable stereotype.

To overcome barriers in forming a partnership with all families, schools need to commit to a new set of beliefs about homes and parents including the six principles below:

1. All families have strengths and weaknesses.
2. There are all kinds of families and each can be successful.
3. All parents want their children to succeed.
4. Parents know a lot about what works and what doesn't with their child.
5. Parents can learn new skills and techniques for raising their children.
6. A child's development depends on the strength of the parent, as well as the school.

Based on this new belief system, here are more successful ways that schools can involve and collaborate with emerging new family forms:

- Show respect for all families.
- Provide parenting classes to help single parents understand and deal with the effects of divorce on a child.
- Show parents how to integrate learning activities into their daily routine and how to prepare a home environment which supports learning.
- Provide support groups for single parents and family transition groups for children adjusting to life in a divorced family.
- Eliminate any practice which discriminates against nontraditional families.
- Develop a list of suggestions which single parents can use at home to facilitate learning and foster positive behavior.
- Use positive, nonjudgmental parent communications at all times. Avoid patronizing comments.
- Schedule evening and weekend conferences.

- Consider holding neighborhood (on-site) conferences and information/counseling meetings.
- Provide parent transportation to school activities and events.
- Arrange for free instrument rental and music lessons for children who can't afford them.
- Provide child care at all school functions.
- Provide family snacks or meals at school events when needed.
- Pay parents a small stipend for participating in selected school activities, if necessary.
- Make home visits a regular practice.
- Use a third party (church, social service agency, and so forth) to initiate parent-school collaboration.
- Serve as a broker for social services. Help families get whatever kind of help they need. (For many families, the bureaucratic maze of social services is aloof, confusing, contradictory, fragmentary, and incomplete.)
- Search out "home-alone" kids and establish a telephone care network to check regularly on each child's welfare.
- Use Community Education funds to hire case managers and coordinators to work directly and on-site with families in housing projects or low-rent apartment complexes.
- Use minority staff members to hold meetings for concerned minority parents.
- Hold small group meetings of at-risk parents and their children to solve mutual problems. School personnel are often surprised by how much these parents care and by the real-world solutions they can offer. It often works well to have students sit in an inner circle surrounded by an outer circle of parents who listen to their children discussing important issues, and then reversing the roles so that the students listen in on their parents' discussion of the same issues. Both groups frequently learn from each other.
- Develop home-school contracts to pinpoint the responsibility of all parties in addressing problems of discipline, attendance, and so on.

Schools and families can't operate in isolation. They need each other to achieve both respective and mutual goals. Collaboration with all families is the only avenue to effective schoolwide discipline!

WHAT IT TAKES TO GET COMMUNITYWIDE INVOLVEMENT

Some forward-looking school leaders have begun to expand the concept of partnership one step further by involving the entire community.

When supporting families, nurturing children and establishing positive behavior standards become communitywide issues, good discipline is almost a certainty. The old African proverb, "It takes a whole village to raise a child" may offer the answer to today's epidemic of violence and misbehavior among youth of all ages.

There is something seriously wrong with a society that allows babies to have babies, who grow up to be violent teenagers, who have more babies. If and when a critical mass in any community gets fed up with hearing bad news about kids and wants to start making some good news, even the worst and most hopeless situations can be turned around. There is some evidence that this is beginning to happen in pockets around the country.

Nationwide, there is a shift toward investing in families and children, initiating court diversion programs for kids, and finding productive alternatives to jail time for youthful offenders. More and more school and civic leaders are agreeing with former Minneapolis mayor, Don Fraser, and his admonition that "...the foremost challenge for this community is to weave a fabric of community support that includes children of all ages and families of all economic and social standing." Any community which acts on this challenge can have the kind of school discipline it wants.

One example of shifting community concern is the effort in some cities to develop a Civilian Children's Panel to deal with problems of youthful lawbreakers. Patterned after the Scottish juvenile justice system of local tribunals for correcting young transgressors, these panels provide an alternative to traditional juvenile courts. Under this approach, offenders can choose to submit to a 3-member local panel. The goal is efficient resolution of juvenile cases using community-based consequences, apart from the gridlock of the current court system.

One of the most promising community partnerships is the fledgling "Children First" initiative in St. Louis Park, MN (see *Sample Mission and Goals*). The Children First movement is a citywide partnership to strengthen families and create a model caring community for children and teenagers. The initiative responds to the growing concern in all communities that many children and adolescents don't receive the support necessary for school success and healthy decision making. The program hopes to involve a multiphased approach including:

- Strong parent education;
- Strengthening preschool and after-school care;
- Building school-family collaboration;
- Developing family-friendly work policies;
- Increasing the impact of youth programs by city agencies, religious institutions, and voluntary organizations;
- Connecting children and teens to many caring adults in the community.

(Sample Mission and Goals)

Children First Partnership

Mission:

To build a community which puts children first in order to create a better tomorrow for everyone.

Proposed Key Results and Goals (draft):

Key Result 1: A safe, caring environment for every child—

- Safe from violence
- Safe to take risks and make mistakes
- Safe from sexual harassment
- Safe from verbal abuse

Goal 1:   More caring.
Goal 2:   More safe places.
Goal 3:   Less conflict.
Goal 4:   Greater respect.

Key Result 2: A broad sense of ownership in the community of the problems facing children and the solutions to these problems.
Goal 1:   A community commitment that children should be first.
Goal 2:   Comfort with diversity.
Goal 3:   Business' support of children and families.

Key Result 3: Families successful in raising children.
Goal 1:   Schools are supportive of families.
Goal 2:   Parents more effective with their children.
Goal 3:   The right social services available and easily accessible to all families.

Key Result 4: An environment where all children are ready and eager to learn.
Goal 1:   Friendlier school climate.
Goal 2:   More accessible preschool experiences.

If successful, the Children First model may serve as a prototype for communitywide partnership to help young people succeed and become good citizens.

Any effective community partnership begins with an all inclusive dialogue—a communitywide conversation about what's working, what's not, and what new needs to be done. If you're interested in conducting such a dialogue in your community, strategic planners suggest a four-step process:

PROCESS FOR COMMUNITY DIALOGUE

1. Invite a cross-section of community leaders to serve as an initial sounding board. Membership should represent the schools, city government, police, the judiciary, religious community, social service agencies, the business and corporate community, senior citizens, parents (including parents of preschool children) and students.

2. Conduct a series of Town Meetings on how to help children and promote better discipline. The entire community should be invited via the media and school notices to attend and participate in the dialogue (see *Protocol for Conducting Town Meetings*). Broader exposure can be realized if Town Meetings are videotaped and replayed over local community access cable TV channels.

3. Use paid staff and/or volunteers to carry out interviews with a wide range of focus groups throughout the community. Suggested interview groups include:

PTAs

PCN (Parent Communication Network) members

Preschool Parents

Single Parents for Kids

Student Council members

Alternative School students

School Board

City Council

Library Staff

Social Service Professionals

Political Representatives

Senior Citizen Advisory Councils

Human Rights Commission

ESL Students and Parents

Police

Ministerial Association

Chamber of Commerce

Youth Ministers

Protocol for Conducting Town Meetings

Purpose: To engage citizens in building a shared vision of a healthy community for children.

- A shared vision exists when many people help create a picture in their minds of something which doesn't currently exist.
- It's not a vision unless others can see it.
- To create a vision, we need to know what many people think the problems are, what strengths exist to build on, and what the future should look like.

Chairs arranged in semicircles (small groups of 3–5 people).

Each person presented with an agenda, a fact sheet, note paper, and "I want to know more" postcards.

Format:
- a.) Small group conversation with reports back to total group.
- b.) Questions and Answers.
- c.) Open microphone.

Questions for Discussion:
- What can we build on? What do we have going for us?
- What are our concerns about children and teenagers in our community? What are we most worried/disturbed about?
- What would a caring community that supports the positive development of children and teens look like?

Youth Service Agencies (Scouts, Campfire Girls, and so on)

School Staffs

Unions

Other Special Groups

The purpose of all the discussion groups should be to identify how everyone and every institution in the community—together with hundreds of other people in the city—can play a role in creating a better present and future for young people.

4. Encourage neighborhood conversation groups involving all interested parties in the community.

The results of all these citizen dialogues should be compiled, reported back to the community and used as the basis for forging a communitywide partnership and a comprehensive action plan in behalf of all children.

The power of a community partnership for helping young people and promoting positive behavior in school and elsewhere is limited only by the creativity and commitment of the participants.

School-home and community partnerships are necessary so that neither parents nor school staff members feel alone in setting and enforcing standards of behavior. Parents become more confident if they are supported by school discipline. Likewise, teachers work more effectively if they feel assured of parental support and cooperation. The stronger the partnership, the more effective the discipline both at home and in school.

CHAPTER TWELVE

LITTLE THINGS
THAT MAKE A DIFFERENCE
IN DISCIPLINE

Good discipline is often a matter of doing lots of little things right every day. Just as some court cases are lost because of a minor technicality, many discipline programs fail because of inattention to detail. Success lies in nuance.

This chapter deals with some of the nitty-gritty considerations and the little "extras" which can make or break any school's discipline plan.

WAYS TO WORK SMARTER IN SOLVING DISCIPLINE PROBLEMS

Discipline is labor-intensive and time-consuming. It takes lots of time and energy to develop policies and strategies, monitor behavior, investigate incidents, impose consequences, and hold endless rounds of conferences. At the same time, every school is always short-handed when it comes to dealing with discipline.

Creative staffing and scheduling can help, but there will never be enough hours or enough help to carry out all desirable discipline functions. Likewise, there is a point at which teachers and administrators can't work productively any longer, harder, or faster. To maintain positive discipline, school personnel have to find ways to work smarter.

Most discipline issues can't or won't wait until a more convenient period. They have to be dealt with now. If no additional time or help is available, the only alternative is to discover or invent ways to get more and better results with the resources at hand.

231

It starts with a "work smarter" attitude. The anchors for such an attitude are a wariness of bureaucracy and a willingness to question *every* routine or procedure. Other important tenets include:

- Doing the right things first.
- Doing things right the first time.
- Understanding that more isn't always better.
- Believing that people-work is more important than paperwork.
- Having a reason for everything you do.

The right attitude can change the way you do business and enable you to do more with the same time and effort. The following are 33 success secrets which have helped many administrators work smarter in dealing with discipline and can help you too:

1. Get by with as few rules as possible.
2. Tackle big ticket items first (for instance, a weapons offense is more important than an attendance problem). Prioritizing should always be your first priority.
3. Work through other people by letting co-workers do what they do best. (If you have a Chemical Health Specialist, don't spend your time trying to assess whether or not a student has a dependency problem.) Delegation is an act of orchestration, not abdication.
4. Beat procrastination by breaking down complex situations or processes into manageable bits.
5. Be a goal-setter, not just a go-getter. Have a plan every day.
6. Always try to do routine items quickly.
7. Use your waste basket more than your file cabinet.
8. Listen more. Talk less.
9. Use tickler files to stay organized and to track all due process steps.
10. Train your secretary to complete routine discipline records and reports.
11. Don't do other people's work. Insist that teachers try some interventions of their own before referring troublesome students to the administration.
12. If you have some bad rules, work as hard to change them as you do to enforce them.
13. Do the hardest things when you're freshest.

14. Be sure all employees know and understand school policy and legal requirements. It may save time in damage control later on.

15. If a course of action doesn't "feel right," hold off for awhile.

16. Deal with groups of offenders and/or their parents when possible and appropriate. You don't always have to repeat the same lecture several times over.

17. Don't try to solve all problems yourself. Brainstorm possible scenarios and solutions with colleagues.

18. Don't waste time trying to walk on eggs or soft pedal consequences. Say what has to be said and move on.

19. Save some time for reflection every day.

20. Refuse to use all your time putting out fires.

21. When your plate is full, don't take seconds. Learn to say, "No." Some administrators post a sign saying, "What part of the word, 'No' don't you understand?"

22. Build in flexibility by overallotting time for meetings and appointments. The minutes saved provide time to deal with each day's surprises.

23. Stay focused by managing visitors and interruptions (see tips that follow).

Tips on Handling Visitors and Interruptions

- Set aside a specific time to receive and return phone calls each day.
- Don't make your office so comfortable that students and adults tend to linger.
- Remain standing when unexpected visitors drop in.
- Don't feel compelled to always follow an open door policy. Sometimes, a "door ajar policy" is sufficient.

---

24. Find an up-side to downtime by using it for good purpose (for example, review mail while waiting for a parent to come to the phone).

25. Avoid getting sidetracked by office politics (for instancce, don't agonize over the consequences of disciplining a Board member's daughter or the Superintendent's son). Follow policy and be consistent.

26. Make conferences, committees, and meetings work for you (see tips).

Tips for Handling
Committees and Meetings

- Don't tie up several people in a meeting when a simple memo would do.
- Don't schedule meetings or conferences at the wrong time (late Fridays, just before a holiday, immediately preceding a major work deadline).
- Don't ask a committee to reach an important decision without sufficient background information.
- Don't involve too many people or the wrong people in any meeting or committee.
- Don't permit meetings or committees to settle for superficial solutions. Make them deal with the real issues.
- Don't call meetings or conferences on short notice when participants can't prepare properly.
- Don't schedule too many conferences or committee meetings close together.
- Respect your time and everyone else's by starting and ending meetings on time.
- Always have an agenda for every meeting. Distribute it in advance if possible.
- Schedule meetings well in advance so that participants can collect any necessary data.
- Pay attention to seating at meetings or conferences. No party should feel outnumbered, overwhelmed, or intimidated.

27. Use computer technology to track attendance, record referrals, and so on.
28. Try never to get caught without a contingency plan.
29. Pick your discipline team carefully. Some well-intentioned staff members have a proclivity for making things worse and becoming part of the problem instead of part of the solution.
30. Learn ways to win the paper shuffle (see tips that follow).
31. Maintain perspective. Keep in mind all the good things kids do when dealing with the bad things some kids do.
32. Remember that discipline is an important part of the curriculum for all students. It will help you do what you have to do.
33. Take care of yourself so you can take care of business. Use your strengths, pace yourself, and try not to take work home.

Tips for Taming the "Paper Tiger"

- Handle every paper once only.
- Use form letters wherever feasible.
- Save old reports as models for future ones.
- Always write with a specific reader in mind.
- When writing reports, keep it simple and use plain language. Don't try to show off or be cute.
- Have someone else open and sort your mail.
- Don't feel compelled to read all the junk mail you receive.

Many intelligent administrators do lots of dumb things in dealing with discipline. This usually happens because they don't evaluate their own behavior or analyze the tasks which have to be done. In many situations, "working smarter" is the only way to stay afloat in today's rising tide of discipline problems and expectations.

HOW TO DOCUMENT DISCIPLINARY ACTION

Nobody likes paperwork; but proper documentation of all disciplinary action is more important than ever before. Careful notes, records, and reports are essential to support actions, validate due process, guard against faulty memory and maintain a paper trail in case of future problems or legal actions.

Documentation is a survival tool for the nineties. In today's litigious society, proper notes and records may constitute your best defense against subsequent investigations, law suits, or penalties. Battles won today may be lost tomorrow because of insufficient or improper documentation. (In fact, improper documentation may be worse than no documentation at all.)

Many educators are hesitant about putting things in writing. Most are also unaccustomed to recording conversations and events. All hate red tape. Nevertheless, record keeping is the name of the game in discipline today.

Inexperienced administrators often ask, "What kinds of things must be documented?" When dealing with discipline, the best answer is, "Almost everything." Below is a partial list of discipline areas requiring some form of documentation:

- Allegations/charges of impropriety on the part of students or staff members.
- Incident reports.

- Summaries of disciplinary conferences with either students, parents, or staff members.
- Warnings issued.
- Notifications sent to students or parents.
- Telephone logs of conversations about discipline cases.
- Correspondence related to discipline.
- Behavioral contracts.
- Interview notes.
- Procedures followed in conducting investigations.
- Reprimands.
- Disciplinary action taken (even lesser forms of discipline should be noted/recorded).

Since discipline notes and records often take on legal significance, experienced school attorneys offer the following guidelines for maintaining proper documentation:

1. Record notes and summarize conferences as soon as possible while memory is fresh. Timeliness is sometimes an issue.
2. Proofread your own records or notes carefully. Check for accuracy and legibility.
3. The most important information to document is who, what, where, when, how, and why.
4. Wherever possible, always include dates, times, locations, names of witnesses, phone numbers, and addresses.
5. Record only facts. Don't editorialize, speculate, reach conclusions, or make judgments in writing.
6. Interview notes should include exact quotes whenever possible.
7. Retain receipts of all certified/registered mail related to disciplinary action.
8. Have the party involved or a witness sign-off that pertinent documents have been delivered, reviewed, and/or received.
9. It sometimes helps to have one administrator conduct a conference or interview while a second administrator records what is said.
10. Never assume that your personal notes are private. The power of subpoena is far-reaching.
11. Except for formal/legal papers, most disciplinary notes and records do not have to be placed in pupil cumulative records or in personnel files.

12. Retain records indefinitely, particularly in cases of sexual harassment or abuse (see Chapter 8).

The primary purpose of all disciplinary documentation is to establish a paper trail showing a sequence (chronology) of events and actions. In today's court-conscious society, it's better to err on the side of overdocumentation than to document too little.

WHEN AND HOW TO USE LEGAL COUNSEL

Most school districts can't afford to retain an attorney on staff, but no school district can afford to operate today without close and frequent legal counsel, particularly for discipline matters. The missing link in the discipline procedures of many schools is securing adequate input and assistance from qualified legal counsel. A legalistic world requires sophisticated legal advice.

In times of trouble, a lawyer can be an administrator's best friend. Consequently, principals should have authorization to contact the school's attorney directly without having to go through a central office administrator for clearance. Sometimes, legal counsel is needed immediately.

Choosing a competent legal advisor is one of the most important decisions any school board makes. Here's what to look for in a school attorney:

Characteristics of an Effective Legal Advisor

- Experience in processing school discipline cases, including suspensions and expulsions.
- Sound knowledge of school law and legal precedents related to students' rights and disciplinary procedures.
- Understanding of school cultures and how schools work.
- Ability to draft clear policies and guidelines.
- An instinct for anticipating problems.
- Effective communication and listening skills.
- Impeccable integrity and credibility.
- Sense of humor.

Once you have qualified legal counsel available, don't be afraid to use it. The following are some of the most common ways in which skilled attorneys can help every administrator:

- Clarify what you can and cannot do within the law.

- Explain exactly what a specific law says.
- Interpret complicated and/or confusing statutes.
- Review policies and procedures.
- Discover legal precedents and recent court decisions regarding issues you may be facing.
- Draft policies, procedures, letters of reprimand, suspension, and expulsion notifications, and other legal documents related to disciplinary functions.
- Conduct interviews and investigations.
- Respond to grievances, charges, allegations, and complaints.
- Negotiate settlements in disputes regarding disciplinary actions.
- Brainstorm solutions to sensitive issues and find out how others have handled similar situations.
- Arrange for hearing officers, mediators, and arbitrators when needed.
- Test whether proposed actions are legal and/or defensible.
- Help to prepare you to give testimony.
- Conduct a legal audit of student control policies.
- Take depositions.
- Represent the school in confrontational conferences and situations.
- Research pertinent legal issues.
- Serve as official spokesperson or advise on public statements as needed.
- Provide staff development on new laws, legal limits of punishment, risk management, interview techniques, incident reporting, and so forth.

Never be bashful about contacting counsel, but realize that legal expertise doesn't come free of charge. Expect to pay for all advice. Even phone conversations are subject to billing. It's not a racket—it's how lawyers make their living.

There's no excuse for taking any disciplinary action today which is illegal or violates any student's due process rights. Help is just a phone call away. Failure to double check with legal counsel before taking action is one of those little things that can come back to haunt any administrator. Don't let it happen to you.

The best credo to follow in handling complex discipline situations is: "When in doubt, check it out (with legal counsel)."

WHERE TO GO FOR HELP

No matter how good you are, some discipline problems can't be handled alone. Fortunately, there are lots of resources available to assist, and winning principals make use of all of them.

Some principals, however, are reluctant to ask for support or assistance because they don't want to be perceived as weak or incompetent. No one ever said that leadership had to be a solitary act. Effective leaders actively seek out help and take it wherever they can get it.

Positive student behavior and successful learning are communitywide, state, and national issues. It takes combined resources from all three levels to ensure safe, orderly, and productive schools.

If you're like many administrators, you may be surprised by the amount of help available to every school. Of course, three of the best resources are always close at hand:

1. *Staff.* Always make maximum use of staff members in resolving schoolwide discipline issues. This includes everyone on your discipline team (assistant principals, deans, police liaison officers, hall monitors, security aides) and regular staff members as well. Special education teachers, especially those licensed to work with emotional and behavior disorders (EBD), can be particularly helpful with many problems. Likewise, Teacher Assistance Teams and Peer Coaching Programs can often bolster discipline efforts throughout the school. Discipline is everybody's responsibility. It's not your job to shield professionals from their duty.

2. *Parents.* Every school has lots of parents who are willing to help with discipline. Many have special expertise which can assist with special problems. In addition, PTAs, PTOs, Parent Advisory Committees and Site Councils often have both human and financial resources to help tackle specific issues. Parental involvement is essential to good discipline. Make the most of it.

3. *Students.* Don't forget about the kids as a source of help with discipline problems. Even in the worst schools, many students want to do what's right and want a school that works. In every school, students can tell you best what's going on, what will work, and what won't. Listen to your students, ask for their cooperation, and take their advice when it fits.

In addition to these common sources of help, other agencies and individuals which can sometimes lend a hand in solving discipline issues include the following:

- District specialists (school psychologists, district nurse, social workers)
- Youth Ministers
- Probation Officers
- Child Protection Agencies
- Family Counseling Centers
- Crisis Intervention Centers

- Juvenile Court Judges
- United Way Agencies
- Civic Clubs (often the best source of money for special projects)
- Youth-Serving Agencies (Y.M.C.A., Y.W.C.A., Boys and Girls Club, Camp Fire Girls)
- Big Brother and Big Sister Organizations
- Safety Councils
- Police
- Public Health Department
- State Department of Education
- Bureau of Alcohol, Tobacco, and Firearms
- Minority Advocates and Organizations (NAACP, Bureau of Indian Affairs)
- Child Psychologists
- Adult Activist Organizations (MADD)
- Student Activist Organizations (SADD)
- Police Reserve Units
- Administrative Interns
- Help "Hot Lines"
- 12-Step Recovery Programs
- Sheriff's Office
- City Government
- State Attorney General's Office
- Highway Patrol
- Psychiatrists
- Pediatricians
- State Teachers Association
- College and University Personnel
- Runaway Shelters
- County Commissioners
- Ad Hoc Task Forces (Governors' Task Forces on Drugs, Violence, Bus Safety)
- State Bureau of Investigation
- Safe Houses
- Ex-Gang Members (can be invaluable advisors)
- Case Workers

- Treatment Centers
- Booster Clubs
- Local Bar Association
- FBI
- Chamber of Commerce
- Support Groups (inside and outside of the school)
- Alumni Groups
- U. S. Department of Education
- Center for Disease Control
- State Education Association
- American Federation of Teachers
- National Education Association (NEA)
- Retired Teacher Groups
- Faculty Wives Club
- Fellowship of Christian Athletes
- Homeless Shelters
- Future Teachers of America (FTA)
- Phi Delta Kappa (and other professional fraternal organizations)
- Local and State Political Figures
- Insurance Investigators
- Local Media
- Educational Research Service (ERS)
- Professional Books on Discipline (see *bibliography* at the end of this text)
- Security and Alarm Specialists
- Neighborhood Associations
- Block Clubs
- Arson Investigators
- Private Surveillance Firms
- National Institute on Drug Use
- Guardian Angels
- Jacob Wetterling Foundation (and other missing children organizations)
- Commercial Consulting Firms (Lee Cantor and Associates)
- Handwriting Experts
- National Principals Associations

- National Institute on Alcohol Abuse and Alcoholism
- Volunteer Mentors and Role Models
- Children's Defense Fund

In addition to the more formal resources listed above, many leaders find that their best source of help and advice on discipline comes through *networking* with other professionals and practitioners in the field. Every school leader needs to maintain contacts and linkages with a wide variety of professional colleagues across the country. Computer networking now offers almost limitless opportunities for staying connected with other principals and administrators. Peer support and assistance can be an invaluable force in fostering effective leadership for improved student behavior and enhanced school climate.

Tapping all potential resources is one of the little success secrets that separates winners from losers in school discipline. The best principals know what help is available and never hesitate to call for it when needed.

WHAT KIND OF STAFF DEVELOPMENT HELPS DISCIPLINE

Staff development is no longer a luxury in education. It's an imperative. There are no good schools today without an active program of continuous in-service training. Just as worldclass companies invest heavily in research and development (R and D), successful schools upgrade programs continually and reinvent their professional staff through staff development.

Almost every facet of education (curriculum, delivery systems, technologies, and so on) has changed dramatically in recent years. Likewise, the attitude and actions of students are strikingly different today, as are the requirements and expectations regarding school discipline. Rapid and radical change requires far-reaching, on-going staff development.

Even recent graduates need additional education. No training is recent enough to keep up with the changing world of kids, schools, and schooling. Despite years of study, many inexperienced teachers don't have a clue as to how to discipline today's youth. The naiveté of many beginners is well-illustrated in the story of the newcomer in one school who announced proudly one day, "My class was so noisy this morning that I just walked out. That should show them." Obviously, this neophyte had a lot to learn and there are many more just like him.

Veterans and beginners alike need staff development covering everything from new curriculum and assessment programs to what gangs are all about, to personal protection and defense techniques (see *Sample Inservice Course Announcement*). The menu of training needs is extensive and growing.

(Sample Inservice Course Announcement)

**Self Defense for Teachers
(Not Just Kicks and Punches!)**

- Recognize an attack in the making.
- Avert potential trouble.
- Learn simple, practical self-defense strategies anyone can use.
- Identify options for avoidance, deescalation and action.

March 1   4–5:30 p.m.

High School Gymnasium
$5 registration fee

Instruction provided by certified crime prevention specialists.

Any upgrading which helps teachers become more effective in the classroom (skills in handling learning styles, cooperative learning, whole language instruction) helps improve discipline at the same time. The best guarantee against disruptive behavior is simply good teaching.

Most modern instructional improvement programs concentrate on emerging trends in curriculum and teaching (see *Trends in Curriculum and Instruction*). Of course, all teachers also need specific training in the changing youth culture and the latest discipline techniques.

Trends in Curriculum and Instruction

What's Hot	*What's Not*
Active learning	Reliance on lecture
Identifying patterns	Memorization
Analyzing data	Topics taught in isolation
Situational problems	Follow-the-example exercises
Open-ended questions	A single right answer
Emphasis on connections	Isolated skills
Variety of instructional settings.	Single response tests
Communication skills in all subjects	Teaching out of context

The best staff development programs are "home-grown" and "home-owned" (training designed to meet the specific needs of a specific school or staff). Other commonly accepted characteristics of an effective training program follow. The program:

- Involves teachers in identifying needs and planning appropriate activities.
- Incorporates/integrates several components.
- Accommodates varying levels of readiness and different learning styles.
- Provides for practice, feedback, and follow-up (one-shot shows don't "take" and don't make a difference over time).
- Stresses "nuts and bolts" as well as philosophy.
- Features choices for professionals.
- Uses varied delivery systems (released time, weekend workshops, summer sessions, dinner/study meetings).
- Provides some "pay off" for teachers.
- Uses in-house experts (teachers teaching teachers).
- Is well-timed (not too much too fast).
- Starts with those who are most ready.
- Relates clearly to the school's vision and mission.
- Allows time (3–5 years) to institutionalize new programs.
- Includes opportunities for real evaluation (see *Sample Evaluation Form*).

Some school leaders think they can't afford staff development. If this is true, they can't afford to succeed. Staff training and retraining is not a "little thing" you can cut back or overlook. Proper training is absolutely essential to the success of any school discipline program today. Never introduce a new system of discipline without providing the staff development necessary to make it work.

There's no room for complacency in running a school. Very often, discipline deteriorates bit by bit. It has to be built back and maintained the same way. Pay attention to details. Little things make a difference.

Staff Development Evaluation Form

Please fill out this evaluation and return to principal.

Name of Program: _____ **Date:** _____

Instructor: _____ **Location:** _____

	High		Low

1. Rate usefulness of the
   program for you.   3 _____ 2_____ 1

2. Rate amount and quality
   of information you received.   3 _____ 2_____ 1

3. Rate the instructor.   3 _____ 2_____ 1

4. What was best about the program? _____

   _____

   _____

5. What would you change? _____

   _____

   _____

_____
Your name (optional)

CHAPTER THIRTEEN

A FINAL WORD

Change is "messy, bloody, weepy, nasty, and just plain scary" according to Middle School Principal, Marilyn Willis (Calloway County, KY). Nevertheless, change has become routine in school discipline today.

Modern school leaders are dealing with discipline challenges unheard of a decade ago. Student behavior problems have increased and intensified. New sets of antisocial behaviors have emerged in school settings at all levels. Student behavior is shifting toward more violent and destructive kinds of activities and some schools are out of control.

Obviously, traditional discipline techniques aren't enough anymore. Principals and other school officials must rethink their discipline policies and procedures and seek new ways to address today's unprecedented behavior problems. The good news is that it's already happening. It can happen in your school, too. This guide can help you get started.

Despite the negative scenarios being played out in a few schools across the country, the intended tone of this guide is *positive, optimistic, and hopeful*!

Certainly, students and problems are radically different today and many old ways don't work anymore, but that doesn't mean that *nothing* will work.

It's still possible to take back our schools where things have gotten out of control, to have safe, orderly schools in all communities and to create an environment where all kids can learn.

In fact, that's what's happening in many schools today. Things aren't as bad as some naysayers would have us believe. Considering the tumultuous nature of contemporary society, the schools are doing remarkably well and they're about to get even better.

It's Better than Most People Think

Most people get their news and views of schools second hand. Unfortunately, their most frequent sources of information (rumor, gossip, the "grapevine," and media reporting) tend to dwell on the extreme, the unusual, the dramatic and/or the spectacular. ("Normal" isn't news.) Because of this, all the common communication channels have contributed to a distorted public perception of the current status of discipline in the public schools. Even administrators, who work almost exclusively with discipline and delinquency, sometimes fall prey to a narrow misconception of what's really happening in schools. Actually, things are a lot better than many people think they are.

It's true that students are more streetwise, disrespectful, "mouthy," and even violent than in the past. It's true that all schools have discipline problems today and that some schools have a lot of serious, even dangerous, student behavior problems. But it's also true that:

- Most students want a safe, orderly school where they can learn successfully and have fun;
- Most parents want their children to be good and do well in school;
- Most students follow the rules everyday;
- Most teachers care and know what they're doing;
- Most schools are doing their jobs.

The common view of schools in chaos is overdrawn. Critics who want to write off public schools because of unruly, antisocial student behavior give up too easily.

There may be a few hard-core schools scattered throughout the country which need to be dissolved and reconfigured to get a fresh start. The *vast majority* of schools, however, continue to be under control, to be safe havens, and to help students learn more, better, and faster than ever before.

People who know schools know this to be true. Unbelievers need only to visit schools firsthand and to observe today's teachers and students in action to become convinced.

Not only are things better than most people believe, there are also lots of significant signs of improvement-in-process:

- Gang behavior has crested in some of the most hard-hit core cities in the nation.

- Most states have adopted or are adopting major reform measures designed to improve learning for all pupils.

- Public/community awareness of children's issues (drugs, violence, suicide) is increasing daily.

- Many communities are experiencing a rebirth of the partnership between the home and the school.

- More and more people are realizing that strengthening families is the first step toward strengthening schools.

Even in the worst schools, most of the ingredients for success are present. What is most often lacking is impassioned leadership and teamwork (community-wide teamwork). These are the areas where you and other school leaders can make the greatest difference.

Schools have problems; but they won't succumb to chaos. Society can't afford it and we won't let it happen!

WE'RE ALL IN THIS TOGETHER

School discipline isn't just a student or teacher or principal or parent issue. It's everybody's issue. Every member of the community, whether a parent or not, has a stake in the safety and success of the schools. If the public schools unravel because of dysfunctional discipline, the dreams and future of society crumble away at the same time.

Solutions to today's discipline problems won't be found in state capitols or the halls of congress. The best that government can do is to provide seed money, band-aids, and back-up. The real answers can only come through *local action* rooted in *individual responsibility.* "It takes a whole village to educate a child." It also takes a whole village to support and sustain disciplined schools.

The pathway to better discipline lies in communitywide networks, bridges, partnerships, and collaboratives all focused on providing a healthy, structured and orderly environment (inside and outside of school) in which all children can grow, learn, and thrive. It starts with reinforcing and supporting family structures of all kinds.

Although there are no pat formulas or perfect prototypes, a model community with a comprehensive action plan to support children, families, and schools would probably include the following (some of these elements are already beginning to appear piecemeal in places around the country):

- Schools teaching parenting skills to parents at all levels.

- Businesses adopting individual schools.
- Schools serving as one-stop centers for social services.
- Safe Houses for kids in every block.
- Parents helping to supervise school campuses and parking lots.
- Schools facilitating support groups for parents of children of all ages.
- Neighborhoods providing safe corridors (walking routes) to and from school.
- Police and firefighters serving lunch at school on a regular basis as a means of fostering trust, rapport, and communication with children and teenagers.
- Schools doing lots of things (exhibits, demonstrations, performances, celebrations) in the neighborhoods.
- A strong parental presence in every classroom.
- Parents, businesses, and city government working together to discourage children from staying out late and/or spending a lot of unsupervised time on the streets.
- School-sponsored Adopt-A-Park programs.
- Parent networks agreeing on guidelines for TV viewing, work hours for minors, and so on.
- Community-oriented policing (cops on the beat and in the neighborhoods.)
- Schools, churches, city officials, and service agencies cooperating to enrich children's free time with supervised positive activities.
- Community groups providing free music instruments and lessons to needy children.
- On-going communitywide dialogue about children's issues.
- Fire stations serving a dual purpose as drop-in centers for teens (always open, always supervised).
- Profamily policies in the work place.
- Schools sponsoring day care and after-school care accessible and affordable to all families.
- All students involved in community-service programs.
- Use of a mobile City Hall to take local government into the neighborhoods.
- Schools setting up Family Resource Centers.
- Parents, teachers, and students signing a covenant to support learning and to work for better schools.
- Businesses helping to establish computer labs in subsidized housing projects.
- Volunteer projects involving entire families.
- Planned intergenerational interaction.

- Public transportation system designed to "de-ghetto" the community by allowing poor kids to get to the same places and do the same things as rich kids.

Parents, schools, and communities work best in partnerships. We're all in this together. The means to guarantee positive discipline in all schools exists in most communities today. The main thing missing is *will*!

MAKING IT WORK

There are lots of things school leaders can do to improve discipline as outlined throughout this guide. The most powerful and long-lasting approaches, however, build on existing student strengths and support systems. That's why the culture of the school and the presence of a viable family are so important in children's lives. Too many children and teen-agers today lack hope and optimism. They have no faith in tomorrow, and so have little incentive to play by the rules today.

The Search Institute (Minneapolis, MN) has identified *30 internal and external assets* (family support, positive school climate, self-esteem, friendship skills, values of helping people, involvement in church or synagogue, parental standards) and *20 at-risk factors* (school absenteeism, weapon use, binge drinking, depression, and so on) which influence students' abilities to make healthy, positive behavior choices.

After surveying thousands of young people, their research clearly demonstrates that the more of these assets that exist in children's lives, the fewer at-risk behaviors they exhibit.

To improve discipline, it's just as important to connect kids to positive influences, as it is to protect them from bad ones. Self-discipline is as much a result of affirmations as it is of punishments and penalties.

Discipline is at the heart of what schools are all about. It constitutes, in some ways, the most enduring curriculum. Positive discipline is both the goal and the daily life-blood of every school. Its attainment requires the best efforts of an active, on-going coalition of teachers, administrators, parents, and the community-at-large.

The once-popular image of the "hero principal" who tames the school by stalking the corridors brandishing a baseball bat sends all the wrong messages. The measure of a principal's effectiveness today is measured by how well he or she can organize and energize schoolwide and communitywide coalitions to foster positive discipline.

Whatever happens to schools in the years ahead will be either created, prompted, or allowed by today's school leaders. You have the means to make good things happen and to create an environment where all kids can learn. By following the wealth of suggestions, directions, and principles spelled out throughout this guide, positive discipline is within the reach of every school, including yours!

APPENDICES

APPENDIX A:
SAMPLE DISCIPLINE POLICIES

School discipline policies are more than words on paper. Good policies: (1) make a statement; (2) send a message; (3) define limits; (4) set standards; (5) spell out consequences; and (6) guide action. Behind most successful discipline programs stands a set of definitive policy statements which spell out the rules by which the school operates.

The model policies contained in this appendix show how effective schools get their act together on paper first, before taking any ill-advised, random, or inconsistent action. Each of these policies has been selected for inclusion because of its positive approach, unusual subject matter, specific language, detailed directives, or notable absence of ambiguity. These examples, as well as others throughout the guide, may be adapted or adopted in any school system.

Educational and Personal Rights
Howard County (MD) Schools

I. Definitions

A. *Harassment.* A pattern of actions or statements directed at an individual or identifiable group ... which are intended to or which a reasonable person would understand are intended to ridicule or to demean the other ...

B. *Defamation.* False and unprivileged statements ... about an individual or identifiable group of individuals that harm the reputation of the person ... by demeaning him, her, or them in the estimation of the community or deterring others from associating with or dealing with him, her, or them.

E. *Intimidation.* Actions or statements that are willful in nature and which put an individual in fear of bodily harm.

F. *Signal incident.* Use of race, cultural identity, national origin, religion, socioeconomic status, gender, sexual orientation, or physical or mental disability as a basis for treating another in a negative manner, including epithets based on those characteristics used by individuals engaged in a conflict situation.

—Any signal incident brought to the attention of the principal, whether or not such incident was reported in conjunction with an alleged violation of this policy, shall be reported to the Office of Human Relations. The school principal ... shall assess the incident in the context of the school environment to determine what immediate and/or long term educational efforts may be called for.

II. Regulations

A. It shall be a violation ... to harass, defame, intimidate, threaten, use profanity toward, assault or engage in an act of violence directed against an individual or identifiable group of individuals ...

B. Mere expression of views, no matter how offensive or unpopular, which does not constitute harassment, defamation, intimidation or involve threats or use of profanity ... is not a violation of this policy..., however, expression of such views may constitute a *signal incident.*

C. Any student who violates this policy shall be disciplined, including possible suspension or expulsion ... In addition to any discipline imposed for violation of this policy, the student will receive appropriate counseling by the school system regarding the behavior in question.

---

*(*Author's Note:* This policy represents an up-to-date approach to problems of harassment, defamation, and intimidation. The concept of a "signal incident" is unique in terms of heading off, as well as handling, problem behavior.)

(Sample Policy)*

Ombudsman
Yorktown Heights (NY) High School

Yorktown High School created the Ombudsman position as a result of student requests to have a person responsible to guarantee student rights ... The Ombudsman will help to maintain a more positive atmosphere in the school. Experience has shown that students are more likely to respect the rules and be more responsible for their own actions and for the actions of their peers when they know there is a fair and equitable way of processing their own grievances and complaints....

The role of the Ombudsman is to ensure that students' rights are protected. Students who feel they have been treated unfairly or illegally by anyone on the high school staff should discuss their case with the Ombudsman and he/she will utilize all possible administrative procedures to help resolve the grievance ... The Ombudsman will take his/her case to the School Board or Commissioner of Education if it is necessary to ensure that students are treated fairly.

---

*(*Author's Note:* The Ombudsman position described represents a novel approach to protecting students' rights and ensuring due process.)

(Sample Policy)*

Student Conduct Off School Grounds
Putnam (CT) Public Schools

Students are subject to discipline, up to and including suspension and expulsion, for misconduct even if such misconduct occurs off school property and during non-school time.

Such discipline may result:

- if the incident was initiated in the school building or on school grounds;
- if the incident occurred or was initiated off school grounds and on nonschool time and if after the occurrence there was a reasonable likelihood that return of the student would contribute to a disruptive effect on the school's educational program or threaten the health, safety, or welfare of students and of school property.

Examples of the type of off-school property misconduct that may result in such discipline include but are not limited to:

- use, possession, sale, or distribution of dangerous weapons, including knives or guns;
- use, possession, sale, or distribution of controlled substances;
- use of physical force.
  The Board may impose discipline ... if it is determined that a student's:
- use, possession, or sale of controlled substances in the community has a reasonable likelihood of endangering the safety of students or employees because of the possibility of sales in the school;
- use of weapons or violent conduct in the community presents a reasonable likelihood of repeating itself in the school environment;
- similar type of misconduct in the community has a reasonable likelihood of being continued or repeated in school or of bringing retaliation or revenge into the school scene for such misconduct off school grounds.

---

*(*Author's Note:* This policy extends school discipline beyond the immediate school grounds. Most school rules overlook conduct off school property.)

(Sample Policy)*

Summer School
Anoka-Hennepin (MN) School District

A. Summer school is not a state or federally mandated program and students are not required to attend ... participants must make up every day of absence from summer school in order to complete the necessary minimum number of hours for course credit. Excessive absence could result in a student being dismissed from a summer school credit course.

Parents and students should be aware that summer school also differs from the regular school year in that alternative programs are not provided for students who exhibited attendance and/or behavior problems. Students will be dropped from summer school for violations of the student code of conduct.

B. Anoka-Hennepin School District recognizes its obligations to provide students with the elements of due process. Due process is the implementation of procedures which when adhered to guarantees the protection of equal rights. Before a student is dropped from summer school, the appropriate due process components will be followed. These include:

1. The summer school discipline policy will be provided to all students at the beginning of the summer session.

2. Students will be terminated from summer school only after a fair and objective investigation.

3. For any student subject to termination, an opportunity for a hearing will be provided for the student to discuss the infraction, the evidence, and the punishment with summer school authorities.

---

*(*Author's Note:* This policy recognizes the distinction between discipline during the regular school year and in summer school. Many districts fail to have a separate policy governing summer school discipline.)

(Sample Policy)*

Speical Situations—Substance Abuse
Plymouth-Canton (MI) Community Schools

The abuse of drugs is a highly complex problem for which no single solution will suffice. It is clear, therefore, that programs designed to modify substance use habits among students will have to be multifaceted and multileveled. The overriding goal of a systematic and integrated substance abuse intervention program ... will be to combat drug usage among our youth by providing appropriate learning experiences which will favorably alter students' health, knowledge, and habits. Research data suggests that, among students who have a firm sense of self-respect, the strongest dissuader available is accurate understanding about risks of heavy and sustained drug use.

The Plymouth-Canton Community School's program will include the following:

A. To teach decision making as a process in order to improve decision-making capabilities when faced with drug-related choices.

B. To present viable alternatives to students for the use of mood-modifying drugs.

C. To provide students with information about substance use and abuse in a factual manner facilitating ability to reach intelligent decisions regarding their own use of drugs.

D. To provide access to substance abuse counseling when appropriate.

E. To monitor and curtail the flow of illicit substances in the school for the protection of all students and to use the full force and the powers of this school district to interdict and curtail the possession, use, and flow of illicit substances in schools where appropriate.

F. To increase interagency and community involvement with the school on substance use and abuse issues.

G. To provide information to parents and teaching staff about all aspects of substance use and abuse and involve them when appropriate in coping with the problems related to use and abuse.

H. To increase community's perception that the schools are in the process of assuming a strong proactive stance in combating substance use and abuse.

I. To improve the consistent administration of appropriate cause/effect consequences for substance possession and use within the school premises.

HIGH SCHOOL SUBSTANCE ABUSE DISCIPLINE PROCEDURES

PENALTY FOR *POSSESSION OR USE* OF ANY SUBSTANCE, FOR ILLICIT PURPOSES, INCLUDING ALCOHOL, DRUGS OR MEDICATION

1st Offense:

—Parent contact

—Minimum of two days out-of-school suspension and one day in-school suspension.

—Issue suspension letter and counseling referral letter to parents

—Assign student to intervention program

—Contact appropriate teacher/consultant for all certified students

2nd Offense:

—Parent contact

—Minimum 4-day out-of-school suspension

—Implement one of the following:

A. Issue suspension letter for five days suspension and counseling letter to parents. Mandatory parent conference in order for student to return to school.

B. Issue suspension letter for three days out-of-school suspension and one day in-school suspension if parent and student attend in-school intervention together.

C. Issue suspension letter for five days suspension and counseling referral letter to parents. The parents may reduce the suspension by one day if they contact an outside-of-school resource designed to address the problem of substance abuse.

3rd Offense:

1. Parent Contact.
2. Petition to the Board of Education for expulsion.
3. Begin expulsion proceedings ...
4. Schedule conference involving student, parent, area coordinator, building principal and staff person specializing in substance abuse prevention. At this conference, review charges, evidence, and intervention steps taken previously. Explore options available for further assistance....

5. If Special Education student is involved, contact appropriate teacher/consultant. Proceed to examine records and convene Individual Educational Planning Conference.

6. The Superintendent will schedule expulsion hearing and inform parents.

PENALTY FOR *SALES OR DISTRIBUTION* OF ANY SUBSTANCE, FOR ILLICIT PURPOSES, INCLUDING ALCOHOL, DRUGS, OR MEDICATION

1. Police involvement when in the judgment of the administrator in charge, such police involvement is warranted.

2. Suspension and automatic petition for expulsion to the Board of Education.

3. Formulate charges—contact parents—contact building principal—suspend for five days. Schedule return conference with parents. During the five-day interim, establish expulsion process ... Establish Special Education procedure.

4. Convene the return conference ... Review charges, evidence, rationale, and other pertinent data. Offer alternatives in view of expulsion.

5. The Superintendent will schedule expulsion hearing and inform parents.

(Author's Note: The policy which follows is included because it emphasizes positive preventative measures, as well as penalties and punishments.)

APPENDIX B
BIBLIOGRAPHY

Benson, Peter. *The Troubled Journey: A Profile of American Youth,* Search Institute, Minneapolis, MN, 1993.

Caroll, Charles R. *Drugs In Modern Society,* Wm. C. Brown Pub., Dubuque, IA, 1985.

Chernow and Chernow. *Classroom Discipline and Control,* Parker Pub. Co., Inc., West Nyack, NY, 1981.

Chernow and Chernow. *The Classroom Discipline Survival Guide,* Center for Applied Research in Education, West Nyack, NY, 1989.

Edelman, Marian Wright. *The Measure of Our Success: A Letter to My Children and Yours,* Beacon Press, Boston, MA, 1992.

Ianni, Francis, A. J. *Violent Schools—Safe Schools, U.S.D. Hew,* Washington, D. C., Dec., 1977.

Karlin and Berger. *Discipline and the Disruptive Child,* Parker Publishing Company, West Nyack, NY, 1992.

Minnesota Police and Peace Officers Association. *Street Drugs/Gang Violence,* Stuart-Bradley Prod., Inc., Nevada, 1990.

Myrick and Every. *Youth Helping Youth,* Educational Media Corporation, Minneapolis, MN, 1985.

New Jersey Department of Education. *Violence and Vandalism Prevention Task Force Report,* January, 1994.

Petersen and Straub. *School Crisis Survival Guide,* The Center for Applied Research in Education, West Nyack, NY, 1992.

Ramsey, Robert D. *Secondary Principals Survival Guide,* Prentice Hall, Englewood Cliffs, NJ, 1992.

Rich, John M. *Innovative School Discipline,* Charles C. Thomas Pub. Co., Springfield, IL, 1981.

South Carolina Department of Education. *Executive Summary Report of the Task Force on School Violence in South Carolina,* April, 1993.

Sprick, Randall. *Discipline in the Secondary Classroom,* The Center for Applied Research in Education, West Nyack, NY, 1985.

Sturkie and Gibson. *The Peer Helpers' Pocketbook,* Reserve Publications, Inc., San Jose, CA, 1992.

Wolfgang and Glickman. *Solving Discipline Problems: Strategies for Classroom Teachers,* Allyn and Bacon, Inc., Boston, MA, 1986.